Lonely Planet Publications
Melbourne | Oakland | London | Paris

W9-APS-876

Simon Richmond

Cape Town

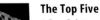

The Top Five

1 Cape Point
Discover the dramatic scenery of the peninsula's rugged tip (p76)

2 Table Mountain
Look down on the city from more than 1000 vertical metres (p64)

3 Robben Island
Visit Nelson Mandela's former cell at this infamous prison (p67)

4 City Bowl
Explore museums and markets in downtown Cape Town (p60)

5 Kalk Bay
Browse the village's fish market and antique shops (p75)

Contents

Published by Lonely Planet Publications Pty Ltd
ABN 36 005 607 983

Australia Head Office, Locked Bag 1, Footscray,
Victoria 3011, ☎ 03 8379 8000, fax 03 8379 8111,
talk2us@lonelyplanet.com.au

USA 150 Linden St, Oakland, CA 94607,
☎ 510 893 8555, toll free 800 275 8555,
fax 510 893 8572, info@lonelyplanet.com

UK 72–82 Rosebery Ave, Clerkenwell, London,
EC1R 4RW, ☎ 020 7841 9000, fax 020 7841 9001,
go@lonelyplanet.co.uk

France 1 rue du Dahomey, 75011 Paris,
☎ 01 55 25 33 00, fax 01 55 25 33 01,
bip@lonelyplanet.fr, www.lonelyplanet.fr

Printed through SNP SPrint Singapore Pte Ltd at
KHL Printing Co Sdn Bhd, Malaysia

The Author

SIMON RICHMOND

'I could live here', thought Simon after his first two-month-long visit to Cape Town in 2001 to research the Lonely Planet guides to *South Africa, Lesotho & Swaziland* and *Cape Town*. Coming from Sydney, he understood the similarities people noticed between the two cities, but also keenly sensed the differences and how the city was struggling to reinvent itself in the post-apartheid era. Three years later, and back in town for a month to research this guide, he sublet a flat in Rondebosch, shopped for groceries at the local Woolworths and roamed from Cape Point to the Winelands in a shiny red Toyota Tazz. He reckons that getting under the skin of this magnetic, stunning city is all about indulging in life's pleasures, be it savouring a gourmet meal and fantastic wines, hiking through the magnificent *fynbos* covering Table Mountain, sunning yourself on the beach, or meeting people who believe passionately in the possibilities and future of the Mother City.

PHOTOGRAPHER

Belgian-born photographer Ariadne van Zandbergen has been Johannesburg based since overlanding from Europe in 1994. She has trained her lens, often in rudimentary conditions, on remote landscapes and peoples in 25 African countries. Cape Town, with its sophisticated blend of cultures, made for a refreshingly urbane change, although encounters with cantankerous baboons, inquisitive penguins and loony motorists kept her on her toes!

Introducing Cape Town

When it comes to ranking the world's most beautiful cities Cape Town is right up there with the best of them. A major part of the attraction is a 1073m-high mountain slap-bang in the centre of the city. Table Mountain and its attendant peaks – Devil's Peak and Lion's Head – are the city's most enduring image. As beautiful as the surrounding white beaches and verdant vineyards are, it's this rugged wilderness, covered in a unique flora, that is the focus of everyone's attention.

Next you'll most likely notice how vibrantly colourful everything is, from the beaded dolls and patterned shirts in the tourist shops to the Victorian bathing chalets at St James' beach and the pastel-painted façades of the Bo-Kaap. The many different faces on the city streets provide visual proof of South Africa's status as a rainbow nation and a reminder of the Mother City's tumultuous recorded history of more than 350 years. Walk through the lovely Company's Gardens and you are literally walking through that history. Here is the vegetable garden planted by the city's founder, Jan van Riebeeck; the graceful Cape Dutch architecture of the 18th-century Tuynhuis; the awful reality of the old Slave Lodge; the staunch majesty of St George's Cathedral, focus of Archbishop Desmond Tutu's struggle against the madness of apartheid; and the houses of parliament, where Nelson Mandela was proclaimed the country's first democratically elected president. It's soul-stirring stuff.

The scars of the republic's violent birth and apartheid adolescence still run deep. The culture of the original inhabitants the San and Khoikhoi has vanished, leaving Cape Town, like all South African cities, with a dual nature – European but not European, African but not African; a potentially volatile mixture of the Third and

---

Lowdown

Population 2.9 million

Time Zone GMT + two hours

3-star room Around R600

Glass of wine R10-15

Shared taxi ride R2

Essential accessory Wola Nani safety-pin and bead bracelet

No-no Not tipping the guys who look after your car

Essential Cape Town

- **Robben Island** (p67)
- **South African National Gallery** (p64)
- **Kirstenbosch Botanical Gardens** (p72)
- **Table Mountain** (p64)
- **Drum Café** (p105)

first Worlds. Apartheid allowed whites to reserve some of the world's most spectacular real estate, and the stark contrast between poverty-stricken Crossroads and ritzy Clifton remains – black and white.

And yet you must visit the ever-growing Cape Flats townships, home to an estimated 1.5 million people, to truly understand this city and to glimpse its future. Not everything you see will appal you. On the contrary, it can be argued that a stronger sense of optimism and pride are found in the shacks of Khayelitsha than in the mansions of Tamboerskloof. The experience of the city's large coloured community, rooted in slavery, is presented movingly in the District Six Museum (p61) and is equally fascinating and essential for putting Cape Town fully into context.

For all the city's contradictions you'll find Capetonians amazingly likeable, open-minded and ultra-relaxed. Like many of the world's ports, Cape Town is a long time master of showing visitors a good time. The range and quality of accommodation is brilliant with a particularly strong showing for unique luxury guesthouses. Its mix of trendy restaurants and bars compares favourably with those in other cosmopolitan cities. There's a lively cultural scene, particularly when it comes to music, which seems to pervade every corner of the city. If outdoor activities and adrenaline buzzes are your thing, then you've also come to the right place.

The capital of Western Cape province and the parliamentary capital of the republic, Cape Town works as a city in a way that so few on the African continent do. Historic buildings have been saved, businesses are booming, crime is coming under control and you'll seldom be stuck for a parking space. Factor back in those stunning mountains, magnificent surf beaches and outstanding vineyards and you'll soon discover – like many before you – that it's easy to lose track of time while exploring all the wonders of this unique Southern African city.

SIMON'S TOP CAPE TOWN DAY

It's 7am and I'm parking the Tazz by the cable car and starting the long, steady slog up the mountain before the sun rises too high in the sky. Two hours later, exhausted but elated I stand atop the mountain, surveying the many possibilities Cape Town holds for the day. First, breakfast. I return by cable car to the motor and wheel it downhill for breakfast with the cool customers at Vida e Caffé on Kloof St; their cappuccinos and egg sandwiches are the best. Next it's over to Constantia for a spot of wine tasting. It's very tempting to hang out at Buitenverwachting for a gourmet picnic on the immaculate lawn, but the charms of Kalk Bay beckon and, in particular, lunch at Olympia Café. Having browsed the antique and craft shops I head back over to the Atlantic coast towards Noordhoek and the famed Chapman's Peak Drive around to Hout Bay. There's time for an hour's sunbathe at Sandy Bay (no need for a swimming costume!) before meeting with mates for sundowner drinks at Eclipse in Camps Bay. A quick shower and change and it's back into town for a fun-filled dinner at Cara Lazuli (what is that belly dancer doing with the snake?!), followed by a trawl of the Long St bars and grooving into the early hours at Rhodes House.

City Life

City Life

CAPE TOWN TODAY

You can say practically whatever you like to friendly, laid-back Capetonians about them or their city and they will just smile, confident in the undisputable fact that they are living in one of the most successful and beautiful cities in Africa. 'A fool's paradise' is what the writer Rian Malan calls it; a place so seductive and attractive that it's easy to ignore the hard and violent realities of the country in which it is based.

Anyone who reads the shock-horror headlines of the local newspapers or, worse, makes the wrong turn in the more lawless suburbs of the Cape Flats, will quickly discover that these realities are a lot closer to home than you might realise while sipping cocktails at Camps Bay or shopping in the Waterfront. But then those carefree activities are just as much a part of Cape Town life as crime or AIDS statistics. It's just one of the mildly perplexing, always fascinating contradictions of life in the Mother City. Besides, Capetonians wouldn't expect Jo'burgers like the writer Malan to think of Cape Town in anything other than negative terms. They know this certainly doesn't stop their Gauteng cousins from flocking here for their holidays just like everyone else.

And why wouldn't they? It's so easy to enjoy the lush outdoor life that Cape Town provides – the splendid beaches, the magnificent geography and unique flora of Table Mountain National Park (covering three quarters of the peninsula), the beauty of well-preserved heritage architecture, as well as centuries-old vineyards and their grand estates. Initiatives between local government and business are helping control crime and increase security in the city centre, where property developers are putting their efforts into loft-style apartments and ritzy new shopping centres such as the Cape Quarter in the Waterkant.

Here you'll find evidence of how far Cape Town has come in the last 10 years since democracy reopened the country to global consumption. Its restaurants, bars and clubs have picked up on the latest styles of New York, London and Paris, adding a distinctively African twist. There's a growing local fashion scene. Arts and crafts businesses, born in the desperate circumstances of the townships, add liberal dashes of colour and creativity that really do make you feel that this is the rainbow city of the rainbow nation. Is it any wonder that the beautiful people of the northern hemisphere, having spent their winters sunning themselves on Cape Town's beaches, are now buying up property and staying year round?

Life might be considerably tougher for large sections of the city's population, but you only have to spend some time in the townships to realise that it might not be quite so uniformly awful as depicted by the broad brush strokes of the media. There's still a long way to go, but at least two thirds of people in the townships now have formal housing. These may not be much more than concrete Reconstruction and Development Programme (RDP) houses but they're certainly better than the flimsy, fire-prone shacks that people called homes before. There's an increasingly visible black and coloured middle and upper class, too – just as there are white beggars and trashy white areas of the city, such as Brooklyn.

With house prices on the rise, the chances are that Brooklyn may get its day in the sun. The real estate revival is already happening in once down-and-out Muizenberg on False Bay, which was rediscovered as a fine

---

Hot Conversation Topics

- **Property** – should I sell? Can I afford to buy?
- **AIDS babies** – who will care for South Africa's generation of orphans?
- **Chapman's Peak Drive** – money well spent or an environmental disaster?
- **Price rises** – how much did you say our restaurant bill was?!
- **Patricia de Lille** – could this feisty politician be the next South African president?

place to live when the houses along the fashionable Atlantic coast soared out of reach of your average Capetonian. Rising prices are a problem, as is the worry that Cape Town may now be killing off the cash-cow of tourism by becoming too greedy, jacking its prices too high for it to appeal even to the international jet set it so actively courts.

CITY CALENDAR

Hardly a week goes by in Cape Town without some event or celebration happening somewhere in the city and its immediate surroundings, from outdoor arts performances in January to Carols by Candlelight in the Company's Gardens in time for Christmas. For a full rundown call **Cape Town's Events Office** (☎ 487 2764; www.capetownevents.co.za). See p173 for a list of public holidays.

JANUARY & FEBRUARY

CAPE TOWN NEW YEAR KARNAVAL
☎ 637 0873

If you haven't headed out of town, like most Capetonians do for the New Year holidays, go and see this colourful carnival held on the streets of the City Bowl and Bo-Kaap on 1 January and the following three Saturdays at Green Point and Athlone stadiums. Cape Town's longest-running annual street party was first officially documented in 1907, but dates back to the early 19th century when slaves enjoyed a day of freedom over the New-Year period. The carnival was inspired by visiting American minstrels, hence the face make-up and colourful costumes that are all part of the ribald song-and-dance parades. The highlight is the 1 January parade, which culminates at Green Point Stadium. Around 13,000 revellers organised into separate troupes participate in the parade, and each troupe competes to win trophies in various categories over the course of the carnival, including for best dressed, most flamboyant, best band and best singer.

STANDARD BANK CAPE TOWN JAZZATHON
☎ 683 2201; www.jazzathon.co.za

The largest free open-air jazz festival in South Africa runs for four days in early January at the Waterfront, drawing more than a million people to see top acts such as Hugh Masekela and Sibongile Khumalo. Check their Web site for details of the special concerts also held on Robben Island.

SPIER ARTS SUMMER SEASON
☎ 809 1100; www.spier.co.za

From January through to March the Spier wine estate near Stellenbosch runs a series of top-class concerts, operas and plays at its outdoor amphitheatre. Every other year there is a sculpture exhibition in the surrounding grounds too.

CAPE TO RIO YACHT RACE

This major yacht race is held every even-numbered year and starts on the first week in January. It draws contestants from around the world.

J&B MET
☎ 426 5775 South Africa's biggest horse race, with a jackpot of R1.5 million, is a time for big bets and even bigger hats. Head to Kenilworth Racecourse to catch the action. In 2004 it was moved to April due to an equine flu scare, but it's generally held on the last Saturday in January.

OPENING OF PARLIAMENT

A grand parade with military marching bands halts the traffic down Adderley and Parliament Sts when parliament opens in early February. Come to see the MPs and dignitaries in their finest outfits, to glimpse celebrities such as Nelson Mandela and to groove with the public at the pop concert traditionally held in Greenmarket Square afterwards.

MARCH & APRIL

CAPE ARGUS PICK 'N' PAY CYCLE TOUR
☎ 083 910 6551; www.cycletour.co.za

Held on a Saturday in the middle of March this is the world's largest timed cycling event, attracting more than 30,000 contestants. The route circles Table Mountain, heading down the Atlantic Coast and along Chapman's Peak Drive. Forget driving around town on the day.

CAPE TOWN FESTIVAL
☎ 082 899 8791; www.capetownfestival.co.za

Begun in 1999, this is becoming a major annual arts event held in the middle of March throughout the City Bowl and at the Waterfront. It includes comedy, drama, debates, an African short film festival and a food festival in the Company's Gardens.

OUT IN AFRICA SOUTH AFRICAN GAY & LESBIAN FILM FESTIVAL
☎ 465 9289; www.oia.co.za

With screenings at Cavendish Square and the Waterfront, the Out in Africa film festival offers up a smorgasbord of queer cinema from around the world.

NORTH SEA JAZZ FESTIVAL
☎ 083 123 5299; www.nsjfcapetown.com

This is the big one, attracting all the big names in jazz from both South Africa and abroad. In 2004 it was held at the Cape Town International Convention Centre at the end of March with performances across four stages. It often includes a free concert.

JUST NUISANCE DAY

No, this is not an April Fools' joke. Every 1 April a dog parade is held through Jubilee Square in Simon's Town to commemorate Able Seaman Just Nuisance, the Great Dane who was a mascot of the Royal Navy during WWII.

OLD MUTUAL TWO OCEANS MARATHON
☎ 671 9407; www.twooceansmarathon.org.za

Held on 10 April in 2004 (it's often held at the end of March) this 56km marathon kicks off in Newlands on Main Rd and follows a similar route to the Pick 'n' Pay Cycle Tour around Table Mountain. It generally attracts about 9000 competitors.

MAY
CAPE GOURMET FESTIVAL
☎ 465 0069; www.gourmetsa.com

For two weeks from early May, Cape Town comes over all gourmet with various food-focused events. A highlight is the Tastic Table of Reconciliation and Unity where a table for 700 diners of varying ethnicities is set up at the top of Table Mountain.

JULY & AUGUST
CHILLI FIESTA
☎ 419 1881; www.chillifiesta.co.za

Held in the City Bowl in either July or August, this two-week celebration of chillies sees scores of restaurants battling to outdo each other in a red hot and sizzling cook-off. Patrons get to vote for their favourite chilli dish; in 2003, Madame Zingara's beef fillet in a chilli and chocolate sauce took top honours.

NATIONAL WOMEN'S DAY
www.capewow.co.za

South African women get their own day of celebration on 9 August. Around this time there's usually a Cape Wow (Women of the World) arts and culture festival, too.

SEPTEMBER & OCTOBER
FLOWER SHOWS
www.capetownevents.co.za

Spring comes to the Cape in September. The wildflowers bloom, and festivals are held in their honour up and down the province. See the Cape Town Events Web site for full details. There's usually a spring flower show at the Waterfront, too.

CAPE TOWN INTERNATIONAL KITE FESTIVAL
☎ 447 9040; www.kitefest.co.za

Held in mid-September, in support of the Cape Mental Health Society, this colourful gathering of kite enthusiasts at Zandvlei near Muizenberg is big, entertaining and for a good cause.

SMIRNOFF INTERNATIONAL COMEDY FESTIVAL
☎ 685 7880

This is a justly popular event held over a week at the end of September at the Baxter Theatre and a few other venues around town. It features local talent as well international comedians.

CAPE ARGUS/WOOLWORTHS GUN RUN
☎ 426 5775; www.gunrun.co.za

Starting from Beach Rd in Mouile Point, this popular half-marathon is the only time that the noonday gun on Signal Hill gets fired – the idea is to have finished the race before the gun goes off. It's generally held at the end of September.

Top Five Quirky Holidays & Events

- **Cape Town New Year Karnaval** (p9) – dancing in the streets with lively jazz music and many shiny satin suits.
- **Cape Argus Pick 'n' Pay Cycle Tour** (p9) – get on your bike or at least along the route and cheer on the thousands of frantically turning pedals.
- **Chilli Fiesta** (p10) – fire up your taste buds with the chilli-hot culinary creations of Cape Town's top chefs.
- **Cape Town International Kite Festival** (p10) – watching this multicoloured aerial show is as good a reason as any to spend a breezy day down in Muizenberg.
- **Mother City Queer Project** (p11) – camp as a row of tents, this is the hottest dance event of the year with compulsory fancy dress.

STELLENBOSCH FESTIVAL
☎ 883 3891; www.stellenboschfestival.co.za
From the end of September to early October, Stellenbosch enjoys three festivals celebrating music and art, food and wine, culture and local history.

HERMANUS WHALE FESTIVAL
☎ 028-313 0928; www.whalefestival.co.za
Hermanus gets into its stride as the Cape's premier whale watching location at the end of September with this family-focused arts festival incorporating a range of events around town.

NOVEMBER & DECEMBER
MOTHER CITY QUEER PROJECT
☎ 426 5709; www.mcqp.co.za
Everyone is as queer as folk at this must-attend dance party held in early December. Check out the theme and run yourself up a fabulous costume – they won't let you in unless you're dressed appropriately. See p103 for details.

KIRSTENBOSCH SUMMER SUNSET CONCERTS
☎ 799 8782; www.nbi.ac.za
The Sunday afternoon concerts, usually held from 5pm, are a Cape Town institution. Bring a blanket, a bottle of wine and a picnic and join the crowds enjoying anything from arias performed by local divas to a funky jazz combo. There's usually a special concert for New Year's Eve, too.

CULTURE

Culturally, Cape Town is South Africa's most cosmopolitan city, and it always has been. The foundations of the melting pot began with the Dutch who imported slaves from around Africa and Asia to assist them in building up the colony. Those slaves' descendants, plus what's left of the area's original inhabitants, the San and Khoikhoi, make up the city's majority coloured population today.

The black population brings its culture to the table, too, with *sangomas* (traditional African healers) and initiation ceremonies (p12) which are a common part of township life. There is a prominent Muslim community and a small but influential Jewish community. Even within the white community there are differences (not always celebrated, mind you) between those of British and Afrikaans heritage. There's the gay community which, with impeccable taste, has adopted Cape Town as its very own Mother City. And then there are the most recent arrivals – Europeans and people from across the whole continent of Africa, seduced by Cape Town's promise of the good life.

IDENTITY

The racial mix in Cape Town is different from the rest of the country. Out of its population of 2.9 million more than half are coloured; blacks account for about a third of the total, and whites and others comprise the balance.

In this book we make use of the old apartheid terms: white, black, coloured and Indian. It is impossible to pretend that these distinctions, as distasteful as they may seem, have disappeared from South Africa. Many South Africans proudly identify themselves with one or other of these groups – for example, you'll meet black South Africans who happily refer to themselves as black rather than South Africans or Africans (which is the African National Congress's preferred collective expression for all people of African, Indian and mixed-race origin).

Coloureds

Coloureds, sometimes known as Cape coloureds or Cape Malays, are South Africans of long standing. Although many were brought to the early Cape Colony as slaves, others were political prisoners and exiles from the Dutch East Indies. People were brought from countries as far apart as India and modern Indonesia, as well as East Africa, but their lingua franca was Malay (at the time an important trading language), which is how they came to be called Cape Malays.

Although Islam could not be practised openly in the colony until 1804, the presence of influential and charismatic political and religious figures among the slaves helped a cohesive Cape Muslim community to develop. The Cape Muslim culture has survived intact over the centuries, and has even resisted some of the worst abuses of apartheid. The strongest evidence of it is in Cape Town's Bo-Kaap district; in the circle of 20 or so *karamats* (tombs of Muslim saints) that circle the city; and, to a lesser extent, in Simon's Town; for more details see p46.

The slaves who moved out with the Dutch to the hinterland, many losing their religion and cultural roots in the process, had a much worse time of it. And yet practically all the coloured population of the Western Cape and Northern Cape provinces today are bound by Afrikaans, the unique language that began to develop from the interaction between the slaves and the Dutch over three centuries ago. One of the oldest documents in Afrikaans is a Koran transcribed using Arabic script.

The most public, secular expression of Cape-coloured culture today is the riotous Cape Town New Year Karnaval also known as the Cape Minstrel Carnival (p9). At the end of Ramadan thousands of Muslims pray on Cape Town's Sea Point promenade, where they gather to sight the new moon.

Blacks

Although most blacks in Cape Town are Xhosa hailing from Eastern Cape province, they are not the only group in the city. Cape Town's economy has attracted people from all over Southern Africa including a fair few immigrants from the rest of the continent, as you'll discover strolling around the craft markets outside the train station and at Green Point.

Xhosa culture is diverse, with many clan systems and subgroups. Politics makes for another division, with most people supporting the African National Congress but a sizable minority supporting the more hardline Pan-African Congress (PAC, see also p19). There are also economic divisions, with some owning their own houses in the townships; and subgroups based on culture, such as the Rastafarian community.

Few Xhosa in the Cape Flats maintain a traditional lifestyle on a daily basis, but among the women, in particular, different subgroups wear different costumes, colours and arrangements of beads. *Sangomas* are often approached if a person suffers an illness and traditional methods might be followed to deal with this. At important junctions in life, such as birth, coming of age (p12) and marriage, various old rites and customs are followed, too.

Whites

Within the white community the culture depends on whether you are a descendant of the Boers or the British. The Boers' history of geographical isolation and often deliberate cultural seclusion has created a unique people who are often called 'the white tribe of Africa'.

Initiation Ceremony

While in the townships or travelling to and from them you may notice makeshift tents erected amid the wastelands. Rather than accommodating newcomers to the townships this is quite likely to be the place where male initiation ceremonies are being carried out. In the past, boys would go away around the age of 16 (although they may be older) from their families for up to three months to be circumcised, live in these tents and learn what it is to be a man in tribal society. The period of separation is likely to be a month or less these days, but the initiates still have to shave off all their hair and daub themselves in white clay before being circumcised. When they return to their families they wear smart clothes – often a sports jacket and cap.

Dealing with Racism

Visitors to South Africa will find that, although the apartheid regime has been dismantled, cultural apartheid still exists. To an extent, discrimination based on wealth is replacing that based on race (so most visitors will automatically gain high status), but there are still plenty of people (mainly whites) who sincerely believe that a particular skin colour means a particular mind-set. A few believe it means inferiority.

If you aren't white, many white South Africans will register this. The constant awareness of race, even if it doesn't lead to problems, is an annoying feature of travel in South Africa, whatever your skin colour. Racial discrimination is illegal, but it's unlikely that the overworked and underresourced police force will be interested in most complaints. Tourism authorities are likely to be more sensitive. If you encounter racism in any of the places mentioned in this book, please let us know.

African

If you are of African descent, you may well encounter some white resentment. The lies perpetuated about blacks during the apartheid era are taking some time to wear off. On the other hand, do not assume a special bond with black South Africans. The various indigenous peoples of South Africa form distinct and sometimes antagonistic cultural groups. The hardline Pan-Africanism is a force in politics here, but not the dominant force. Thus travellers of African descent from France or the USA will not necessarily receive a warmer welcome than anyone else.

White

If you are of European descent, it will be assumed by most white South Africans that you are essentially the same as them. However, if you've saved for your trip by, say, cleaning offices or working in a petrol station, you will get some startled reactions from some white South Africans. You may also find yourself having to listen to some obnoxious racist remarks.

Indian

Although Indians were discriminated against by whites during apartheid, blacks saw them as collaborating with the whites. If you are of Indian descent this could mean some low-level antagonism from both blacks and whites.

Asian

East Asians were a problem for apartheid – Japanese were granted 'honorary white' status, and people from other East Asian countries are probably indistinguishable from the Japanese to insular South Africans. Grossly inaccurate stereotyping and cultural ignorance will probably be the main annoyances you will face.

The ethnic composition of Afrikaners is difficult to quantify but it has been estimated at 40% Dutch, 40% German, 7.5% French, 7.5% British and 5% other. Some historians have argued that the '5% other' figure includes a significant proportion of blacks and coloureds.

Afrikaans, the only Germanic language to have evolved outside Europe, is central to the Afrikaner identity but it has also served to reinforce their isolation from the outside world. The Afrikaners are a religious people and the group's brand of Christian fundamentalism based on 17th-century Calvinism is still a powerful influence. Urbanised middle-class Afrikaners tend to be considerably more moderate and the further the distance between the horrors of the apartheid era and the 'new South Africa', the more room there is for Afrikaners to be proud of their heritage. You'll find Afrikaans a much stronger presence in the northern suburbs of Cape Town and in the country towns of the Cape, including the Winelands around Stellenbosch which has a prominent Afrikaans university.

Most other white Capetonians are of British extraction. Cape Town, as the seat of British power for so long, is somewhat less Afrikaner in outlook than other parts of the country. Liberal Capetonians were regarded with suspicion by more conservative whites during the apartheid years, and today the city is tantalisingly cosmopolitan.

LIFESTYLE

There is no such thing as an 'average' Capetonian lifestyle – the city's range of cultures and ethnicities puts paid to that. Pious Muslims in the Bo-Kaap head to the mosque for morning prayers while, in the nearby Waterkant, hedonistic partygoers are on their way home.

Places of Worship

- **Groote Kerk** (p61) Dutch Reform
- **Great Synagogue** (Map p206; ☎ 465 1405; 88 Hatfield St, Gardens) Jewish
- **Lutheran Church** (p62) Lutheran
- **Palm Tree Mosque** (Map pp200–2; ☎ 447 6415; 185 Long St, City Bowl) Muslim
- **St George's Cathedral** (Map pp200–2; ☎ 424 7360; 1 Wale St, City Bowl) Anglican
- **St Mary's Cathedral** (Map pp200–2; ☎ 461 1167; Roeland St, City Bowl) Roman Catholic

The life of a black live-in maid (average monthly salary R800 to R1000 including board and lodging), her children looked after by her mother or grandmother in the countryside, is radically different from that of the middle-class white family she works for (average monthly salary R15,000 with both husband and wife working).

This is not to say that the 'dream' lifestyle of the Capetonian doesn't exist, only that it's a lot rarer than might be imagined. A fortunate family will live in one of the more salubrious suburbs, say Vredehoek or Newlands, in a multimillion rand home with a pool. They have a holiday home elsewhere in the Western Cape, perhaps up at Paternoster or down around Hermanus. There's a car or two to get the family around, and at least one maid/nanny to take care of the more tedious bits of housework and childcare. There are school fees to consider and the cost of keeping a dog – typically a large one – which will act as an extra security device alongside the locked gates, window bars and rapid response alarm systems that are dotted throughout the home. The fear that someone could take all this away is naggingly constant. Still, it's a good life, with restaurant meals, nights at cinemas and theatres, and frequent visits to the beach.

What this dream family might spend on groceries every month could keep the much more numerous 'average' black family in the Cape Flats going for many months, if not a year. These families might be lucky and live in a concrete and brick home, but chances are that they are in a self-built shack that cost about R2700 for all the materials. The furniture is likely to be second-hand; it is highly unlikely that they have a car (if they do it is also likely to be second-hand) just as it is rare to have a fully plumbed bathroom in the house. For water and ablutions there's a standpipe and toilets shared with several other families on the block. The mother will be working in a low-paid job out of which she'll have to find a large chunk of cash for transport and smaller amounts for childcare and the kid's fees at school. A holiday is likely to be a trip once a year on a deathtrap of a bus back to the Eastern Cape to visit relatives in the countryside.

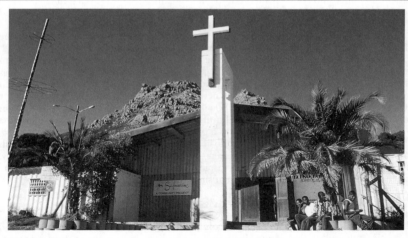

Church built from shipping containers, Imizamo Yethu (p66), Hout Bay township

Gay Talk

Cape Town has a special place in South African gay culture as the home of a unique gay language. 'Moffie', the local derogatory term for a homosexual, is the Afrikaans word for glove and is also the word used for the leader of a perform-ance troupe in the Cape New Year Karnaval (p9). These leaders wear gloves and are often gay, hence moffie's alternative meaning. South African gays have now reclaimed moffie as a word to use among themselves, in much the same way that many gays have appropriated 'queer' in an effort to repudiate its negative connotations.

Gay Capetonians also developed a code language, called Gayle, in which women's names stand in for certain words. For example, a Cilla is a cigarette; Nadia means no; Wendy, white; Priscilla, police; and Bula, beautiful. So if you hear someone talking about Dora in a bar, you'll know they're after a drink (they could also be calling someone a drunk!). To learn more about this fascinating underground language read Ken Cage's *Gayle – The Language of Kinks and Queens* which includes a dictionary of the most popular code words. For more information on gay and lesbian Cape Town, see p172.

FOOD & DRINK

Cape Town has a deservedly good reputation for its cuisine. Apart from the home-grown traditional dishes of Cape Malay and Afrikaner cooking (p15), there is a strong movement towards modern South African cuisine which uses local ingredients in creative ways. The city's restaurants and cafés also offer up a world of eating possibilities from Turkish and Mid-dle Eastern to Chinese, Japanese and Indian. Some of the Italian restaurants, in particular, are excellent, and there's also a mouth-watering range of delis, often with attached cafés.

As you'd expect in a city by the water, seafood is plentiful. In many places you'll see 'line fish' advertised – this means the catch of the day. Meaty local fish such as *kingklip* and *snoek* are often served; search out the freshest speci-mens at the Waterfront, Kalk Bay (with its marvellous fish market) and Hout Bay.

Restaurants serving African dishes, most of which don't originate in South Africa, are popular – try a meal at the exceptional Africa Café or the lively Marco's African Place, both in the City Bowl. For a slightly less touristy experience, head out to one of the growing number of places serving food in the Cape Flats. You'll find here that the staple for most blacks is rice or mealie meal (maize), often served with a fatty stew. It isn't especially appetising, but it's cheap. The same goes for the sheep's heads, or *smilies*, that you'll see boiled up and served on the streets.

Traditional Afrikaner cuisine shows its Voortrekker heritage in foods such as *bil-tong* (the deliciously moreish dried meat) and rusks, perfect for those long journeys into the hinterland. *Boerewors* (farmers' sau-sage) is the traditional sausage, and must be 90% meat, of which 30% can be fat.

There are plenty of fast-food options. Among the local chains are Steers for burg-ers, Spur for steaks and salad bar, and the internationally known Nandos, which pur-veys spicy Portuguese-style chicken.

It's OK to drink the tap water. There are plenty of good local fruit juices, and in-ternational soft-drink brands are sold eve-rywhere. Note that cans of fizzy drink are called cool drinks.

Cape Malay Cuisine

Although some will undoubtedly find it overly stodgy and sweet, the unique Cape Malay cuisine (along with its close cousin Afrikaner cuisine) is well worth trying. This intriguing mix of Malay and Dutch styles origi-nated in the earliest days of European settlement and marries pungent spices with local produce.

The Cape Malay dish you'll come across most often is *bobotie*, a kind of shepherd's pie made with lightly cur-ried mince topped with savoury egg custard, and usually served on a bed of turmeric-flavoured rice with a side dab of chutney. There is a variety of *bredies* (pot stews of meat or fish, and vegetables); one unusual example is *waterblommetjie bredie*, a mutton dish with faintly pep-pery water-hyacinth flowers and white wine. Plenty of recipes make use of game; some include venison, which will be some type of buck.

Desserts are *malva* pudding, a delicious sponge tra-ditionally made with apricot jam and vinegar, and the very similar brandy pudding (note that true Cape Malay cuisine – which is strongly associated with the Muslim community – contains no alcohol). You might also want to try *koesisters*, a doughnut-like confection.

Among the places to sample this type of food are **Biesmiellah** (p87) and the **Noon Gun Tearoom & Restaurant** (p88) in Bo-Kaap; **Jonkerhuis** (p94) at Groot Constantia and **Jonkershuis Restaurant** (p38) at the Spier wine estate near Stellenbosch, which offers a fine Cape Malay buffet.

Top Five Cape Cookbooks

- *Leipoldt's Food & Wine*, C Louis Leipoldt (2003) – Although he died in 1947, doctor, botanist and man of letters C Louis Leipoldt is still remembered for his early contribution to the understanding of Cape cuisine. This anthology brings together a trio of his books: *Cape Cookery*, *Culinary Treasures* and *Three Hundred Years of Cape Wines*.
- *Cape Flavour – A Gastronomic Meander Through the Winelands*, Myrna Robins (2003) – Gorgeously photographed collection of the best restaurants, recipes and food sensations of the Cape Winelands, from Stellenbosch to Robertson.
- *The Savoy Cabbage Cookbook*, Janet Telian (2002) – The chef who made the **Savoy Cabbage** (p89) a famous eatery may have departed the restaurant but her culinary creations live on in this delectable book. Learn how to make mango and yoghurt soup with smoked mussels and papaw, and butternut and pistachio-stuffed cabbage.
- *The Africa Café Experience*, Portia de Smidt (2003) – A colourful and tempting book that documents the legend that is the **Africa Café** (p87). Recipes are gathered from all over the continent including *tà amiya* bean and herb patties from Egypt and chilli chicken wings as done in Mozambique.
- *Cape Town Food*, Phillippa Cheifitz (2002) – Award-winning cookery book that focuses on dishes made with local ingredients such as Cape Town's vast variety of seafood. Learn how to use *waterblommetjies* (indigenous water flowers) in a traditional slow-cooked lamb stew.

You should sample some of the excellent Cape wines while you're in town; see the Wine chapter (p33) for recommendations of specific wineries.

Draught beers are served in large (500mL) or small (250mL) glasses. Usually you will be sold lager-style beer in cans or *dumpies* (small bottles) for around R8. Black Label and Castle are popular brands but Amstel and Carlsberg are also good. Look out for Mitchell's and Birkenhead's beers, which come from a couple of small breweries. Windhoek beer, brewed in Namibia, is made with strictly natural ingredients. The alcohol content of beer is around 5%, stronger than UK or US beer. Even Castle Lite has 4% alcohol.

FASHION

Cape Town is beginning to make a name for itself with its fashions. The first Cape Town Fashion week in 2003 was a huge success and is being followed up by an even bigger show at the Cape Town International Convention Centre in 2004. Don't expect anything particularly original or even African influenced – the casual styles on offer take their inspiration from global street fashion trends and wouldn't look out of place on the streets of Sydney or San Francisco.

Designers of note include Geoff Hobbs and Erwin Overkamp, the guys behind the brand ICuba; Jenny Le Roux at Habits; and Kathy Page-Wood and Cheryl Arthur at Hip Hop. Creating the most heat is Maya Prass, a talented young designer known for her use of boldly feminine colours, textures and patterns in her clothes. Find them at **India Jane** (p130) among other places.

Greenmarket Square is a good place to hunt around for more African styles of clothing, such as the colourful, highly patterned 'Madiba' shirts popularised by Nelson Mandela. Here you'll also find the cheeky T-shirts of Justin Nurse's **Laugh It Off** (www.lio.co.za) company, which satirise the logos and catchphrases of global brands and multinationals. Also enquire at **Monkeybiz** (p128) about having items of clothing, such as denim jeans and jackets, custom beaded.

SPORT

Capetonians are just as mad about sport as other South Africans. In terms of drawing the crowds the biggest game in town is soccer. Cape Town has three teams in South Africa's national Premier Soccer League: Santos, the national champions in 2001/2002; Hellenic; and Ajax Cape Town. The first two teams' home base is at Athlone Stadium while Ajax, affiliated with the Dutch club Ajax Amsterdam, plays home games at Newlands Rugby Stadium. The national squad is known as 'Bafana Bafana' (literally 'Boys Boys', meaning 'Our Lads'). Professional games are played during the period from August to May with teams competing in the Premier Soccer League and the knockout Rothman's Cup.

The game of rugby (union, not league) is traditionally the Afrikaners' sport, although the 1995 World Cup, hosted and won by South Africa, saw the entire population go rugby mad. Cross-race support for the game has waned somewhat in the face of efforts to introduce greater balance in the ethnic composition of teams, and things haven't been helped by scandals involving allegations of racial intolerance between team members. The most popular games to watch are the Super 12 tournament, in which teams from South Africa, Australia and New Zealand compete from late February until the end of May. If you're in town when one of these is on it's worth getting a ticket, all games are held at the Newlands Rugby Stadium.

Cricket fans tend to be English-speaking South Africans, but for a period after South Africa's return to international sport in the 1992 World Cup, cricket occupied centre stage. The game was the first of the 'whites only' sports to wholeheartedly adopt a non-racial attitude, and development programmes in the townships are now beginning to pay dividends. The sport took a knocking in South Africa in 2000 when Hansie Cronje, the youngest captain in the nation's cricketing history, admitted taking bribes to rig matches. He was banned for life, but had public opinion softened when he died in a plane crash in 2003. In 2003 Cape Town hosted the Cricket World Cup.

The top national and international games are played at Newlands. Cape Town's second test ground opened in the township of Langa in 2000. Local cricketers to watch out for include Jacques Kallis and Mkya Ntini.

For details of all sporting stadiums and how to get tickets for matches see the listings on p123). The first horse races in Cape Town were held at Green Point in 1795. The sport took hold from then and today Cape Town has two courses, Kenilworth (see p123) with two tracks and Durbanville northeast of the city. Kenilworth is the location of South Africa's fanciest race-meeting, the J&B Met, usually held at the end of January.

MEDIA

Cape Town newspaper readers can pick up the *Cape Times* in the morning and the *Cape Argus* in the afternoon. Specialising in flashy headlines, usually highlighting a sports story or crime incident, they are both tabloids masquerading as broadsheets and print practically the same news – hardly surprising since both are in the stable of one of South Africa's largest media organisations, Independent News and Media.

The best weekly read, although it can at times take itself too seriously, is the *Mail & Guardian*. Its arts review supplement contains good listings and reviews of what's going on in Cape Town. The two Sunday newspapers, the *Sunday Times* (www.sundaytimes.co.za) and the *Independent on Sunday,* are also worth a look.

Local magazines include the bi-monthly *Cape Etc* arts and listings magazine and the *Big Issue,* a good read that helps provide an income for the homeless. For a satirical *Private Eye*–style look at South African politics and business dealings check out the monthly magazine *Nose Week* (www.noseweek.co.za). Published monthly, *Wine* (www.winemag.co.za) is a glossy magazine devoted to the local wine industry, and *Getaway* is a good travel-focused magazine with lots of features on African destinations.

Although not nearly so bland as during apartheid when blasphemy was assiduously edited out of imported programmes, South African television is still nothing to get excited about. The local commercial channel, e-tv, may set pulses racing with its soft-porn movies late on Saturday night, but you could still channel-surf yourself into a coma in a matter of minutes most other days – the breakfast advertorial and shopping shows are particularly awful. The national broadcaster SABC offers up three channels with precious little to choose between them other than the language content.

Zapiro

The cartoons of Capetonian Jonathan Shapiro, aka Zapiro, brighten up the pages of both the *Mail & Guardian* and the *Sunday Times*. He takes pointed and witty swipes at all political sides and current events in his work which has lampooned, among other things, the South African government's approach to the AIDS crisis and Cape Town losing its 2004 Olympic bid to Athens. Collections of his cartoons can be bought at all major Cape Town bookshops. You can also view them at the Web site of the *Sunday Times* on www.sundaytimes.co.za/zapiro.

Top Five Media Web sites

- **www.mg.co.za** – the *Mail & Guardian*'s site with a fee payable for premium content.
- **www.iol.co.za** – allows access to all of Independent News & Media's Web sites including those for the *Cape Times* and *Cape Argus* and the Tonight arts and culture listings.
- **www.noseweek.co.za** – catch up on the latest political and economic stories that other media are loath to print.
- **www.getawaytoafrica.com** – read some of Getaway magazine's content online, take part in competitions and search past issues.
- **www.eatout.co.za** – the annual *Eat Out* restaurant guide to South Africa, with a searchable database of reviewed Cape Town eateries.

LANGUAGE

In the Cape Town area three of South Africa's 11 official languages (all equal under the law) are prominent: Afrikaans (spoken by many whites and coloureds), English (spoken by nearly everyone) and Xhosa (spoken mainly by blacks).

As early as 1685 there are reports of a corrupted version of Dutch being spoken in the Cape in the area where Paarl is today. It was in Paarl, two hundred years later, that this new language, taking bits and pieces from German, French, Portuguese, Malay and indigenous African languages, was first codified with consistent spellings and uniform grammar (p155). In 1905 as the Second Language Movement got into its stride, Afrikaans was stripped of its coloured roots when Dutch words were substituted for those with an African or Asian origin. In the Cape though, where Afrikaans is the predominant language of the coloured community, a version called Cape Taal has persisted and developed along its own special lines.

The languages of the Cape's indigenous peoples, the San and Khoikhoi, have all but disappeared, like the races that once spoke them. The **South African Museum's** (p64) rock art gallery has some fascinating exhibition materials on these languages. Meanwhile, as ever more Xhosa speakers move to Cape Town, the language is increasingly noticeable and more people (ie whites and coloureds) are learning how to get their tongues around the various clicks that are part of Xhosa pronunciation. For more information on languages, see p179.

ECONOMY & COSTS

Western Cape accounts for about 15% of the country's total GDP, and many of South Africa's petroleum, insurance and retail corporations are based in Cape Town. Viticulture, clothing, textiles, agriculture and fishing are all important sectors of the local economy, as is tourism, increasingly. The opening of the Cape Town International Convention Centre has given a significant boost to this sector of the economy and several high-profile hotel developments are under way, including an ultra-luxury hotel complex at the Waterfront by entrepreneur Sol Kerzner of Sun City fame.

Cape Town's economy has been on something of a roll over the last few years, and is rapidly catching up with similar cities abroad. This in turn means that it's not quite the bargain that it used to be – especially as the rand strengthens in value. There have been accusations that Capetonian businesses have been overcharging, particularly at the high end of tourism where some hotel prices have shot up in excess of international levels. Finance Minister Trevor Manuel has complained publicly about one (unnamed)

How Much?

Copy of the *Cape Argus* R3.80

Cocktail at Eclipse, Camps Bay R20

Beer at a backpackers R8

Movie ticket R35

One hour's parking in the city centre R6

36-print camera film R30

Ticket to Robben Island R150

Litre of unleaded petrol R4.10

Monkeybiz doll R150-500

Entry to Rhodes House nightclub R50

Responsible Tourism

In a country so riven by economic inequality you might want to make an effort to spend your rands where they'll help most. For instance, take a township tour run by township people, not a big company; stay at one of the township B&Bs; buy your souvenirs from the people who make them, not a dealer; shop for fruit at road-side stalls rather than supermarkets. All such businesses need your support. For details of shops such as Monkeybiz, Streetwires and Wola Nani – all of which produce goods that help people in the townships – see the Shopping chapter, p125-32.

One very worthy project that you can get involved in is the **Tourism Community Development Trust** (www.tcdtrust.org.za). This was started in 1999 by the owners of the Backpack who wanted to help build a crèche in the Cape Flats' townships. This has been achieved and the trust has since grown and become a major organisation taking on other education projects, with board members from Ashanti Lodge and Daytrippers and Grassroutes tour companies. At either the Backpack or Ashanti you can leave your old clothes so they can be sold to raise money for the trust.

Remember to pay the guys who look after cars around town; in general, they're helping to make the streets safer for everyone. And don't forget to tip waiting and hotel staff and petrol pump attendants – they rely on this income to supplement their low wages (see p168).

South Africa's national parks and reserves are well managed but, in general, environmental laws are weak, and some activities permitted here wouldn't be allowed in other countries. Shark-diving, sand-surfing and 'adventure' 4WD tours, for example, can have a negative effect on the environment, so try to get a feel for operators' commitment to treading lightly on the earth before you make arrangements.

hotel charging R120 for a toasted sandwich. In reality, this type of pricing is quite rare, with the average mid-range hotel room going for R600 and the average light meal still less than R100. In some respects, Cape Town's prices are just catching up with those of equivalent cities in the world – what still makes the city decent value is the high quality of products and services you get for your cash.

GOVERNMENT & POLITICS

Cape Town is one of the three capitals of South Africa. Pretoria is the administrative capital, Bloemfontein is the judicial capital and Cape Town is the seat of the nation's parliament. There are two houses of parliament: the National Assembly with 400 members and the National Council of Provinces (NCOP) with 100 members.

The head of state is the president, currently Thabo Mbeki, leader of the ANC. The president is elected by the National Assembly (and thus is always the leader of the majority party) rather than directly by the people. A South African president has more in common with a Westminster-style prime minister than with a US president, although as head of state he or she does have some executive powers denied most other prime ministers.

Cape Town is also the capital of Western Cape province, which has its own legislature and premier – currently Marthinus van Schalkwyk of the New National Party (NNP), which shares power at the province's government with the ANC. It may seem astounding that one of the most liberal areas of South Africa should cast so many votes for the NNP – the successor to the party that created and enforced apartheid. However, those who identify themselves as coloured make up the largest voting group in Western Cape province. Coloureds are largely Afri-

New Constitution

South Africa's constitution is one of the most enlightened in the world – not surprising when you consider the people's long struggle for freedom. Apart from forbidding discrimination on practically any grounds, among other things it guarantees freedom of speech and religion, and access to adequate housing, adequate health care and basic adult education.

kaans-speaking and under apartheid they received slightly better treatment than blacks. It's believed many coloureds voted for parties other than the ANC out of fear of a black government. Many blacks resented the coloureds' favoured status and perceived them as uncommitted to the struggle against apartheid.

Patricia de Lille

Patricia de Lille is one of that rare breed of politician of whom it can be said that no matter what political party she would belong to, one cannot help liking and admiring her.

Nelson Mandela (in the foreword to Patricia de Lille: My Life *by Charlene Smith)*

The saintly Mandela aside, politicians are just as mistrusted and maligned a breed in South Africa as anywhere else in the world. One who gets more respect than raspberries is Patricia de Lille, a Capetonian coloured woman who created a new political party the Independent Democrats (www.id.org.za) in June 2003. De Lille became involved in politics in the 1980s when she was a trade union leader in the chemical industry. Moving into national politics she became a board member of the Pan-African Congress and was involved on their behalf in the constitutional negotiations that led up to the first democratic elections in 1994. While in parliament she has been a resolutely independent MP and has campaigned on issues including AIDS and prison reform – she famously met the killer of her sister in jail. She gained most respect for helping to uncover and bring to national attention corruption involving African National Congress (ANC) ministers and the arms industry. With the Independent Democrats she is aiming to offer a credible alternative to the ANC. Despite her personal popularity in the Cape, most political bystanders reckon she has a long way to go to gain a significant national standing, but as South African politicians go, De Lille is certainly shaping up as a presence to watch.

This hasn't stopped the ANC, ever the savvy political party, from teaming up with the NNP to run Western Cape province and the local Cape Town city council, where the executive mayor is the black female ANC politician Nomaindia Mfeketo.

ENVIRONMENT

THE LAND

Cape Town is at the northern end of a peninsula that juts into the Atlantic Ocean on the southwest tip of Southern Africa. The peninsula has a steep, high spine of mountains, beginning at Devil's Peak in Cape Town and running all the way down to Cape Point. Table Mountain, the most prominent feature of these mountains, is more than 1000m high, starting close to sea level. The escarpment running down the Atlantic (west) coast south of Table Mountain forms a striking series of buttresses known as the Twelve Apostles (although there are more than 12 of these formations).

The suburbs and towns on the Atlantic coast, and those on False Bay, west of Muizenberg, cling to a very narrow coastal strip. East of these mountains the land slopes more gently down to the Cape Flats, a sandy plain. Looking east across the Cape Flats you can see more mountain ranges rising up around Stellenbosch and, to the southeast, the Hottentots Holland area. There is no major river in the city area, although there is a system of estuarine lakes northeast of Muizenberg, near the Cape Flats.

Some 600 million years ago, all of what today is Cape Town lay beneath the sea. Volcanic activity pushed the land briefly out of the ocean but it wasn't until roughly 400 million years later that another series of cataclysmic earth movements would force the land back up again for good. The continent of Africa began to form around 125 million years ago, and the plateau around Cape Town gradually eroded to leave behind Table Mountain.

All this geological activity has left the Cape Peninsula with three main types of rock. The lower reaches of the mountains are made up of Malmesbury shale, a soft, finely textured rock that is easily weathered. Under the shale, and sticking out in places such as Simon's Town and along the Atlantic coast, is granite. The mountains themselves are Table Mountain sandstone, which is a combination of sandstone and quartzite that starts off grey and weathers to red-brown. The sandy deposits that make up the Cape Flats are a comparatively recent addition.

Best Five Green Spaces in Cape Town

- Company's Gardens (p61)
- Kirstenbosch Botanical Gardens (p72)
- Rondevlei Nature Reserve (p74)
- Table Mountain National Park (p64)
- Tokai Arboretum (p73)

Cape Floral Kingdom

Cape Town and Western Cape are home to the fascinating Cape floral kingdom, the richest and smallest of the world's six floral kingdoms, with nearly 8500 plant species – more than three times as many per square kilometre as in the whole of South America! Table Mountain and the peninsula alone contain 2285 plant species, more than all of Britain. In part this is a result of ecological isolation, as South Africa's mountain ranges harbour mini-universes of biodiversity. At least as impressive as the number of species is their colour; the profusion of hues could drive a would-be post-impressionist back to the banks of the Seine.

The most common type of vegetation is *fynbos* (literally 'fine bush', from the Dutch). *Fynbos* somehow thrives in the area's nitrogen-poor soil – it's supposed that the plants' fine, leathery leaves improve their odds of survival by discouraging predators. *Fynbos* is composed of three main elements: proteas (South Africa's national emblem), heaths and reeds. On Signal Hill and the lower slopes of Devil's Peak you'll find *renosterbos* (literally 'rhinoceros bush'), a vegetation type that is composed predominantly of a grey ericoid shrub, and peppered with grasses and rich in geophytes (plants that grow from underground bulbs). In the cool, well-watered ravines on the eastern slopes of Table Mountain you'll also find small pockets of Afro-montane forest and thicket.

GREEN CAPE TOWN

So special is the environment of the Cape Peninsula that the whole area has been nominated for UN World Heritage status. Yet four centuries on from European settlement it is also an environment that has been radically and often detrimentally changed, with the indigenous flora and fauna now surviving mainly in reserves and on agriculturally unviable land.

Dense evergreen forests that were once home to large mammals have long since vanished. Forests of non-indigenous trees such as oak, pine and eucalypt have been planted in their place. In the Cape's kind climate these aliens have thrived, but have also wreaked havoc on the environment. For example, the wind-sculpted pines that coat the lower slopes of Table Mountain are draining the Cape of its precious water supplies; the whole peninsula regularly suffers water shortages. Their presence also contributes to the devastating forest fires that regularly sweep across the mountain.

The Cape's unique *fynbos* (see boxed text above) is also under attack from water-hungry alien flora, which include black wattle (*Acacia mearnsii*) and Port Jackson wattle (*Acacia saligna*). Sydney golden wattle (*Acacia longifolia*), introduced to the Cape early last century, has also become a pest. Probably the worst offender is *Hakea sericea* (known locally as silky hakea), imported as a hedge plant in the 1830s and now declared a noxious weed in South Africa. In 1997 an alien-clearance programme was started within and around what has now become the Table Mountain National Park. It is the largest programme of its type and has shown positive results so far.

In the huge townships and squatter camps on the Cape Flats, Third-World economic imperatives result in poor environmental standards. The most obvious sign is the smoke that sometimes drifts around the mountain and

Protea brenda (see p72)

over the city, building up into quite heavy pollution after a few windless days. Luckily for those on the city side of the mountain, successive windless days are uncommon. The airport is close to the townships and planes sometimes have to make instrument landings because of the smoke.

Most of the smoke is from fires used for cooking and heating (people trudging back to the townships carrying loads of wood is a common sight on the roads east of the city) but some is from burning tyres. A few scraps of metal can be gleaned from a tyre and then sold.

Pollution is also a threat to the marine environment, as demonstrated by an oil spill in Table Bay in June 2000, the worst ever suffered along the notoriously treacherous Cape coast. Over 40% of the African penguin population on Robben and Dassen Islands were threatened, causing conservation bodies, the local authorities and even the army to mount the world's biggest rescue operation of its kind to save 21,000 oiled birds.

There are good things being done to help Cape Town's environment. The City of Cape Town is the first local authority in the country to adopt an integrated metropolitan environmental policy. The first three strategies will deal with coastal zone, biodiversity and environmental education and training. The **Oasis Centre** (www.oasisrecycling.org.za/backgroundhome.htm) runs a recycling depot and encourages recycling across the Cape, cleaning up after big events such as the J&B Met and the Two Oceans Marathon. The **Fairest Cape Association** (☎ 462 2040) runs the 'Keep the Cape in Shape' campaign, which gets clean-ups going and educates communities about how best to deal with waste. In supermarkets customers have to pay for plastic bags which encourages people to reuse them or bring their own shopping bags.

URBAN PLANNING & DEVELOPMENT

To a large extent Cape Town is shackled with the legacy of apartheid's notion of 'urban planning' – designated areas for blacks, whites and coloureds. These, of course, no longer exist, but the infrastructure – or lack of it – that goes with them cannot be changed overnight, as the millions who live in the benighted Cape Flats know only too well. A large share of the City of Cape Town's resources goes into improving the lot of townships such as Khayelitsha and Crossroads with new homes and community facilities, but the council is also aware that it needs to keep its eye on the money-generating city centre and Atlantic coast area, too.

Wanting to avoid the devastating white flight to the suburbs experienced in Jo'burg, it is now working to secure the future development of the city centre through the Cape Town Partnership, an initiative between business and local government. Since 1999, this body has had a huge success in improving security and cleanliness in the City Bowl area. It has been instrumental in setting up City Improvement Districts across the central suburbs and is now beginning to focus on the bigger picture. Its aim is to make the City Bowl more pedestrian friendly, get more people living in the city centre (hence all those loft apartment developments in old city buildings and warehouses) and to introduce social programmes that deal with the problem of street kids. It's quite likely the city will be working with Jan Gehl, a Danish architect, whose past projects include city centre improvements in Copenhagen, Melbourne and Adelaide.

The rebuilding of homes on the long-vacant land of District Six (p44) is certainly a step in the right direction, as is the improved use of land along the Foreshore where the Cape Town International Convention Centre and new residences between the city and the Waterfront now stand. For more information about modern Cape Town architecture see p23.

Capetonian Fauna

The closest you'll get to an elephant in Cape Town these days is by spotting its nearest living relative, the ubiquitous dassie, also known as the rock hyrax, on Table Mountain. Apart from the cuddly little dassies, Table Mountain is home to 111 invertebrates and one vertebrate (the Table Mountain ghost frog) not found anywhere else on Earth. The birdlife is particularly impressive.

Among the feral population of introduced fallow deer that roam the lower slopes of Table Mountain around the Rhodes Memorial, you may spot an animal long regarded as extinct: the quagga. This partially striped zebra was formerly thought to be a distinct species, but DNA obtained from a stuffed quagga in Cape Town's South African Museum showed it to be a subspecies of the widespread Burchell's zebra. A breeding programme, started in 1987, has proved successful in 'resurrecting' the quagga.

Mammals in the Cape of Good Hope section of the national park include eight antelope species, Cape mountain zebras and a troupe of Chacma baboons. Many signs warn you not to feed the baboons (and you shouldn't – they're potentially dangerous). At Rondevlei Nature Reserve, hippos have been reintroduced.

Both the southern right whale and the humpback whale breed in False Bay and along the southern coast (p159). Dolphins can also be spotted in False Bay, while Cape fur seals entertain visitors at the Waterfront and can be seen in a more natural environment at Duiker Island, which can be reached from Hout Bay.

Arts &
Architecture

Arts & Architecture

From the 17th-century Castle of Good Hope to the late-20th-century redevelopment of the Victoria & Alfred Waterfront, Cape Town's wealth of interesting architecture is one of its most attractive features. Although the city has been extensively developed, much that might have been destroyed has been preserved, and a walking tour of Cape Town's City Bowl (p82) is a great way to get a feel for the history of the city. At the same time you'll gain an insight into the city's vibrant visual arts scene, from kaleidoscopic and inventive crafts to arty, challenging photography and sculptures.

Music is part of the lifeblood of the Mother City, which has a particularly strong reputation for jazz. The performing arts scene is also relatively healthy, with comedy and small fringe productions offering up the best dividends. If there's one area of the arts that's not as well as endowed, it is literature – despite the plethora of bookshops, Capetonians are by and large not huge readers. Still, there are a handful of volumes that shed light into the dark, hidden corners of the city's soul.

ARCHITECTURE

DUTCH COLONIAL

When the Dutch colonists arrived in 1652 they brought their European ideas of architecture with them, but they also had to adapt to the local conditions and materials. There was plenty of rugged stone on hand from Table Mountain to build the **Castle of Good Hope** (p60) between 1666 and 1679.

Although the castle is frequently cited as South Africa's oldest surviving colonial structure, Jan van Riebeeck's vegetable garden, forerunner of the **Company's Gardens** (p61), actually predates it by 14 years. And the first incarnation of the **Slave Lodge** (p63) at the gardens' northern end was built in 1660 as a single-storey building to house up to 500 wretched souls. (It was substantially changed under later British administrations.)

To begin with, houses were utilitarian structures, such as the thatched and white-washed Posthuys in Muizenberg, dating from 1673. This simple rustic style of building is one that you'll still find today along the Western Cape coast, particularly in fishing villages such as Paternoster (p163).

> ### Architecture Books
>
> - *Cape Dutch Houses & Other Old Favourites*, Phillida Brooke Simons – good photographs and lively text enhance this fine review of the Cape's most elegant old homes.
> - *Shack Chic*, photography by Craig Fraser – all the vibrant colours and inventive design of township architecture is displayed in this coffee-table book.

Thanks to Britain's wars with France, the British turned to the Cape for wine, so the Dutch colonists prospered and, during the 18th and 19th centuries, were able to build many of the impressive estates that can be seen today. Governor Simon van der Stel built his quintessential manor house, Groot Constantia, in 1692, thus establishing the prototype for other glorious estates to follow in the Winelands further inland, such as **Vergelegen** (p39) and **Boschendal** (p39).

Bordering the Company's Gardens is the lovely Tuynhuis dating from 1700; you can see the monogram of the Dutch East India Company (Vereenigde Oost-Indische Compagnie, or VOC) on the building's pediment. Now the official residence of the republic's president (thus off limits to visitors), the building was altered during the British administration of the 19th century.

On Strand St, the fancy façade of the late-18th-century **Koopmans-de Wet House** (p61) is attributed to Louis Thibault, who, as the VOC's lieutenant of engineers, was responsible

Design of the Cape Dutch Manor

The main features of a Cape Dutch manor are the stoep (a raised platform, the equivalent of a veranda) with seats at each end, the large central hall running the length of the house, and the main rooms symmetrically arranged on either side of the hall. Above the front entrance is the gable, the most obvious feature, and there are usually less elaborate gables at each end. The house is covered by a steep thatched roof and is invariably painted white.

The front gable, which extends above the roof line and almost always contains a dormer window, shows the influence of 18th-century Dutch styles. The large ground-floor windows have solid shutters. The graceful plaster scrolls of the gable are sometimes reflected in the curved moulding above the front door (above which is a fanlight, sometimes with elaborate woodwork). Sometimes the doorway shows neoclassical features such as Doric pilasters or a simple pediment.

Inside, the rooms are large and simply decorated. The main hall is often divided by a louvred wooden screen, which is thought to have derived from similar screens the Dutch would have seen in the East Indies. Above the ceilings many houses had a *brandsolder*, a layer of clay or brick to protect the house if the thatching caught fire. The roof space was used for storage, if at all.

for the design of most of Cape Town's public buildings in this period. Thibault also had a hand in the handsome **Rust en Vreugd** (p62) which dates from 1778, famous for its delicately carved rococo fanlight above the main door and its double balconies and portico.

Of course, not everyone lived in such a grand manner. In the city centre, the best place to get an idea of what Cape Town looked like during the 18th century to ordinary folk is to take a stroll through the Bo-Kaap (p60). You'll notice flat roofs instead of gables, and a lack of shutters on the windows. These features are the result of building regulations instituted by the VOC in the wake of fires that swept the city.

BRITISH COLONIAL

The Dutch ran a tight and orderly ship in Cape Town, but when the British took over in the early 19th century, they had their own ways of doing things and this extended to the architectural look of the city. British governor Lord Charles Somerset made the

Castle of Good Hope, pentagonal fort built 1666–79 (p60)

biggest impact during his 1814–26 tenure. It was he who ordered the restyling of the Tuynhuis to bring it into line with Regency tastes for verandas and front gardens.

Built in about 1840, the two-storey brick **Bertram House** (p63), at the southern end of Government Ave, is an example of late Georgian style.

As the British Empire reached its zenith in the late 19th century, Cape Town boomed and a whole slew of monumental buildings was erected. Walk down Adderley St and through the Company's Gardens and you'll pass the 1880 Standard Bank with its pediment, dome and soaring columns; the 1884 **Houses of Parliament** (p61), outside which stands a marble statue (1890) of Queen Victoria; and the Byzantine-influenced **Old Synagogue** (p64) dating from 1862 (the neighbouring and much more baroque Great Synagogue with its twin towers dates from 1905).

Long St is where you can see Victorian Cape Town at its most appealing, with the wrought-iron balconies and varying façades of shops and buildings such as the **Long St Baths** (p62). In the adjacent suburbs of Tamboerskloof and Oranjezicht many mansions of that era still survive.

Sir Herbert Baker

Born in Kent, England in 1862, Herbert Baker arrived in South Africa in 1891. Through his cousin, a Royal Navy admiral based in Cape Town, he was introduced to the colony's richest and most powerful man, Cecil John Rhodes. A carefully cultivated relationship with Rhodes was to be a prevailing influence on Baker's life.

Apart from his work on various houses and monuments belonging to or related to Rhodes, Baker is also responsible for the design of St George's Cathedral in Cape Town as well as many other impressive civic and private buildings around the country. Among his most famous constructions are the imposing Union Buildings in Pretoria.

Baker left for India in 1913, eventually returning to England where he worked on South Africa House in London's Trafalgar Square. He died in 1946 and was buried at Westminster Cathedral.

Cecil John Rhodes, prime minister of the Cape Colony from 1890 to 1896, commissioned a young English architect, Sir Herbert Baker, to redesign his home, **Groote Schuur** (p70), in Rondebosch in 1898, thus kicking off the style known as Cape Dutch Revival. Another famous Baker building is **Rust-en-Vrede** (p75) by the sea at Muizenberg, also commissioned by Rhodes but completed in 1902 just after the statesman died at the neighbouring cottage.

As the Victorian era came to a close, Cape Town's grandest public building, the Old Town Hall, rose on the southwest side of Grand Parade in 1905; it was from the balcony here that Nelson Mandela made his first public address as a free man in 1990.

EARLY TWENTIETH CENTURY

Edwardian Cape Town is best represented by the **Centre for the Book** (Map pp200–2), which opened in 1913 as the headquarters of the now-defunct University of Good Hope. More recently it has become an annexe of the National Library of South Africa, and gained some notoriety as the venue for the inquiry into cricket match fixing in 2000.

A second building boom in the 1920s and '30s led to the construction of many fine examples of Art Deco architecture, which can be seen in the city centre. Prime examples include the buildings around Greenmarket Square and the handsome 1940 **Mutual Building** (Map pp200–2), the continent's first skyscraper, decorated with friezes and frescoes, all with South African themes. To get acquainted with the best of Cape Town's Art Deco architecture follow the walk on p80.

Clock tower, Victoria & Alfred Waterfront (p67–8)

Meanwhile, the economic boom that was causing the city centre buildings to sprout up was also stoking demand for cheap coloured and black labour. These people needed somewhere to live and the solution was found out on the bleak Cape Flats. Langa, meaning 'sun', was established in 1927 and is South Africa's oldest planned township. As in all townships, the roads are wide and in excellent condition, thus allowing for quick access for the authorities should there be trouble. The type of dormitory accommodation that would become common for migrant labourers was first built here.

Under the pass laws (which stated that those who didn't have a job outside the Homelands were not allowed to leave), such hostels were for men only. They lived in basic units, each accommodating 16 men, who shared one shower, one toilet and one small kitchen. Tiny bedrooms housed up to three men each. After the pass laws were abolished, most men brought their families to live with them. So each unit became home to up to 16 families, each room sleeping up to three families. It's no wonder that people moved out and built shacks.

MODERN

Due to the economic recession brought on by sanctions, there was little architectural development in Cape Town during the apartheid era. Examples of rationalist architecture include Artscape and the adjoining Civic Centre on the foreshore (see p27), which demonstrate the obsession with concrete that was typical of international modernism (we would call it concrete brutalism at its worst). The best building to come out of this era is the **Baxter Theatre** (p106) in Rondebosch. Designed by Jack Barnett, its flat roof is famously dimpled with orange fibreglass downlights which glow fabulously at night.

The less said about the total lack of planning or official architectural concern for the townships the better, although it is worth mentioning the tremendous ingenuity and resilience that residents show in creating livable homes from scrap. A visit to the townships today reveals colourfully painted shacks and murals, homes and churches made from shipping crates, and more recent imaginative structures such as the **Guga S'Thebe Arts & Cultural Centre** (p78) in Langa.

For the vast majority of visitors, contemporary Capetonian architecture is summed up in the redevelopment of the **Victoria & Alfred Waterfront** (p67), which has recently been graced by the Nelson Mandela Gateway and Clock Tower Precinct, built in 2001 as the new departure point for Robben Island. The **Cape Town International Convention Centre** (p60), with its ship-like prow and sleek glass-and-steel hotel, is another new building drawing favourable nods and helping push the City Bowl back towards the waterfront from which it has been cut off for decades.

Architectural Bouquets & Blunders

The Best

- **Baxter Theatre** (p106) – one of the best pieces of architecture to come out of the 1970s.
- **Groote Schuur** (p70) – the Cape-Dutch revival started here with the work of Sir Herbert Baker.
- **Guga S'Thebe Arts & Cultural Centre** (p78) – colourful and creative example of the best of township architecture.
- **Mutual Building** (Map pp200–2) – now luxury apartments, this old insurance company building is an Art Deco treasure.
- **Rust en Vreugd** (p62) – the finest surviving example of an 18th-century Cape Dutch Townhouse.

The Rest

- **Civic Centre** (Map pp200–2) – ugly bulky building that is so badly located that the road running under it has been known to turn into a savage wind tunnel able to flip cars over.
- **Unfinished Highway** (Map pp203–5) – beloved by action movie directors as a ready-made set, this is one less highway to cut off downtown Cape Town from the sea.
- **Disa Park** (Map pp198–9) – known as the Tampon Towers, these three cylindrical towers mar the view to Devil's Peak from the city.
- **Good Hope Centre** (Map pp200–2) – now that the Cape Town International Convention Centre has arrived, perhaps this hideous concrete tent-like structure can be pensioned off?

ARTS

LITERATURE

Apart from fellow Capetonian JM Coetzee (p28), the contemporary fiction writer most associated with the Mother City is André Brink. Coetzee, the foremost literary opponent of apartheid, depicts the end of that appalling era in *Age of Iron*, which is about the lives of the homeless, known as Bergies in Capetonian vernacular. Also worth reading are Brink's *A Chain of Voices*, about slavery in the 18th-century Cape and *The Rites of Desire* set in modern-day Cape Town.

Cape Town's Man of Letters

For a man who carefully shuns the media spotlight, JM Coetzee has an uncanny knack of drawing attention to himself. First he won the coveted Booker Prize, not once but twice, with *The Life and Times of Michael K* in 1983 and *Disgrace* in 1999. Then he was awarded the Nobel Prize for Literature in 2003, with the Swedish Academy hailing him for being a 'scrupulous doubter, ruthless in his criticism of the cruel rationalism and cosmetic morality of Western Civilisation'.

For some clues into what informed this world view you could start by reading JM's childhood memoir *Boyhood*. Born in Cape Town in 1940, Coetzee (the J and M stand for John Maxwell) studied at Cape Town University and began writing fiction in the early 1970s while he was teaching in the US. He now lives in Adelaide, Australia, but Cape Town still makes brief appearances as a backdrop in novels such as *Disgrace* and *Youth*.

The books of Alex la Guma, a coloured writer who died in exile in 1985, are worth reading; they include *A Walk in the Night*, a collection of short stories set in District Six. Sindiwe Magona is a black female writer whose *Mother to Mother* is a fictionalised account of the correspondence between the mother of Amy Biehl, a white American woman murdered in the Cape Flats in 1993, and the mother of her killer.

Occupying the region between travel literature and an objective review of the issues facing contemporary Cape Town is Mike Nichol's *Sea-Mountain, Fire-City*. It's an especially good read if you want to get the measure of white paranoia post apartheid and the vicissitudes of building a house. In *The Promised Land*, British rave-generation journo Decca Aitkenhead comes to Cape Town in search of the perfect E (ecstasy tablet) but instead finds a city in the grip of vicious gang warfare.

Many travel writers have been drawn to Cape Town as a starting or finishing point on their tours of South Africa, or, as in the case of Peter Moore in *Swahili For the Broken-Hearted* and Paul Theroux in *Dark Star Safari*, an epic journey across the continent itself. The city itself tends to come off favourably but, along with Dervla Murphy in *South From The Limpopo* and Gavin Bell in *Somewhere Over the Rainbow*, both Theroux and Moore are keen to beat a path to Khayelitsha to observe the grim challenges of township life close up.

Top Five Novels Based in Cape Town

- *Sachs Street*, Rayda Jacobs (2001) – Jacobs, winner of the Herman Charles Bosman Prize in 1997, turns her talents to a tale from the Bo-Kaap about a young girl growing up in Cape Town in the 1950s, listening to stories from her grandmother.
- *A Time of Angels*, Patricia Schonstein (2003) – magical realism comes to Cape Town in the form of this tender and witty tale about a Jewish clairvoyant who reads people's futures on Long St. It also boldly tackles bigger themes including the Holocaust, love and betrayal.
- *'Buckingham Palace', District Six*, Richard Rive (1986) – Rive died in 1989 but his book remains a testament to those like him who lived in the central Cape Town area known as District Six. His stories about the inhabitants of five houses in the heart of the area are thought-provoking and highly readable.
- *You Can't Get Lost In Cape Town*, Zoë Wicomb (2000) – coming-of-age story that paints a complex and evocative picture about the experience of the coloured community in Cape Town during the apartheid era.
- *The Reluctant Passenger*, Michael Heyns (2003) – lively satire penned by a Stellenbosch English professor about a mad plan to develop Cape Point and the efforts of the protagonist to save the baboons (leading to a scene where the baboons run wild in Cavendish Square!).

VISUAL ARTS

A wander around any of Cape Town's major public and private galleries (p29) demonstrates that the contemporary art scene is tremendously exciting and imaginative. There are also many examples of public art including murals, monuments and memorials. It's amazing how many of the old statues and icons of the apartheid era remain, testament to the tolerance of the black majority. Contrast these with the bright murals of the townships or Brett Murray's amusing *Africa* sculpture in St George's Mall (p29).

Another irreverent white artist to watch is Conrad Botes, who has collaborated with Murray on designing the Boogie Lights series. Botes came to notice with the strange and weird cult comic *Bitterkomix*, founded along with Anton Kannemeyer. His colourful images, both beautiful and horrific, displayed in 2003 in a New York exhibition, can be seen at **Photographers Gallery** (p129).

Other local artists to look out for include Sanell Aggenbach, winner of the ABSA Atelier Award in 2003, Willie Bester whose mixed media creations of township life are very powerful, and the more conventional John Krammer who captures the ordinary, serene quality of the South African landscape. The Web site www.artthrob.co.za is a good place to find out about the best in South African contemporary art

Going back a bit further, some people come to Cape Town in search of works by the world-famous, Russian-born artist Vladimir Tretchikoff, who still lives (in ill health) in the leafy suburb of Bishopscourt.

Arts & Architecture – Arts

Top Five Galleries

- **AVA Gallery** (p127)
- **Irma Stern Museum** (p71)
- **Michael Stevenson Contemporary** (p130)
- **Photographers Gallery** (p129)
- **SA National Gallery** (p64)

His signature images – portraits of amazing blue-faced Eurasian and African beauties – have become icons of the kitsch lounge music generation. You won't find any of the originals in the main Cape Town galleries, but check into the **Head South Lodge** (p141) and you'll find a fantastic collection of his prints, which are increasingly rare.

South Africa's oldest art is undoubtedly that of the San, who left their mark on the landscape in the form of rock paintings and subtle rock engravings. Despite having been faded by aeons of exposure, these works of art are remarkable; a fantastic example is the Linton Panel in the **South African Museum** (p64). Today, San motifs are commonly employed on tourist art such as decorative mats and carved ostrich eggs.

The art of the Bantu-speaking peoples is similar to that of the San as a result of their long history of cultural interaction. Their traditional nomadic lifestyle led to their artefacts being portable and generally utilitarian (p30). Headrests, spoons and bead-work are not created as mere commodities: they are individual statements of self and have always entailed long hours of careful labour.

Brett Murray

When Brett Murray's iconoclastic statue *Africa* was placed in St George's Mall, Cape Town was fairly split between those who thought it fantastic and those who wondered what the hell it was. The giant African fetish object with a rash of Bart Simpson heads popping out of it still turns heads today, and the artist's work has become so popular and prevalent around the city that it's almost as if Cape Town has caught the Brett Murray bug.

Born in Pretoria, but trained at the University of Cape Town, Murray's best known works are his 'Boogie Lights' series which can be bought at various shops around the city (p127). His designs capture the beauty and weirdness of living on the southern tip of Africa, and his love/hate relationship with US cultural imperialism.

There are also pieces by Murray in the **SA National Gallery** (p64) but to date his most significant work is the 6.5-tonne artwork *Baobabs, Stormclouds, Animals and People* that hangs in the **Cape Town International Convention Centre** (p60). This collaboration with the late San artist Tuoi Steffaans Samcuia, of the !Xun and Khwe San Art and Cultural Project, is astonishing in its scale and design – huge steel figures, animals and trees standing out against the maple wall panels. It's the highlight of the Convention Centre.

South African Crafts

For decades, African art was dismissed by European colonisers as 'mere craft', as distinct from 'art'. Be prepared to surrender this artificial Western distinction as you root around the craft shops and markets of Cape Town. The following are a few things to look out for:

Pottery

The master potters of the Venda people, who live in the northeastern corner of Northern Province, are all women. Their hand-fashioned pots come in 10 different sizes and designs. Each one has a different function: cooking, serving food or liquids, or storage. The pots feature brightly coloured geometric designs and are more ornamental than functional.

Bead-work

Zulu bead-work is now mainly used for decoration, and sometimes in traditional ceremonies. It takes many forms, from the small, square *umgexo*, which is widely available and makes a good gift, to the more elaborate *umbelenja*, a short skirt or tasselled belt worn by girls from puberty until they are married. *Amadavathi* (bead anklets) are worn by men and women.

Beads are also traditionally used as a means of communication, especially as love letters. Messages are 'spelled out' by the colour and arrangement of the beads. For example, red symbolises passion or anger; black, difficulties or night; blue, yearning; white or pale blue, pure love; brown, disgust or despondency; and green, peace or bliss.

A modern interpretation of this style of bead-work is that produced by **Monkeybiz** (p128).

Basketwork

Zulu hand-woven baskets, although created in a variety of styles and colours, almost always have a function. The raw materials vary depending on seasonal availability – a basket could be woven from various grasses, palm fronds, bark, even telephone wire.

Two decorative basket patterns predominate: the triangle, which denotes the male, and the diamond, which denotes the female. A design on the basket of two triangular shapes above one another in an hourglass form indicate that the male owner of the basket is married; similarly, two diamonds so arranged mean the female owner of the basket is married.

Township Crafts

New and imaginative crafts have sprung up in the townships, borrowing from old traditions but using materials that are readily available. For example, old soft-drink cans and food tins are used to make hats, picture frames and toy cars and planes, while wire and metal bottle tops are used for bags and vases. Complex wirework sculptures and mixed-media paintings and collages are common. Printing and rug-making are also taking off.

Woodwork

Venda woodcarvings are also popular. Traditionally, woodcarving was a men-only occupation, but these days expert female woodcarvers can be found. A number of local woods are used, including *mudzwin*, *mutango* and *musimbiri*. Carved items include bowls, spoons, trays, pots, walking sticks, chains attached to calabashes, and knobkerries (sticks with a round knob at one end, used as clubs or missiles).

PERFORMING ARTS

Fame at the Cape Town International Convention Centre; *African Footsteps* and *Phantom of the Opera* at Artscape; *The Rocky Horror Picture Show* at the Spier Summer Arts Season – it's easy to think the performing arts scene in Cape Town is beginning to resemble that of any other major world city. In an environment where government subsidy for European cultural expressions has dried up, it's no wonder that tried-and-tested shows are the order of the day.

Despite this, Capetonians are proving adept at creating both their own crowd-pleasing plays and musicals as well as more challenging productions that reflect South Africa as it is today. *Enfant terrible* Brett Bailey's theatre company Third World Bunfight is certainly one troupe to watch. He specialises in using black actors to tell uniquely African stories in

Cape Town in the Movies

You'll search in vain at Cape Town's multiplexes for locally made movies. So what are all those film makers doing every time you turn a corner in Cape Town? Well, most of them are making commercials, and most of those are for overseas clients – they like Cape Town's bright weather, its picturesque and quirky locations, and most of all its high-quality labour and low costs.

This said there have been some excellent recent movies that have been set in Cape Town or feature local identities. The American documentary *Long Night's Journey into Day* was nominated for a best documentary prize at the 2001 Oscars. This very moving Sundance Film Festival winner follows four cases from the Truth & Reconciliation Commission hearings, including that of Amy Biehl, the white American murdered in the Cape Flats in 1993.

Scooping up the prizes at the Sundance festival in 2002 was the documentary feature *Amandla*, a South African–US co-production about the role of protest songs in the country's struggle to rid itself of apartheid. Among the many star South African performers testifying in the film is Cape Town's world famous jazz pianist Abdullah Ibrahim, who coins the immortal phrase that South Africa is the only country in the world to have undergone 'a revolution in four part harmony'.

productions such as *Mumbo Jumbo*, which explores the interaction between the realms of theatre and ritual. The production, which has also been performed at London's Barbican Theatre, hit the front pages of the South African newspapers in a storm of controversy when the cast sacrificed a real chicken at its season finale in Cape Town.

Of the three musicals that David Kramer and Taliep Peterson have worked on together, the biggest hit has been their jazz homage *Kat & the Kings*, which swept up awards in London in 1999 and received standing ovations on Broadway. Other local successes include *Meet Joe Barber*, a comedy by Oscar Petersen and David Issacs, and Petersen's *Suip!*, a play about the homeless which has had outings in Australia and London. Pieter-Dirk Uys (p107) continues to get audiences at home and abroad laughing and thinking with his cabaret shows based on the tough topics of apartheid and AIDS.

MUSIC

Cape Town is one of the world's jazz capitals and is home to some internationally known musicians, including the elder statesmen of the scene – Abdullah Ibrahim (also once known as Dollar Brand, see p105), Robbie Jansen, and Winston 'Ngozi' Mankunku. All these musicians occasionally play in town (your best chance of catching them will be at a jazz festival such as the Jazzathon at the Waterfront in January or the North Sea Jazz Festival in March, see p10). Other respected locals artists to watch out for include the guitarist Jimmy Dludlu, pianist Paul Hanmer and singer Judith Spehuma.

Techno, trance and jungle have all found their way from the mixing boards of London to Cape Town dance clubs. Here you can also tune in to kwaito, the local dance-music sensation that's a mix of mbaqanga jive, hip-hop, house and ragga. The music of the late local singing superstar Brenda Fassie, who died in May this year, had a strong *kwaito* flavour. Hip-hop is also big; Moodphase 5ive is one of the better groups around that mixes hip-hop with soul.

Plush at Jo'burg bar (p99)

Top Five Cape Town Soundtracks

- *Jika Jika, Freshly Ground* – the cool multi-racial funk, folk, pop combo has produced a sublime album that is guaranteed to get you dancing.
- *A Moment in Cape Town* – live modern jazz album recorded at the local Beach Rd studios and featuring Robbie Jansen and Mac McKenzie.
- *Luxury, Robin Auld* – recorded at his Kommetjie studios, Auld's latest offering is a shining example of African acoustic rock and pop.
- *Cape Town 2am* – Café del Mar–style chill-out album, the perfect mood music for sundowners on Clifton beach.
- *Kat and the Kings*, David Kramer & Taliep Peterson – soundtrack album to the award-winning show that began in Cape Town and went on to take London's West End by storm.

On the rock and pop scene Cape Town has also produced some notable acts – look out for concerts by Fetish, Valiant Swart and the Blues Broers (pronounced brews – it's slang for brother), an immensely popular five-piece Afrikaner blues band. Hot rock bands include Sugar Drive and Boo!

Singer-songwriters include the immensely talented Robin Auld, one-time championship surfer, now doing his best to become the Mother City's Elvis Costello with an African lilt. Before he hit the international big time with his musical *Kat and the Kings* (p31) David Kramer was already hugely popular as the journeyman guitarist who sang in Afrikaans about and for all the people of South Africa.

Wine

Wine

South Africa is the eighth largest wine producer in the world. The industry began in Cape Town more than 340 years ago and, today, within a day's drive of the city you can visit more than 200 wineries. The bulk of these are found around Stellenbosch (see p148), but there are also several within Cape Town's boundaries at Constantia (see p36).

Several wineries are capitalising on the industry's popularity by adding restaurants, accommodation and other attractions. We've reviewed some of the more notable of these in this section, along with vineyards that are renowned for their fine wines. With so many nice wines to sample it's understandable that you might not want to drive yourself around all these wineries. To the rescue come several tour companies which run from Cape Town and Stellenbosch; we list some options on p58 and p150.

If you're looking to take your knowledge of the local wines further than amateur sampling, you can take one of the wine-appreciation courses run by the **Cape Wine Academy** (☎ 809 7597; www.capewineacademy.co.za). You'll need about six weeks to complete a course. The headquarters are in Stellenbosch, but it also occasionally runs courses in Cape Town. the **Nose Wine Bar** (see p100), in Cape Town, also offers a six-week course for R250.

The annual *John Platter's South African Wine Guide* (www.platterwineguide.com) is *the* book to consult if you want full tasting notes on the thousands of different local wines. If you don't have time to get out to the wineries, there are several wine shops in Cape Town with excellent selections (see p130).

HISTORY

'TODAY, PRAISE BE THE LORD, WINE WAS PRESSED FOR THE FIRST TIME FROM CAPE GRAPES.'

Jan van Riebeeck, 2 February 1659

Although the founder of the Cape Colony, Jan van Riebeeck, planted vines and made wine himself, it was not until the arrival of Governor Simon van der Stel in 1679 that wine-making began in earnest. Van der Stel created Groot Constantia, the superb estate on the flanks of Table Mountain, and passed on his wine-making skills to the burghers who settled around Stellenbosch.

Between 1688 and 1690, some 200 Huguenots arrived in the country. They were granted land in the region, particularly around Franschhoek, and, although only a few had wine-making experience, they gave the infant industry fresh impetus.

For a long time, Cape wines other than those produced at Groot Constantia were not in great demand and most grapes ended up in brandy. But the industry received a boost in the early 19th century as war between Britain and France meant more South African wine was imported to the UK.

Apartheid-era sanctions and the power of the Kooperatieve Wijnbouwers Vereeniging (KWV; the cooperative formed in 1918 to control minimum prices, production areas and quota limits) didn't exactly encourage innovation and instead hampered the industry. Since 1992 the KWV, now a private company, has lost much of its former influence.

Many new and progressive wine makers are leading South Africa's re-emergence onto the world market. New wine-producing areas are being established away from the hotter inland areas, in particular in the cooler coastal areas east of Cape Town around Mossel Bay, Walker Bay and Elgin.

WORKERS' WINES

Black empowerment in the wine industry is happening, but slowly. **Thabani** (☎ 882 8790; www .thabani.co.za; not open to the public), in Stellenbosch, is South Africa's first wholly black-owned wine company. It hit the big time in the US when Oprah Winfrey served its lively sauvignon blanc at a party for poet Maya Angelou. Students of Thabani wine maker Jabulani Ntshangase are now being snapped up by big vineyards, including KWV.

The **Fair Valley Workers Association** (Map p19; ☎ 863 2450; tastings and sales at Fairview, see p41) is a 17-hectare workers' farm next to Fairview. It's still developing its own vineyards, but has already produced four seasons of chenin blanc (sold through the UK wine chain Oddbins) made with grapes bought in from Fairview, as well as a sauvignon blanc and a pinotage.

At **Nelson's Creek** (see p41), north of Paarl, the owner has donated part of the estate to his workers to produce their own wines. Under the label New Beginnings, these wines – a classic dry red, a rosé and a dry white – are being sold in the UK, the Netherlands and Japan.

Other worker empowerment wines to look out for include **Thandi** (☎ 844 0605; www.cluver.co.za; ⏲ 9am-5pm Mon-Sat)

Wine – Varieties of Wine

Top Five Wineries

The following are our favourite five wineries:

- **Boschendal** (p39) – this classic estate has a fairytale location and fine wine, food and architecture.
- **Buitenverwachting** (p36) – enjoy a lovely picnic on an immaculate lawn, and wash it down with the quaffable chardonnay or Rhine riesling.
- **Cabrière Estate** (p39) – attend the Saturday morning cellar tour to witness the owner skilfully slice off the top of a sparkling bottle of wine with his sabre.
- **Fairview** (p41) – sample from a selection of some 23 wines, including the workers' empowerment wine Fair Valley, as well as many goat's and cow's milk cheeses.
- **Vergelegen** (p39) – the wineland's most elegant estate produces some equally stylish wines, the flagship being its very fruity Vergelegen red.

from the Elgin area, which is available at Tesco in the UK, and **Tukulu** (☎ 809 8305; www. tukulu.co.za; not open to the public) from the Darling area. This highly successful operation has won awards for its pinotage and is receiving rave reviews for its chenin blanc.

All this has to be balanced against the reality of a black and coloured workforce numbering some 350,000 toiling in vineyards owned by 4500 whites. The average monthly cash wage is R544, with women workers receiving even less. The infamous 'tot' system, whereby the wages of labourers are paid partly in wine still happens and the consequences, socially and physiologically, have been disastrous.

VARIETIES OF WINE

The most common variety of white wine is chenin blanc, or *steen*. In the last decade or so, more fashionable varieties such as chardonnay and sauvignon blanc have been planted on a wide scale. Other widely planted whites include colombard, semillon, crouchen blanc (known as Cape riesling) and various sweet muscats. Table whites, especially chardonnay, once tended to be heavily oaked and high in alcohol, but lighter, more fruity whites are now in the ascendancy. For good sauvignon blancs look to wineries in the cooler wine-growing regions of Constantia, Elgin and Hermanus.

Older, more robust red varieties such as shiraz, cabernet sauvignon and the Cape's own pinotage (a cross between pinot noir and *cinsault* or shiraz which produces a very bold wine) are being challenged by lighter blends of cabernet sauvignon, merlot, shiraz and cabernet franc, making a style closer to Bordeaux styles. The reds attracting the highest prices are cabernet sauvignon and the Bordeaux-style blends. A buzz word of the moment is Cape blend, which must contain at least 30% pinotage.

The Worcester region is the country's leading producer of fortified wines, including port, brandy and South Africa's own hanepoot. This dessert wine is made from the Mediterranean grape variety known as muscat of Alexandria to produce a strong, sweet and suitably high-alcohol tipple for the domestic market. In Worcester you'll also find the KWV Brandy Cellar, the largest in the world and the final stop on the Brandy Route, which runs from Van Ryn Brandy Cellar (see p37). For more information contact the South African Brandy Foundation (☎ 886 6381; www.sabrandy.co.za).

WINE REGIONS

CONSTANTIA

Less than 20km south of the Waterfront on the eastern slopes of Table Mountain, Constantia is the oldest of South Africa's wine-growing regions. Groot Constantia, the original estate established by Simon van der Stel in 1685, was divided up after his death in 1712, so today you can also visit Buitenverwachtig and Klein Constantia, both originally part of the Van der Stel estates. Steenberg Vineyards, which also makes wine for the nearby Constantia Uitsig estate, completes the Constantia wine route.

If you're short of time, head for Groot Constantia, which is among the grandest vineyards and homesteads in the Cape. A delightful way to spend a day, though, is to take Downhill Adventures' cycling tour of this lush area (see p110).

CONSTANTIA UITSIG Map pp196–7

☎ 794 1810; www.uitsig.co.za; Spaanschemat River Rd; tastings free; ◷ 9am-5pm Mon-Sat

The wine on sale here is actually made at the nearby Steenberg Vineyards. You can also taste wines from some 60 other estates. It's one for foodies since it boasts three excellent restaurants – Constantia Uitsig, La Colombe and Spaanschemat River Café – and a luxurious hotel, also called Constantia Uitsig (see p142).

BUITENVERWACHTING Map pp196–7

☎ 794 5190; www.buitenverwachting.co.za; Klein Constantia Rd; tastings free; ◷ 9am-5pm Mon-Fri, 9am-1pm Sat

The name means 'beyond expectations', which is certainly the feeling one gets on visiting this estate set on 100 hectares. For R85 per person you can enjoy a picnic lunch in front of the 1786 manor house (book on ☎ 794 1012). The internationally renowned Christine claret usually sells out on the day of its release each year (around November) and the chardonnay and Rhine riesling are among the standout whites produced here. The estate is known to offer good working and living conditions for its employees.

GROOT CONSTANTIA Map pp196–7

☎ 794 5128; www.grootconstantia.co.za; Groot Constantia Rd, High Constantia; tastings incl glass R20; ◷ 10am-6pm daily Dec-Apr, 10am-5pm daily May-Nov

Although it's a bit of a tourist trap (and can get very crowded on weekends with tour buses), Groot Constantia is also a superb example of Cape Dutch architecture, and embodies the gracious lifestyle the wealthy Dutch created in their adopted country. In the 18th century, Constantia wines were exported around the world and were highly acclaimed. Try the sauvignon blanc, riesling and pinotage. The beautifully restored and furnished homestead is

now a **museum** (☎ 795 5140; adult/child R10/1; ◷ 10am-5pm daily); take a look at the tiny slave quarters beneath the main building. The Cloete Cellar, the estate's original wine cellar, now houses old carriages and a display of storage vessels. Tours of the modern cellar run at least twice daily at 11am and 3pm; book ahead. Concerts are held occasionally in the Bertrams Cellar tasting room. There are also a couple of restaurants on the estate (see p94).

KLEIN CONSTANTIA Map pp196–7

☎ 794 5188; www.kleinconstantia.com; Klein Constantia Rd; tastings free; ◷ 9am-5pm Mon-Fri, 9am-1pm Sat

This small winery, part of the original Constantia estate, is famous for its Vin de Constance, a deliciously sweet muscat wine. It was Napoleon's solace on St Helena, and Jane Austen had one of her heroines recommend it for having the power to heal 'a disappointed heart'. We can't guarantee that, but we can say that while Klein Constantia doesn't offer any of the frills and bonuses of other wineries, it's still worth visiting for its excellent tasting room and informative displays. Also try the riesling, sauvignon blanc and Malbrook, a classic Bordeaux-style blend. At the estate's entrance, pause to look at the *karamat* (saint's tomb) of Sheik Abdurachman Matebe Shah; he was buried in 1661.

STEENBERG VINEYARDS Map pp196–7

☎ 713 2211; www.steenberg-vineyards.com; Steenberg Rd; tastings free; ◷ 9am-4.30pm Mon-Fri Mar-Aug, 9am-1pm Sat Sep-Feb

The oldest Cape wine estate after Constantia, Steenberg began life under the name Swaane-weide (Feeding Place of the Swans) in 1682. Its great merlot, sauvignon blanc reserve and semillon are the wines to sample. The estate also encompasses Steenberg Hotel, a five-star country hotel in the original restored manor house, and an 18-hole golf course.

STELLENBOSCH

It was Stellenbosch in the 1970s that first promoted a 'wine route', an idea that has since been enthusiastically taken up by 16 other parts of the country. For details of wineries in this area not listed here, contact the **Wine Route Office** (☎ 886 4310), or the Stellenbosch Publicity Association (see p148).

BERGKELDER

☎ 809 8492; www.bergkelder.co.za; George Blake St; tastings R15; ⏱ 8am-5pm Mon-Fri, 9am-3pm Sat

This is an option if you don't have time to shuttle around the area's wineries, or want an introduction to what's on offer. The cellar tour (available in French and German as well as English) includes a slide show and tastings of up to 12 wines. You pour your own tastings, so take it easy or it might be your last stop for the day! The Bergkelder is a short walk from the train station.

BLAAUWKLIPPEN Map p37

☎ 880 0133; www.blaauwklippen.com; R44; tastings R20; ⏱ 9am-5pm daily

This rustic, 300-year-old estate with several fine Cape Dutch buildings is known for its excellent red wines, particularly its cabernet sauvignon and zinfandel. Cellar tours are by appointment and lunch is available (call for times, as they change according to the season). It's a good one for kids on weekends when it has horse and carriage rides around the estate (R10). Blaauklippen is on the R44 towards Somerset West.

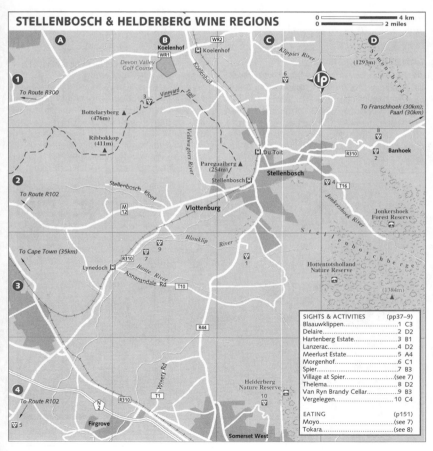

STELLENBOSCH & HELDERBERG WINE REGIONS

SIGHTS & ACTIVITIES	(pp37–9)
Blaauwklippen	1 C3
Delaire	2 D2
Hartenberg Estate	3 B1
Lanzerac	4 D2
Meerlust Estate	5 A4
Morgenhof	6 C1
Spier	7 B3
Village at Spier	(see 7)
Thelema	8 D2
Van Ryn Brandy Cellar	9 B3
Vergelegen	10 C4

EATING	(p151)
Moyo	(see 7)
Tokara	(see 8)

Wine – Wine Regions

DELAIRE Map p37

☎ 885 1756; www.delairewinery.co.za; tastings R10;
⊙ 10am-5pm daily

Known as the 'vineyard in the sky' because of its high altitude location at the top of the Helshoogte Pass on the R310 towards Franschhoek, the views are, naturally, stunning. It's a friendly place with wheelchair access to the restaurant and picnics available October to April (bookings essential). Try the cabernet sauvignon and merlot.

HARTENBERG ESTATE Map p37

☎ 882 2541; www.hartenbergestate.com; tastings free; ⊙ 9am-5pm Mon-Fri, 9am-3pm Sat

Thanks to a favourable microclimate, this estate, founded in 1692, produces many award-winning wines, notably its cabernet sauvignon, merlot and shiraz. Lunch is available from noon to 2pm (bookings essential). The estate is off Bottelary Rd, 10km northwest of Stellenbosch.

LANZERAC Map p37

☎ 886 5641; www.lanzeracwines.co.za; Jonkershoek Valley; tastings R16; ⊙ 9am-4.30pm Mon-Thu, 9am-4pm Fri, 10am-2pm Sat, 11am-3pm Sun

Lanzerac produces a very good merlot and quaffable cabernet sauvignon and chardonnay. The tastings include a free glass and biscuits. Here you'll also find Stellenbosch's most luxurious hotel Lanzerac Manor (see p131).

MEERLUST ESTATE Map p37

☎ 843 3587; www.meerlust.co.za; tastings R60;
⊙ 9am-5pm Mon-Thu, 9am-4.30pm Fri

One of South Africa's most celebrated wine estates (in operation since 1693), Meerlust turns out Rubicon, a wine that John Platter's guide calls the 'pre-eminent Cape claret'. Tastings and cellar tours are by appointment only.

MORGENHOF Map p37

☎ 889 5510; www.morgenhof.com; R44; tastings R10;
⊙ 9am-6pm Mon-Fri, 10am-5pm Sat & Sun Nov-Apr, 9am-4.30pm Mon-Fri, 10am-3pm Sat & Sun May-Oct

An old estate on the slopes of Simonsberg, Morgenhof has fine architecture and a pretty rose garden. Good wines include the chenin blanc and a Bordeaux-style blend. Light lunches are available and the coffee shop serves breakfast from 9am to noon daily. It's on the R44 towards Paarl.

SPIER Map p37

☎ 809 1100; www.spier.co.za; R310; tastings R12;
⊙ 9am-5pm daily

There's something for everyone at this mega-estate which offers steam-train trips from Cape Town (call ☎ 419 5222 for information), horse riding, a performing arts centre, beautifully restored Cape Dutch buildings and several restaurants including the spectacular Moyo (see p151). The only aspect we're unsure

Manor house at Groot Constantia (p36)

about is the cheetah park, where listless animals pose for photos with the tourists. Its wines are nothing to shout about, but in the tasting you can try lots of other vineyards' wines. Check out the annual arts festival that runs from January to March – it's as good a reason as any for coming here. If you want to stay over there's a good Cape Malay–style hotel, the Village at Spier (see p152).

THELEMA Map p37

☎ 885 1924; www.thelema.co.za; R310; tastings free; ☽ 9am-5pm Mon-Fri, 9am-1pm Sat
At the head of the Helshoogte Pass, opposite Delaire, this relatively modern winery has been in business just 20 years. Its sterling reputation for fine cabernet sauvignon, merlot and chardonnay wines suggests a much longer history. Thelema also runs the nearby restaurant Tokara.

VAN RYN BRANDY CELLAR Map p37

☎ 881 3875; www.distell.co.za; Vlottenburg; tastings R15; ☽ 8am-5pm Mon-Fri, 9am-1.30pm Sat
At the start of the Western Cape Brandy Route, three tours generally run daily and include a tasting. In the boardroom you can view fine South African artworks including works by Irma Stern (see p71) and the incredibly lifelike sculptures of Anton van Wouw. It's 8km southwest of Stellenbosch.

HELDERBERG

This area around Somerset West, 20km south of Stellenbosch, has some 20 wineries, including Vergelegen, arguably the most beautiful estate in the Cape. For more information on the area contact Helderberg Tourism Bureau (☎ 851 4022; www.helderbergt ourism.co.za; 186 Main Rd, Somerset West).

VERGELEGEN Map p37

☎ 847 1334; www.vergelegen.co.za; Lourensford Rd, Somerset West; admission R10, tastings R2-10; ☽ 9.30am-4pm daily
Simon van der Stel's son Willem first planted vines here in 1700. The buildings and elegant grounds have ravishing mountain views and a 'stately home' feel to them. On the dining front you can choose from the casual Rose Terrace overlooking the Rose Garden, the upmarket Lady Phillips Restaurant, or a picnic hamper (R180 for two people) – bookings are essential for the last two options.

FRANSCHHOEK

Many of Franschhoek's wineries are within walking distance of the town centre, but to reach Boschendal, on the R310 towards Stellenbosch, you'll need transport. To find out about more wineries in the area see www.franschhoekwines.co.za.

BOSCHENDAL Map p40

☎ 870 4210; www.boschendal.com; Pniel Rd; ☽ 8.30am-4.30pm daily Nov-Apr, 8.30am-4.30pm Mon-Sat May-Oct
Tucked beneath some awesome mountains, this is the classic Winelands estate, with lovely architecture, food and wine. Note the Taphuis wine-tasting area (where tastings cost R12, or R20 for a formal tasting with a guide) is at the opposite end of the estate from the Groote Drakenstein manor house (admission R8) and restaurants. Its reds, including cabernet sauvignon and merlot, get top marks. The blowout buffet lunch (R180) in the main restaurant is mainly a group affair. Far nicer, especially in fine weather, is Le Café where you can have a snack or something more substantial. Also very popular are 'Le Pique Nique' hampers (R87.50 per person, minimum two people) served under parasols on the lawn from mid-October to the end of April (bookings ☎ 870 4274). Boschendal is on the R310 towards Stellenbosch.

CABRIÈRE ESTATE Map p40

☎ 876 2630; www.cabriere.co.za; Berg St; tastings without/with cellar tour R20/25; ☽ 9.30am-4.30pm Mon-Fri, 11am-2pm Sat; tours 11am & 3pm Mon-Fri, 11am Sat
The tastings at this estate include a couple of sparkling wines and one of the vineyard's excellent range of white, red and dessert wines and brandies. No wonder it's so popular. At the Saturday session, stand by for the proprietor's party trick of slicing open a bottle of bubbly with a sabre. Try the wines in paired combinations with food at the Haute Cabrière Cellar (see p153).

CHAMONIX Map p40

☎ 876 2498; www.chamonix.co.za; Uitkyk St; tastings R10; ☽ 9.30am-4.30pm daily; cellar tours 11am & 3pm by appointment
The tasting room at this winery is in a converted blacksmith's; there's also a range of schnapps and mineral water to sample. The pretty La Maison de Chamonix restaurant (Map p19; mains R70-90;

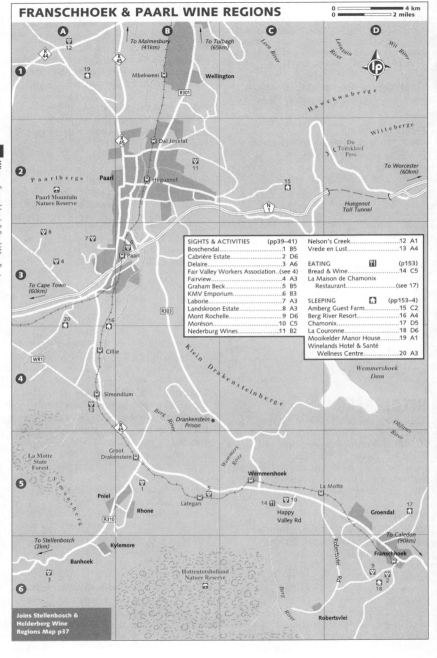

FRANSCHHOEK & PAARL WINE REGIONS

0 ——— 4 km
0 ——— 2 miles

To Malmesbury (41km)

To Tulbagh (65km)

Leeu River

Leeutuin River

Wit River

Mbekweni

Wellington

R301

Hawekwaberge

Dal Josefat

Witteberge

Du Toitskloof Pass

To Worcester (60km)

Paarlberge

Paarl

Huguenot

Paarl Mountain Nature Reserve

Huegenot Toll Tunnel

N1

Paarl

To Cape Town (60km)

R303

R303

WR1

Cillie

Klein Drakensteinberge

Wemmershoek Dam

Simondium

Berg River

Drakenstein Prison

Olifants River

La Motte State Forest

Groot Drakenstein

Wemmers River

Wemmershoek

La Motte

Simonsberg

Pniel

Lategan

Happy Valley Rd

Groendal

Rhone

R310

To Stellenbosch (2km)

Kylemore

Banhoek

Hottentotsholland Nature Reserve

Berg River

Robertsvlei Rd

To Caledon (90km)

Franschhoek

Robertsvlei

Joins Stellenbosch & Helderberg Wine Regions Map p37

SIGHTS & ACTIVITIES	(pp39–41)
Boschendal	1 B5
Cabrière Estate	2 D6
Delaire	3 A6
Fair Valley Workers Association	(see 4)
Fairview	4 A3
Graham Beck	5 B5
KMV Emporium	6 B3
Laborie	7 A3
Landskroon Estate	8 A3
Mont Rochelle	9 D6
Moréson	10 C5
Nederburg Wines	11 B2

Nelson's Creek	12 A1
Vrede en Lust	13 A4

EATING	(p153)
Bread & Wine	14 C5
La Maison de Chamonix Restaurant	(see 17)

SLEEPING	(pp153–4)
Amberg Guest Farm	15 C2
Berg River Resort	16 A4
Chamonix	17 D5
La Couronne	18 D6
Mooikelder Manor House	19 A1
Winelands Hotel & Santé Wellness Centre	20 A3

noon-4pm daily & 6.30pm-9pm Fri) has a reasonably priced lunch menu. You can stay in self-catered cottages amid the vineyards.

GRAHAM BECK Map p40
☎ 874 1258; www.grahambeckwines.co.za; R45; tastings free; ☺ 9am-5pm Mon-Fri, 9am-2pm Sat

As with its main estate out at Robertson (see p41), the buildings here are all determinedly modern with some striking contemporary sculptures to match. Its eminently drinkable products include fizzers that give French champagnes a run for their money and a muscat that is heaven in a glass. It's located on the R45 just before you cross the Berg River on the way to Franschhoek.

MONT ROCHELLE Map p40
☎ 876 3000; montrochelle@wine.co.za; tastings R15; ☺ 10am-5pm Mon-Fri, 11am-5pm Sat year-round, 11am-3pm Sun Sep-Apr only

Mont Rochelle vineyard is also in a beautiful location, and offers great wines. It's one of only a handful of vineyards owned by a black businessman – Miko Rwayibare from the Congo. You can combine your wine tasting with a cheese tasting for an extra R10, and cellar tours (R10) are by appointment.

VREDE EN LUST Map p40
☎ 874 1611; www.vnl.co.za; Simondium; tastings R10; ☺ 10am-4pm daily

The first vintage for this replanted vineyard was released in 2002, although the estate dates back to 1688 when original owner Jacques de Savoye named it 'Peace and Eagerness'. It specialises in blends. The location and buildings are very attractive and there's a deli and restaurant where you can try locally made cheeses and bread.

PAARL

For information about wineries in the area other than those listed here, contact **Paarl Vintners** (☎ 872 3841).

KWV EMPORIUM Map p40
☎ 807 3007; www.kwv.co.za; Kohler St; tastings R20; ☺ 9am-4pm Mon-Sat

Although it is no longer the all-controlling body it used to be, KWV remains one of the best known of the country's wineries since its products are mostly sold overseas. Some KWV port and sherry is available inside South Africa, and its fortified wines, in particular, are among the world's best. The firm's impressive offices are at La Concorde on Paarl's Main St, but the cellar tours are at their complex near the railway line. Call for times of cellar tours (R20), which are worth taking if only to see the enormous Cathedral Cellar built in 1930.

FAIRVIEW Map p40
☎ 863 2450; www.fairview.co.za; tastings R10; ☺ 8.30am-5pm Mon-Fri, 8.30am-1pm Sat

This is a small and deservedly popular winery. Peacocks and goats in a tower (apparently goats love to climb) greet you on arrival. The tastings are great value since they include some 23 wines *and* a wide range of goat's and cow's milk cheeses. You can also sample and buy the pinotage and chenin blanc of the Fair Valley Workers Association (see p34) here. Fairview is 5km southwest of Paarl off the R101.

LABORIE Map p40
☎ 807 3390; www.kwv-international.com; Taillefert St; tastings R9; ☺ 9am-5pm daily Oct-Apr, 9am-5pm Mon-Sat May-Sep

Laborie is KWV's attractive showcase vineyard, just off Main Rd. It's known for its shiraz and Alambic Brandy. The **restaurant** (☎ 807 3095; mains R45-70) is in an old Cape Dutch building and serves dishes such as Springbok shanks and kingklip.

Robertson Wine Valley

If you have more time, a trip further afield to Robertson, 150km east of Cape Town, could be rewarding. The area has some 30-odd wineries and its scenery and the general absence of tourist coaches, lends it an appeal that you may find lacking in other popular wine regions. Wineries to check out include **De Wetshof Estate** (☎ 023-615 1853; www.dewetshof.co.za), **Graham Beck** (☎ 023-626 1214; www.grahambeckwines.co.za), **Robertson Winery** (☎ 023-626 3059; www.robertsonwine.co.za) and **Van Louvern** (☎ 023-615 1505). Staying the night in the peaceful village of McGregor is a good way to end a day's tasting; more details of the area can be found in Lonely Planet's *South Africa, Lesotho & Swaziland*, or by calling the office of Robertson Wine Valley (☎ 023-626 3167; www.robertsonwinevalley.co.za).

LANDSKROON ESTATE Map p40
☎ 863 1039; tastings free; ⊗ 8.30am-5pm Mon-Fri, 9am-1pm Sat

Five generations of the De Villiers family have been perfecting their winemaking skills on this pleasant estate. Overlooking the vines, there's a nice terrace on which you can quaff the cabernet sauvignons and celebrated port. The estate is off the R101, 6km south of Paarl.

NEDERBURG WINES Map p40
☎ 862 3104; www.nederburg.co.za; tastings R10; ⊗ 8.30am-5pm Mon-Fri, 10am-2pm Sat

A big but professional and welcoming operation; the vast range of wines here are among the most widely available across the country. The informative food and wine tastings (R17) will teach you which types of flavour the wines will work best with. The picnic lunches cost R80 per person (December to March only, bookings essential) and are very popular. Nederburg is off the N1, 7km east of Paarl.

NELSON'S CREEK Map p40
☎ 869 8453; www.nelsoncreek.co.za; R44; tastings free; ⊗ 9am-5pm Mon-Fri, 9am-2pm Sat

The owner of this forward-looking estate has donated land to workers to produce their own wines under the label New Beginnings. Wines to sample include the pinotage, cabernet sauvignon and chardonnay. Cellar tours are by appointment and cost R20. It's around 15km north of the centre of Paarl on the R44.

History

History

THE RECENT PAST

On 11 February 2004, 38 years to the day since District Six was declared a whites only area, keys to new homes being built in the inner city area were handed over to 87-year-old Ebrahiem Murat and 82-year-old Dan Mdzabela. Removed like thousands of others from District Six because of the colour of their skin, theirs was a long-awaited but triumphant homecoming. The District Six Beneficiaries Trust is planning on building 4000 homes in the next few years, repopulating a slice of prime real estate that has laid barren for three decades.

The returning black and coloured residents of District Six will be rubbing shoulders with the white elite, who are also being tempted to live in the city centre by increased security, lower crime and the development of ritzy, loft-style apartments in grand, old structures such as the Mutual Building and the old Board of Executors building. Together with the gentrification of the Waterkant, this is fuelling a property boom that has seen prices across the city soar to previously unimaginable heights.

Full integration of the city's mixed population, though, is a long way off, if it's achievable at all. The African National Congress (ANC) and New National Party (NNP) are working together on the city council (which, if ever there was a sign of the times is headed up by mayor Nomaindia Mfeketo, a black woman), but this means little to the vast majority of Capetonians who continue to live in the bleak, windswept communities of the Cape Flats, still split along racial lines and suffering horrendous economic, social and health problems. It is here, in areas such as Langa, Crossroads and Khayelitsha, that Cape Town is having to deal with the AIDS pandemic, while in Mitchells Plain crime is rife.

The violence occasionally spills over into the city too – in March 2004 a former soldier was shot dead as he approached Nelson Mandela's house in Bishopscourt while brandishing a stolen rifle. In the same month two men were sentenced to life for the brutal slaying of nine men at a gay massage parlour in Sea Point.

Top Five Books on Cape Town's History

- *Country of My Skull*, Antjie Krog (1998) – poet and journalist Krog won the *Sunday Times* Alan Paton Award for her incisive account of the investigations of the Truth & Reconciliation Commission. The details are gruesome, but you get a sense of the catharsis South Africa went through during the whole harrowing process.
- *South Africa – A Travellers History*, David Mason (2003) – latest edition of an easy to understand historical account of the country, covering a fair amount of historical happenings in Cape Town. It includes a chronology of major events and an A to Z gazetteer.
- *Cape Town: The Making of a City* and *Cape Town in the Twentieth Century*, Vivian Bickford-Smith, Elizabeth van Heyningen and Nigel Worden (1999) – a pair of well-illustrated books on local history written by a trio of academics from the University of Cape Town. The former covers events up to 1899, the latter the following century; they're less dry than you'd expect.
- *The Island – A History of Robben Island 1488–1990*, edited by Harriet Deacon (1996) – long before it gained notoriety as the prison of Nelson Mandela, this island off the Cape Town coast was home to the indigenous Khoikhoi people and later a leper colony, lunatic asylum and military barracks. Learn about it all in this collection of academic essays.
- *Recalling Community in Cape Town*, edited by Ciraj Rassool and Sundra Posalendis (2001) – illustrated account of the District Six area demolished during apartheid and how its memory was kept alive by those who once lived there; the area was eventually revived in the excellent city museum.

TIMELINE	c.100,000 BC	AD 1487	1652
	San people settle Southern Africa	Bartholomeu Dias sails around the Cape of Good Hope	The Dutch establish a settlement in Table Bay (Cape Town)

FROM THE BEGINNING

SAN & KHOIKHOI PEOPLES

Signs of the first humans have been found in several places in South Africa. At Langebaan Lagoon (north of Cape Town), the discovery of 117,000-year-old fossilised footprints prompted one researcher to speculate that 'Eve' (the very first human; the common ancestor of us all) lived here.

Little is known about these first humans, but there are signs that they conducted funerals, an indication of at least basic culture. Academics don't know whether the earliest recorded inhabitants of South Africa – the San peoples – are direct descendants or if they returned to the area after aeons of travel.

The San (also known as Bushmen) were nomadic hunters and gatherers, and the Khoikhoi (formerly known as Hottentot) were seminomadic hunters and pastoralists. However, both groups were closely related, so the distinction was by no means clear, and the term Khoisan is now widely used to describe these peoples. Culturally and physically, they developed differently from the Negroid peoples of Africa.

It is believed the Khoikhoi developed from San groups in present-day Botswana. It is possible that they came into contact with pastoralist Bantu-speaking tribes, as, in addition to hunting and gathering food, they became pastoralists, with cattle and sheep. They migrated south, reaching the Cape of Good Hope about 2000 years ago. For centuries, perhaps even millennia, the San and the Khoikhoi intermarried and coexisted. It was not uncommon for impoverished Khoikhoi to revert to a hunter-gatherer existence, or for the San to acquire domestic animals.

By about AD 500 the Bantu-speaking peoples had settled what is now KwaZulu-Natal Southern Africa. This migration resulted in many Khoisan peoples being dislodged or absorbed in other parts of South Africa, but the Bantu-speaking peoples did not reach the Cape Town area. Their westward expansion halted around the Great Fish River (in Eastern Cape Province, about 700km east of Cape Town) because they were agricultural people and further west there was not enough rainfall to support their crops.

FIRST EUROPEAN VISITORS

The first recorded European visitors were the Portuguese who came to the Cape Town area on their search for a sea route to India and for that most precious of medieval commodities: spice. Bartholomeu Diaz rounded the Cape in 1487, naming it Cabo da Boa Esperanca (Cape of Good Hope), but didn't linger long, as his eyes were fixed on the trade riches of the east coast of Africa and the Indies.

In 1503 Antonio de Saldanha became the first European to climb Table Mountain. But the Portuguese had no interest in a permanent settlement. The Cape offered them little more than fresh water, since their attempts to trade with the Khoisan often ended in violence, and the coast and its fierce weather posed a terrible threat to their tiny caravels.

By the end of the 16th century, English and Dutch traders were beginning to challenge the Portuguese, and the Cape became a regular stopover for their scurvy-ridden crews. In 1647 a Dutch vessel was wrecked in Table Bay; its crew built a fort and stayed for a year before they were rescued.

This crystallised the value of a permanent settlement in the minds of the directors of the Dutch East India Company (Vereenigde Oost-Indische Compagnie; VOC). They had no intention of colonising the country, but simply wanted to establish a secure base where ships could shelter and stock up on fresh supplies of meat, fruit and vegetables.

Jan van Riebeeck was the man they chose to lead a small expedition from the flagship *Drommedaris*. His specific charge was to build a fort, barter with the Khoisan for meat,

1688	c.1690	1795	1806
French Huguenots arrive at the Cape	Boers move into the hinterland around present-day Cape Town	British capture Cape Town	British defeat Dutch in battle at Bloubergstrand

.and plant a garden. He reached Table Bay on 6 April 1652, built a mud-walled fort not far from the site of the stone castle that survives today, and planted the gardens now known as the Company's Gardens (or the Botanic Gardens).

In 1660, in a gesture that took on an awful symbolism, Van Riebeeck planted a bitter-almond hedge to separate the Khoisan and the Europeans. It ran around the western foot of Table Mountain down to Table Bay, and a section of it can still be seen in the Kirstenbosch Botanical Gardens. The hedge may have protected the 120 Europeans, but the settlement, having excluded the Khoisan, suffered a chronic labour shortage. In another move that would have consequences for centuries ahead, Van Riebeeck then proceeded to import slaves from Madagascar, India, Ceylon, Malaya and Indonesia.

THE SETTLEMENT GROWS

The European men of the community were largely employees of the VOC, and were overwhelmingly Dutch. They comprised a tiny official elite and a larger number of little-educated soldiers and sailors, many of whom had been pressed into service. In 1688 they were joined by about 200 Huguenots, French Calvinists who had fled from persecution by King Louis XIV.

There was a shortage of women in the colony, so the female slaves and the Khoisan survivors were exploited both for labour and for sex. In time, the slaves intermixed with the Khoisan. The offspring of these unions formed the basis of sections of today's coloured population.

Under the VOC's almost complete control, Cape Town thrived, providing a comfortable European lifestyle for a growing number of artisans and entrepreneurs servicing ships and crews. Cape Town became known as 'the Tavern of the Seas', a riotous port used by every navigator, privateer and merchant travelling between Europe and the East (including Australia).

THE BOERS BEGIN TO TREK

The white population did not reach 1000 until 1745, by which time small numbers of free (meaning non-VOC) burghers were drifting away from the close grip of the company into other parts of Africa. These were the first of the Trekboers (literally 'Trekking Farmers'),

Islamic Cape Town

Cape Town's Muslim roots extend back to the slaves brought to Cape Town by the VOC from the Indian subcontinent and Indonesia (hence the term Cape Malays, although few of them actually hailed from what is today called Malaysia). The VOC also used Cape Town as a place of exile for Islamic leaders such as Tuan Guru from Tidore, who arrived in 1780, exiled because he was a dissident against the Dutch rule in Indonesia. During his 13 years on Robben Island he accurately copied the Quran from memory. In 1794 he helped establish the Auwal Mosque, the city's first mosque, in the Bo-Kaap, thus making this area the heart of the Islamic community in Cape Town.

Tuan Guru is buried in Bo-Kaap's Tana Baru cemetery, one of the oldest in South Africa, at the western end of Longmarket St. Within the cemetery (which has fallen into disrepair and is subject to a local preservation campaign) his grave is one of the 20 or so *karamats* (tombs of Islamic saints) encircling Cape Town and is visited by the faithful on a minipilgrimage. Other *karamats* are found on Robben Island (that of Sayed Abdurahman Matura), at the gate to the Klein Constantia wine estate, and by the Eerste River in Macassar (that of Sheik Yussof, the most significant Muslim leader of his time).

A sizable Muslim community also lived in Simon's Town before the Group Areas Act evictions of the late 1960s. Its history can be traced at the Heritage Museum in Simon's Town (p76).

1808	1814	1834	1854
Slave trade abolished	Cape Colony ceded to British	Slaves emancipated	Lower house of parliament created in Cape Town

later known just as Boers, who developed a unique culture and eventually their own language, Afrikaans, derived from the argot of their slaves.

They were fiercely independent and their lives were based on rearing cattle. In many ways their lives were not all that different from those of the Khoisan with whom they came into conflict as they drifted into the interior. The timing of their voluntary withdrawal from the outside world is significant. The Boers, many of whom were illiterate and most of whom had no source of information other than the Bible, missed out on the great social, political and philosophical developments of Europe in the 18th century.

The Boers' inevitable confrontations with the Khoisan were disastrous. The indigenous people were driven from their traditional lands, ravaged by introduced diseases and almost destroyed by superior weapons. The survivors were left with no option but to work for Europeans in a form of bondage little different from slavery.

THE BRITISH TAKE OVER

The fourth Anglo–Dutch War was fought between 1780 and 1783. French regiments were sent to Cape Town to help the Dutch defend the city, but the British eventually prevailed at the Battle of Muizenberg in 1795 and took control of the Cape from the VOC, which by then was bankrupt.

Under the Treaty of Amiens (1803) the British ceded the Cape back to the Dutch, but this proved just a lull in the Napoleonic Wars. In 1806 at Bloubergstrand, 25km north of Cape Town, the British again defeated the Dutch. The colony was ceded to the British on 13 August 1814.

The British abolished the slave trade in 1808 and the remaining Khoisan were finally given the explicit protection of the law (including the right to own land) in 1828. These moves contributed to Afrikaners' dissatisfaction and their mass migration, which came to be known as the Great Trek, inland from the Cape Colony.

Despite outlawing slavery, the British introduced new laws that laid the basis for an exploitive labour system little different from slavery. Thousands of dispossessed blacks sought work in the colony, but it was made a crime to be in the colony without a pass – and without work. It was also a crime to leave a job.

CAPE ECONOMY BOOMS

The British introduced free trade, which greatly benefited Cape Town's economy. Cape wines, in particular, were a huge hit, accounting for some 10% of British wine consumption by 1822. During the first half of the 19th century, before the Suez Canal opened, British officers serving in India would holiday at the Cape.

Capetonians successfully managed to stop the British government's attempt to turn the colony into another Australia when their governor, Sir Harry Smith, forbade 282 British prisoners from leaving the ship *Neptune* when it docked in Cape Town in 1849. The *Neptune* continued to Tasmania and the locals, who had challenged the might of the empire, became bolder in their demands for self-government.

In 1854, a representative parliament was formed in Cape Town, but much to the dismay of Dutch and English farmers to the north and east, the British government and Cape liberals insisted on a multiracial constituency (albeit with financial requirements that excluded the vast majority of blacks and coloureds).

In 1860 construction of the Alfred Basin in the docks commenced, finally giving Cape Town a stormproof port. The opening of the Suez Canal in 1869 dramatically decreased the amount of shipping that sailed via the Cape, but the discovery of diamonds and gold

1864	1877	1881	1899
Cape Town–Wynberg railway line completed; links to Kimberley (1885) and Johannesburg (1892) follow	British annex the Boer Republic of Transvaal	Boers defeat British, and Transvaal becomes the South African Republic	Anglo–Boer War starts

in the centre of South Africa in the 1870s and '80s helped Cape Town maintain its position as the country's premier port. Immigrants flooded into the city and the population trebled from 33,000 in 1875 to over 100,000 at the turn of the 20th century.

BOER WAR & AFTER

After the Great Trek the Boers established several independent republics, the largest being the Orange Free State (today's Free State province) and the Transvaal (today's Northern Province, Gauteng and Mpumalanga).

When the world's richest gold reef was found in the Transvaal (a village called Johannesburg sprang up beside it), the British were miffed that the Boers should control such wealth and precipitated war in 1899. The Boers were vastly outnumbered but their tenacity and knowledge of the country resulted in a long and bitter conflict. The British finally defeated them in 1902.

Cape Town was not directly involved in any of the fighting but it did play a key role in landing and supplying the half a million imperial and colonial troops who fought on the British side. The Mount Nelson Hotel was used as headquarters by Lords Roberts and Kitchener.

Bubonic plague in 1901 gave the government an excuse to introduce racial segregation. Africans were moved to two locations, one near the docks and the other at Ndabeni on the western flank of Table Mountain. This was the start of what later would develop into the townships of the Cape Flats.

After the war, the British made some efforts towards reconciliation, and instituted moves towards the union of the separate South African provinces. In the Cape, blacks and coloureds retained a limited franchise (although only whites could become members of the national parliament, and eligible blacks and coloureds constituted only around 7% of the electorate), but did not have the vote in other provinces.

The issue of which city should become the capital was solved by the unwieldy compromise of making Cape Town the seat of the legislature, Pretoria the administrative capital, and Bloemfontein the judicial capital. The Union of South Africa came into being in 1910.

APARTHEID RULES

Afrikaners were economically and socially disadvantaged compared with the English-speaking minority, which controlled most of the capital and industry in the new country. This, plus lingering bitterness over the war and Afrikaners' distaste at having to compete with blacks and coloureds for low-paying jobs, led to strident Afrikaner nationalism and the formation of the National Party.

In 1948 the National Party came to power on a platform of apartheid (literally, 'the state of being apart'). In a series of bitter court and constitutional battles, the right of coloureds to vote in the Cape was removed and the insane apparatus of apartheid was erected.

Mixed marriages were prohibited, interracial sex was made illegal and every person was classified by race. The Group Areas Act defined where people of each 'race' could live and the Separate Amenities Act created separate public facilities: separate beaches, separate buses, separate toilets, separate schools and separate park benches. Blacks were compelled to carry passes at all times and were prohibited from living in or even visiting towns without specific permission.

The Dutch Reformed Church justified apartheid on religious grounds, claiming the separateness of the races was divinely ordained. The *volk* (literally, 'the people', but it means Afrikaners) had a holy mission to preserve the purity of the white race in its promised land.

1901	1902	1905	1910
Ndabeni, Cape Town's first black township, established	Anglo–Boer War finishes	Government commission recommends separate development for blacks, with inferior education	Union of South Africa created, federating the British colonies and the old Boer republics; blacks denied the vote

FICTIONAL HOMELANDS

A system of Homelands was set up, whereby the proportion of land available for black ownership in South Africa increased very slightly to 13%. Blacks then made up about 75% of the population. The Homelands idea was that each black group had a traditional area where it belonged – and must now stay. The government defined 10 such groups, based largely on dubious 19th-century scholarship. The area around Cape Town was declared a 'coloured preference area', which meant no black person could be employed unless it could be proved there was no coloured person suitable for the job.

Apart from the inequity of the land allocation, not to mention the injustice of making decisions about people who couldn't vote, this plan ignored the huge numbers of blacks who had never lived in their 'Homeland'. Millions of people who had lived for generations in other areas were forcibly removed and dumped in bleak, unproductive areas with no infrastructure.

The Homelands were regarded as self-governing states and it was planned that they would become independent countries. Four of the 10 Homelands were nominally independent by the time apartheid was demolished (they were not recognised as independent countries by the UN), and their dictators held power with the help of the South African military.

Of course, the white population depended on cheap black labour to keep the economy booming, so many black 'guest workers' were admitted to South Africa. But unless a black had a job and a pass, he or she was liable to be jailed and sent back to the Homeland. This caused massive disruption to black communities and families. Not surprisingly, people without jobs gravitated to towns and cities to be near their husbands, wives and parents.

No new black housing was built. As a result, illegal squatter camps mushroomed on the sandy plains to the east of Cape Town. In response, government bulldozers flattened the shanties, and their occupants were dragged away and dumped in the Homelands. Within weeks, inevitably, the shanties would rise again.

Deville Wood memorial, Company's Gardens (p61) and South African Museum (p64)

1912	1913	1919	1923
South African Native National Congress established (forerunner to the ANC)	Natives Land Act restricts black ownership of land to 7.5% of the country	Industrial & Commercial Union formed by coloured and African workers in Cape Town	Black Urban Areas Act passed, a main element in the development of segregation and discrimination

MANDELA JAILED

In 1960 the African National Congress (ANC) and the Pan-African Congress (PAC) organised marches against the hated pass laws, which required blacks and coloureds to carry passbooks authorising them to be in a particular area. At Langa and Nyanga on the Cape Flats, police killed five protesters. The Sharpeville massacres in Gauteng were concurrent and resulted in the banning of the ANC and PAC.

In response to the crisis, a warrant for the arrest of Nelson Mandela (see the boxed text below) and other ANC leaders was issued. In mid-1963 Mandela was captured and sentenced to life imprisonment. Like many black leaders before him, Mandela was imprisoned on Robben Island, in the middle of Table Bay.

The government tried for decades to eradicate squatter towns, such as Crossroads, which were focal points for black resistance to the apartheid regime. In its last attempt

Nelson Mandela

No person has been as important in South Africa's recent history as Nelson Rolihlahla Mandela. It is a testament to his force of personality, transparent decency and integrity that Mandela, a man once vilified by the ruling whites, helped unite all South Africans at the most crucial of times.

The son of the third wife of a Xhosa chief, Mandela was born on 18 July 1918 in the small village of Mveso on the Mbashe River. When he was very young the family moved to Qunu, south of Umtata, where he grew up in a mud hut. He attended school in the Transkei before going to Johannesburg where, after a few false starts, he became a lawyer and set up a practice with Oliver Tambo.

In 1944 he helped form the Youth League of the African National Congress (ANC) with Walter Sisulu and Oliver Tambo. Its aim was to end the racist policies of the white South African government. He met Nomzamo Winifred Madikizela ('Winnie') and married her in 1958, after receiving a divorce from his first wife, Evelyn.

In 1956 he was one of 156 ANC and Communist Party members charged with treason; all were found not guilty at the subsequent trial. But in 1963, having established the ANC's military wing and gone underground, Mandela was captured and sentenced to life imprisonment in the infamous Robben Island prison. He remained there until 1982 when he was moved to Pollsmoor Prison on the mainland.

By the time the ANC was declared a legal organisation, Mandela had again been transferred, this time to a house in the grounds of the Victor Vester Prison near Paarl. It was through the gates of this jail that Mandela walked, at last a free man, in 1990. In 1991 he was elected president of the ANC and continued the long negotiations (which had started secretly while he was in prison) to end minority rule. He shared the 1993 Nobel peace prize with FW de Klerk and, in the first free elections the following year, was elected president of South Africa.

The prison years had inevitably taken their toll on the Mandelas' marriage and in 1992, the couple separated, Nelson saying 'I part from my wife with no recriminations'. They were divorced in 1996.

Mandela's gift for reconciliation was best demonstrated by his famous 'Free at last!' speech made on 2 May 1994, when he said, 'This is the time to heal the old wounds and build a new South Africa'.

In 1997, Mandela (or Madiba, his traditional Xhosa name, which is frequently used as a mark of respect) retired as ANC president and on his 80th birthday in July 1998 he married Graca Machel, the widow of a former president of Mozambique. A huge rock concert was organised in his name in December 2003 in Cape Town. Six months later Madiba, who continues to suffer ailments caused by decades of harsh prison life, announced his official retirement from the international stage.

For more information on this charismatic man read his autobiography, *Long Walk to Freedom*, the first draft of which was written while he was still on Robben Island, and Anthony Sampson's exhaustive *Mandela, the Authorized Biography*. Also check out www.pbs.org/wgbh/pages/frontline/shows/mandela, the informative website of a documentary series on Mandela.

1948	1955	1959	1960
National Party wins government and retains control until 1994; apartheid laws begin to be passed	ANC adopts Freedom Charter	Pan-African Congress (PAC) formed	Sharpeville massacre; ANC and PAC banned

between May and June 1986, an estimated 70,000 people were driven from their homes and hundreds were killed. Even this brutal attack was unsuccessful in eradicating the towns, and the government accepted the inevitable and began to upgrade conditions. Since then vast townships have sprung up across the Cape Flats, and are now home to possibly 1.5 million or more people – no one really knows how many. For more about the history of the townships see p77.

THE COLOURED EXPERIENCE

While blacks suffered the brunt of apartheid's madness in the townships, the experiences of Cape Town's coloured communities were mixed but ultimately no less harrowing. District Six, immediately east of the city centre, was the suburb that, more than any other, gave Cape Town its cosmopolitan atmosphere and life. It was primarily a poor, overcrowded coloured ghetto, but people of every race lived there. The streets were alive with people, from children to traders, buskers to petty criminals. Jazz was its life blood and the district was home to many musicians, including the internationally renown pianist Dollar Brand (now called Abdullah Ibrahim, see p105).

Being so close to the centre, District Six infected the whole city with its vitality.

This state of affairs naturally did not appeal to the National Party government, so in 1966, District Six was classified as a white area. Its 50,000 people, some of whose families had been there for five generations, were gradually evicted and dumped in bleak and soulless townships like Athlone, Mitchell's Plain and Atlantis. Friends, neighbours, and even relations were separated. Bulldozers moved in and the multiracial heart was ripped out of the city, while in the townships, depressed and dispirited youths increasingly joined gangs and turned to crime.

The coloured Cape Muslim community of the Bo-Kaap, on the northeastern edge of Signal Hill, were much more fortunate. Home to Cape Town's first mosque (the Auwal Mosque on Dorp St dates back to 1798), the district was once known as the Malay Quarter because it was where many of the imported slaves from the start of the Cape Colony lived with their masters.

Watchtower of the old prison, Robben Island (p67)

In 1952 the entire Bo-Kaap region was declared a coloured area under the terms of the Group Areas Act. There were forced removals, but the residents of the community, which was more homogeneous than that of District Six, banded together to successfully fight for and keep ownership of their homes, many of which were declared National Monuments in the 1960s (so at least they were saved from the bulldozers).

1961	1963	1967	1976
South Africa leaves the Commonwealth and becomes a republic	Nelson Mandela, Walter Sisulu and others jailed for life	Christiaan Barnard carries out world's first heart transplant at Cape Town's Groote Schuur Hospital	Soweto uprisings begin

Noor Ebrahim's Story

'I used to live at 247 Caledon St', begins Noor Ebrahim, pointing at the street map covering the floor of the District Six Museum. Noor is one of the 60,000-plus people forcibly removed from the inner-city district during the 1960s and '70s. His story is one of the many you can discover on a visit to the District Six Museum (p61).

Noor's grandfather came to Cape Town in 1890 from Surat in India. An energetic man who had four wives and 30 children, he built up a good business making ginger beer. Noor's father was one of the old man's sons to his first wife, a Scot called Fanny Grainger, and Noor grew up in the heart of District Six. 'It was a very cosmopolitan area. Many whites lived there – they owned the shops. There were blacks, Portuguese, Chinese and Hindus all living as one big happy family.'

'We didn't know it was going to happen', remembers Noor of the 1966 order declaring District Six a white area under the Group Areas Act. 'We saw the headlines in the paper and people were angry and sad but for a while little happened.' Then in 1970 the demolitions started and gradually the residents moved out.

Noor's family hung on until 1976, when they were given two weeks to vacate the house that his grandfather had bought some 70 years previously. By that time they'd seen families, neighbours and friends split up and sent to separate townships determined by their race. They'd prepared by buying a new home in the coloured township of Athlone – otherwise they'd have been forced to go to Mitchell's Plain, today one of the most violent suburbs on the Cape Flats.

Noor will never forget the day he left District Six. 'I got in the car with my wife and two children and drove off, but only got as far as the corner before I had to stop. I got out of the car and started to cry as I saw the bulldozers move in immediately. Many people died of broken hearts – that's what apartheid was. It was really sick.'

As a way of reclaiming his destroyed past Noor, like several other former District Six residents, wrote a book and, since 1994, has worked as a guide at the museum. He was naturally delighted when the land was officially handed back to former residents in 2000.

'My life was in District Six', he says. 'My heart and home was there. I'm really looking forward to going back.'

PATH TO DEMOCRACY

In the 1980s, amid deepening economic gloom caused by international sanctions and the increasing militancy of black opposition groups (which began with the Soweto student uprising in 1976), it became obvious that apartheid was no longer sustainable.

In 1982, Nelson Mandela and other ANC leaders were moved from Robben Island to Pollsmoor Prison in Cape Town. (In 1986 senior politicians began secretly talking with them.) In 1983, the United Democratic Front (UDF) was formed when 15,000 antiapartheid activists gathered at Mitchell's Plain in the Cape Flats. At the same time the state's military crackdowns in the townships became even more brutal. In 1989 FW de Klerk came to power. In early 1990, President de Klerk began to repeal discriminatory laws, and the ANC, PAC and Communist Party were legalised. On 11 February Nelson Mandela was released. His first public speech since he had been incarcerated 27 years earlier was delivered from the balcony of City Hall to a massive crowd filling the Grand Parade.

From this time onwards virtually all the old apartheid regulations were repealed and, in late 1991, the Convention for a Democratic South Africa (Codesa) began negotiations on the formation of a multiracial transitional government and a new constitution extending political rights to all groups.

Months of negotiations and brinkmanship finally produced a compromise and an election date, although at considerable human cost. Political violence exploded across the country during this time. It's now known that elements within the police and the army contributed to this violence. There have also been claims that high-ranking government officials and politicians ordered, or at least condoned, massacres.

1985	1986	1990	1991
State of emergency declared in South Africa; official murder and torture become rife, black resistance strengthens	Nobel Peace Prize winner Desmond Tutu elected Anglican archbishop of Cape Town	ANC ban lifted, Nelson Mandela freed	Talks on a new constitution begin, political violence escalates

At midnight on 26 April 1994, *Die Stem* (the old national anthem) was sung across South Africa and the old flag was lowered. Then the new rainbow flag was raised and the new anthem, *Nkosi Sikelele Afrika (God Bless Africa)*, was sung – in the past people had been jailed for singing this beautiful hymn. The election was amazingly peaceful and there was an air of goodwill throughout the nation.

The ANC won 62.7% of the vote, less than the 66.7% that would have enabled it to rewrite the constitution. In Western Cape, though, the majority coloured population voted in the National Party (NP) as the provincial government, seemingly happier to live with the devil they knew than with the ANC.

TRUTH & RECONCILIATION COMMISSION

Crimes of the apartheid era were exposed by the Truth & Reconciliation Commission (1994–99). This admirable institution carried out Archbishop Desmond Tutu's dictum: 'Without forgiveness there is no future, but without confession there can be no forgiveness'. Many stories of horrific brutality and injustice were heard by the commission, offering some catharsis to individuals and communities shattered by their past.

The commission operated by allowing victims to tell their stories and perpetrators to confess their guilt, with amnesty offered to those who made a clean breast of it. Those who chose not to appear before the commission face criminal prosecution if their guilt can be proven, and that's the problem. Although some soldiers, police and 'ordinary' citizens have confessed their crimes, it seems unlikely that the human-rights criminals who gave the orders and dictated the policies will ever come forward (former president PW Botha was one famous no-show), and gathering evidence against them has proven difficult.

The catalogue of crimes committed by the apartheid government and its servants is truly horrific, ranging from beatings, torture, murders and massacres to twisted science, including attempts to design poisons that would kill only nonwhite people. Widespread abuses aside, the simple fact remains that apartheid led to tens of millions of people being denied basic human rights because of their skin colour.

Pagad

During the 1990s drugs became such a problem in the Cape area that communities, and in particular the coloured community, began to take matters into their own hands. People against Gangsterism and Drugs (Pagad) was formed in 1995, but the movement quickly turned sour in 1996 with the horrific (and televised) death of gangster Rashaad Staggie. A lynch mob burned then repeatedly shot the dying gangster, and Pagad was labelled as a group of violent vigilantes by both white and black politicians.

Pagad members are mainly coloured Muslims living in the bleak townships of Mitchell's Plain. The group sees itself as defending the coloured community from the crooked cops and drug lords who allow gangs to control the coloured townships. There's also an element of Islamic fundamentalism to the group. A series of bombings of Cape Town police stations in 1999 and a bomb at the Waterfront have been blamed on the group. The trial of five Pagad members for the murder of Staggie only began, after much legal wrangling, in May 2001.

This being South Africa, the Pagad problem is not as simple as it might seem. The gangs in the coloured townships grew out of a desperate need for the coloured community to organise itself against criminals from the neighbouring black townships. Gang members saw themselves as upright citizens defending their community. Many blacks bitterly resented the coloureds because they received 'favoured' treatment from the apartheid government, and weren't perceived as active in the fight against apartheid.

1992	1993	1994	1996
Whites-only referendum agrees to reforms	New constitution enacted, signalling end of apartheid and birth of new South Africa	Democratic elections held; Nelson Mandela succeeds FW de Klerk as South African president	Truth & Reconciliation Commission hearings begin; final constitution signed into law; Robben Island decommissioned

SHIFTING ALLIANCES

In December 1997, Mandela stepped down as ANC president and was succeeded by his deputy, Thabo Mbeki. Jacob Zuma was appointed the new deputy president. In 1999, after five years of learning about democracy, the country held the second free elections in its history. There had been speculation that the ANC vote might drop, but in fact it increased to put the party within one seat of the two-thirds majority that would allow it to alter the constitution.

In the Western Cape elections a year later, however, the ANC fared worse. The pact between the old NP, restyled as the New National Party (NNP) and the Democratic Party (DP) to create the Democratic Alliance (DA), brought them victory not only in the provincial elections but also in the metropolitan elections. Peter Marais, a coloured member of the NNP, became Cape Town's mayor but was sacked in 2001 by Tony Leon, leader of the DA, following a scandal involving the forging of signatures to support a change in the names of the city's main streets. Marais has since become embroiled in a court case accusing him of sexual harassment.

Meanwhile, in a previously unthinkable alliance, the NNP has ditched the DP to join forces with the ANC. Together this alliance now controls both the province and the city.

1997	1999	2000	2004
Mandela retires as ANC president, succeeded by Thabo Mbeki	ANC wins landslide victory in second democratic elections; Robben Island declared a UN World Heritage Site	Oil spill in Table Bay leads to world's largest rescue effort for stricken African penguins	First of returnees to District Six are handed keys to their new homes in the revived area

Neighbourhoods

Neighbourhoods

Cape Town's commercial heart, commonly known as the City Bowl, is squeezed between Table Mountain, Signal Hill and the harbour. Immediately to the west is the Bo-Kaap, to the east Zonnebloem (once known as District Six). Together with the ritzier suburbs of Gardens, Tamboerskloof, Oranjezicht and Vredehoek, all rising up Table Mountain's slopes, this is the area we define as the City Centre.

The rest of the city naturally falls into four other districts. The Atlantic Coast runs from the beachside district of Bloubergstrand and the enormous Canal Walk shopping mall at Milnerton in the northeast past the harbour to the Waterfront. Around here you'll also find Green Point and the trendy enclave of Waterkant. Further along the coast on the west slope of Signal Hill are Sea Point, Bantry Bay, Clifton and Camps Bay. The road heads over the rump of mountains past Llandudno to Hout Bay and continues through the small Atlantic coast communities of Noordhoek and Kommetjie.

Heading west around Table Mountain and Devil's Peak will bring you to the Southern Suburbs, beginning with the bohomenian, edgy areas, Woodstock and Observatory, and moving through to the increasingly salubrious Rondebosch, Newlands and Constantia.

False Bay's string of seaside communities kicks off with Muizenberg and runs through Kalk Bay, Fish Hoek and Clovelly to the naval port of Simon's Town and rocky beach area known as Boulders. Continue in this direction and you'll eventually come to the end of the road at Cape Point.

Stretching along the N2 southeast of Table Mountain are the vast black townships of the Cape Flats: Langa, Guguletu, Crossroads and, the biggest community of all, Khayelitsha.

See each section and the Directory (p166) for transport details.

ITINERARIES
One Day

It's impossible to ignore Table Mountain (p63) so if you only have one day head straight for the cable car. After admiring the view, return to the city and wander through the orderly Company's Gardens (p60), nipping into the South African National Gallery (p63) to sample the best of the country's art. Get a taste of African cuisine at Off Moroka Café (p89) and then head over to the District Six Museum (p61). If you've managed to get a ticket, take an afternoon tour of Robben Island (p67); otherwise Greenmarket Square and Long St beckon for souvenir shopping (p60). If you've been to Robben Island, it's convenient to hang out at the Waterfront in the evening, having dinner at Emily's (p91) or One.Waterfront (p91), then maybe taking in a jazz performance at the Green Dolphin or Mannenberg's (p104). If you've stayed in the City Bowl, then dine at Aubergine (p90), and grab a nightcap at Planet (p99) in the Mount Nelson Hotel.

Three Days

Now that you're not in so much of a rush you might want to kick off your second day with a half-day tour of the Cape Flats townships (p58). These generally include the District Six Museum, thus freeing up more time to relax on day one. Consider having lunch at a township restaurant, such as Eziko in Langa (p96). In the late afternoon, pack your sun cream and towel and hit the beaches at Clifton or Camps Bay (p68); hang out here for dinner and a drink, too – we suggest Eclipse (p100) followed by Blues (p93).

On day three explore the Southern Suburbs, starting with a visit to the Irma Stern Museum (p71) and then a spot of wine tasting in Constantia; the picnic lunch at Buitenverwachting (p36) is lovely. Equally delightful is an afternoon stroll around Kirstenbosch Botanical Gardens (p72). You could have afternoon tea here or at the restaurant beside the nearby Rhodes Memorial (p71), with its sweeping view across the Cape Flats. Put on your dancing shoes in the evening and head over to the Waterkant (p103) to dine, drink and bop the night away with the gorgeous guys and girls.

One Week

Day four: time to get out of town. With fairytale scenery and a fantastic choice of wine and cuisine, the obvious choice is the Winelands around **Stellenbosch** (p148), **Franschhoek** (p152) and **Paarl** (p154). If you plan to stop over, plump for Franschhoek which has some amazing restaurants such as **Le Quartier Français** (p153). On the way there or back drop by **Vergelegen** (p39), one of the most impressive old wine estates. Alternatively, if it's the right season, a trip down to **Hermanus** (p156) is worth considering for either shark-cage diving or whale watching.

On day five explore the communities along False Bay. Go surfing in **Muizenberg** (p75) or walk down the coast to **St James** (p83). Have lunch at the **Olympia Café** (p95) and pick around **Kalk Bay's** many antique shops. Continue to **Simon's Town** (p75) and magnificent **Cape Point** (p76).

Day six, and it's time for some of those outdoor, adrenaline-pumping activities for which Cape Town is famous. Climb Table Mountain then **abseil** off the top (p110). If the wind is playing ball, do a **tandem paraglide** off Lion's Head (p114). Or you could go mountain biking down Table Mountain or in the **Tokai Arboretum** (p73). Join the boho-student set for an evening's carousing in Observatory at **Café Ganesh** (p94) and **Café Carte Blanche** (p101).

Shopping at the Waterfront or back in the City Bowl could easily take up your last day in town; drop by **Monkeybiz** (p128) and **Streetwires** (p128) for unique gifts that also help disadvantaged communities. Wrap it all up with a pan-African feast at the **Africa Cafe** (p87) or the best of modern South African cooking at **Savoy Cabbage** (p89), both in Heritage Square.

ORGANISED TOURS

HARBOUR CRUISES

A cruise into Table Bay should not be missed. Few people nowadays have the privilege of reaching Cape Town by passenger ship, but something of the feeling can be captured by taking a harbour cruise. Some cruises also take place in Hout Bay (p69) and around Cape Point from Simon's Town (p75). Also see Ferdinand's Tours (p58).

WATERFRONT BOAT COMPANY

Map pp203–5

☎ 418 5806; www.waterfrontboats.co.za; Shop 7, Quay 5, WaterfrontOffers a variety of cruises, including the highly recommended, 1½-hour sunset cruises (R170) on its handsome wood and brass–fitted schooners *Spirit of Victoria* and *Esperance*. A jet-boat ride is R250 for an hour.

CITY & GENERAL BUS TOURS

Major tour companies include **Springbok Atlas Tours** (☎ 417 6545) and **Hylton Ross** (☎ 511 1784; www.hyltonross.co.za); their tours are professional but tend to be expensive and are aimed at older travellers.

AFRICA OUTING

☎ 671 4028; www.afouting.com

A professional, gay-friendly operation run by two experienced and knowledgeable guys who can arrange pretty much whatever type of tour or vacation you want in South Africa, including safaris.

CAPE TOWN EXPLORER

☎ 426 4260

For a quick orientation on a fine day, you can't beat this open-top, double-decker bus tour which runs regularly on a circular route from the Waterfront via Cape Town Tourism and Camps Bay. A full trip (you can hop on and off) costs R90/40 per adult/child and takes two hours.

CAPE TOWN ON FOOT

☎ 426 4260

Contact **Cape Town Tourism** (p177) for details of these daily two-hour walking tours of the city centre (R100) or the Bo-Kaap (R75) led by experienced guide Ursula Stevens, Monday to Friday at 11am. The separate Footsteps to Freedom walking tour costs R100.

DAY TRIPPERS

☎ 511 4766; www.daytrippers.co.za

Long-running and very reliable tour company about which we've received excellent feedback. Mountain bikes are taken along on most trips, so you can do some riding if you want to. Most tours cost about R350 and include Cape Point, the Winelands and, in season, whale watching.

WANDERWOMEN TRAVEL

☎ 683 9215, 082 298 2085; www.wanderwomen.co.za

The women who run this tour company cater for all women, while being 'particularly attuned to the needs of our lesbian sisters'. They can organise accommodation bookings, transport and all sorts of tours.

TOWNSHIP & CULTURAL TOURS

Lots of operators offer township tours. A half-day tour is sufficient – the full-day tours tack on a trip to Robben Island that is best done separately and for which you don't need a guide. Consider asking the tour operator how much of what you spend actually goes to help people in the townships, since not all tours are run by Cape Flats residents. Bookings for most tours can be made directly or via Cape Town Tourism. If you're looking for a good individual guide try **Kenny Tokwe** (☎ 790 8704, 083 486 9667).

ADVENTURE KALK BAY
☎ 788 2242, 788 5113; adventure@kalkbay.co.za

This community-based tourism project offers guided walks around Kalk Bay and harbour explaining the fishing culture of the village. You'll need to be up well before dawn to go on a half-day fishing trip, so consider letting them arrange a homestay with one of the local families.

BO-KAAP COMMUNITY GUIDED TOURS
☎ 422 1554

To learn something of the Cape Muslim and Cape coloured experience take this good, history-based walking tour of the Bo-Kaap district (R100), which lasts around two hours.

CAPE TEAM TOURS
☎ 083 310 6454; www.capett.co.za

This company runs township tours (R195) following the usual agenda plus a visit to the open-air meat market in Nyanga. Its full-day winelands tours are R295, along the Whale Route to Hermanus R345.

CHARLOTTE'S WALKING TOURS
☎ 083 982 5692

A good alternative to the standard bus tour around the Cape Flats townships is this walking tour of Masiphumelele, the township on the way to Kommetjie, led by the ebullient Charlotte and starting from the **Two Oceans Crafts and Culture Centre** (p69).

GRASSROUTE TOURS
☎ 706 1006; www.grassroutetours.co.za

This is one of the most experienced operators of townships tours (half/full day R290/450). Its guides are enthusiastic and knowledgeable,

and tours usually drop by **Vicky's B&B** (p144) for a chat with this Khayelitsha legend. It also runs other tours including a walking tour of the Bo-Kaap to learn about Cape Muslims (R240), a full day in the winelands (R430) and another to Hermanus (R465).

NEW WORLD INC
☎ 790 8825

Operators Debbie Bird and Jan Jasone specialise in music tours of the townships. These can include workshops on African instruments or traditional dancing as well as visits to local *shebeens* (unlicensed drinking establishment) and clubs such as Duma's Falling Leaves and Yellow Door.

SAM'S CULTURAL TOURS
☎ 423 5417, 082 970 0564

The charming Sam Ntimba also works for Day Trippers on its township tours. His half-day trip (R250) includes visits to a dormitory and *shebeen* in Langa and a crèche project in Khayelitsha. He can also arrange Sunday tours to see a gospel choir in a Baptist church in Langa.

TANA BARU CULTURAL TOURS
☎ 424 0719

Tana Baru offers a tour of the Bo-Kaap that focuses on people, and includes tea at the guide's home (R150). This company can also arrange B&B accommodation in the Bo-Kaap for R150 per person.

TOWNSHIP TOURS SA
☎ 083 719 4870

Guide Afrika Moni takes you on a two-hour walking tour (R75) of the Hout Bay township Imizamo Yethu, including a visit to a *sangoma*, a *shebeen* and art projects.

WINERY TOURS

Plenty of companies offer day trips to the Winelands, but unless you're tight for time it's better to stay overnight in, say, Stellenbosch and take a tour from there. See p148 for details of a couple of operators.

FERDINAND'S TOURS & ADVENTURES
☎ 421 1660

Larger-than-life Ferdinand became a media star after winning South Africa's first *Big Brother* TV show. He's since cut back on running these tours himself, but they are still a very popular option for backpackers and those who are seriously into their wines. The tours (R335) take in at least four wineries and include lunch. Things can get pretty raucous, which they also do on the regular, catamaran booze cruises (R245) out of Gordon's Bay on the False Bay side of the city.

OTHER TOURS

BIRDWATCH CAPE
☎ 762 5059; www.birdwatch.co.za
Bird expert Richard Grant runs these informative tours pointing out the many unique species of the Cape floral kingdom; a half-day trip costs R270. He also offers trips further afield in the Karoo, the Kalahari and along the Garden Route.

CAPE FASHION TOURS
☎ 083 299 8728
Lee Thomas has 17 years of fashion-buying experience both locally and internationally. She will tailor a half-day tour (R500) exactly to your shopping needs, taking you to up-and-coming boutiques and discount outlets in areas of Cape Town where no tourist ever ventures.

IMVUBU NATURE TOURS
☎ 706 0842; www.imvubu.co.za
Imvubu, meaning hippopotamus in both Xhosa and Zulu, is the name given by Graham and Joy to their nature tour company based at the **Rondevlei Nature Reserve** (p74). Take one of their tours (adult/child R30/15) around the reserve and you might be lucky enough to see the elusive hippos. Increase your chances by arranging to stay on the island bush camp. Boat trips, for a minimum of four people, are held between August and February and cost R30 per person.

Iziko Museums
Fourteen museums in central Cape Town are jointly managed under the umbrella of **Iziko** (www.museums .org.za/iziko), a Xhosa word meaning hearth. The official names of the museums are all now proceeded by Iziko, hence Iziko: South African Gallery. We list the names of the museums here without Iziko. Note that four of the house museums – Bertram House, Koopmans-de Wet House, Rust en Vreugd and Natale Labia Museum – are now open one day a week and then by appointment only.

CITY CENTRE
Eating pp87–91; Shopping pp126–9; Sleeping pp134–8

Cape Town's City Bowl is the oldest European-style urban area in Africa. Here you'll find both the castle and garden set out by the original Dutch settlers, not to mention the infamous Slave Lodge and the Dutch Reform churches – structures representing the economic and spiritual backbone of the colony. It's certainly an atmospheric area to explore, with lots of street life, including art stalls and buskers along the length of St George's Mall and in Greenmarket Square, and the flower sellers at Trafalgar Place off Adderley St – take one of the walking tours we recommend on p79 to see what we mean.

Bustling with commerce during the day, the City Bowl is much quieter at night, although it's readying itself for an influx of loft-style apartment dwellers, as buildings such as the Mutual and the Board of Executors are given radical makeovers. The new Cape Town International Convention Centre and planned development of Duncan Dock on the Foreshore are pushing the focus of the city closer to the seafront.

In the meantime, if you're looking for action day or night, head to Long St, the city's most appealing thoroughfare with its iron-lace balconied Victorian buildings. Long St was once part of the Bo-Kaap, the Cape Muslim area famous for its brightly painted houses. There's a strong sense of community in the Bo-Kaap – listen out for the horn tooted by the mobile fishmonger doing his rounds and the daily calls to prayer booming from the suburb's several mosques, including the Auwal, the city's oldest such building. Pretty as it is in the daytime, this is not an area in which you'll want to be wandering alone late at night.

West of the City Bowl is Zonnebloem (Sunflower in Afrikaans). This largely desolate tract of land used to be District Six, where a poor, multiracial community flourished until the late 1960s when, in the madness of apartheid, it was razed to the ground and redesignated a

Transport

A good way to get around within the City Bowl is by Rikki, which are small Asian-style open vans; these operate from 7am to 7pm Mon-Fri and until 2pm on Saturday. Another cheap and efficient way to get around is in shared taxis, which cover the city in an informal network of routes. At night it may be safer to take a non-shared taxi but these are more expensive.

whites-only area. There are a few buildings here, including old mosques, churches, the Cape Technikon college and the new houses being built for District Six returnees (p44), but it's a forbidding area that you'd be well advised not to wander around alone, especially after dark.

The Company's Gardens, around which are some of the city's top museums, are the verdant conduit linking the City Bowl with the mainly high-class residential areas of Gardens, Tamboerskloof, Oranjezicht and Vredehoek. Here you'll find some of Cape Town's most appealing and individual accommodation options. Need we mention that the area is dominated by the massive bulk of Table Mountain and the adjacent rocky hump of Lion's Head? You'll hardly be able to keep your eyes off it, especially when the famous tablecloth of cloud is tumbling off the flat summit.

Orientation

The City Bowl is bordered by Buitenkant St to the southeast, Buitengracht St to the northwest and Orange St and Annandale Rd to the south. Its main thoroughfare is Adderley St, which continues through the Company's Gardens as Government Ave. Further to the west up the slopes of Signal Hill is the Bo-Kaap, the focus of which is Wale St; to the east, around Tennant St, is Zonnebloem.

Kloof St is the backbone of Gardens. West and up Signal Hill is Tamboerskloof, while Oranjezicht lies to the east behind De Waal Park. Vredehoek is further to the east up the side to Table Mountain.

CITY BOWL, BO-KAAP & ZONNEBLOEM

BO-KAAP MUSEUM Map pp200–2

☎ 481 3939; www.museums.org.za/iziko; 71 Wale St, Bo-Kaap; adult/child R5/2; ◷ 9am-4pm Mon-Sat

The small and engaging Bo-Kaap Museum gives an insight into the lifestyle of a prosperous, 19th-century, Cape Muslim family and a somewhat idealised view of Islamic practice in Cape Town. The house itself, built in 1763, is the oldest in the area.

CAPE TOWN INTERNATIONAL CONVENTION CENTRE Map pp200–2

☎ 410 5000; www.cticc.co.za; Convention Square, 1 Lower Long St, City Bowl

The Cape Town International Convention Centre (CTICC) opened in mid-2003, providing more than 10,000 sq metres of exhibition space, a major theatre, a modern African restaurant and a swanky business hotel. As far as its architecture goes it's a step in the right direction at this depressingly concrete end of the City Bowl.

Big events such as the **North Sea Jazz Festival** (p10) and the **Mother City Queer Project** (p11) have been held here. If nothing else, step inside to admire the bold and distinctive artworks gracing the foyer; the main focus is the giant relief sculpture in the main hall, *Baobabs, Stormclouds, Ani-*

mals and People (p29). There's a water taxi station linking CTICC to the Waterfront (p169).

CASTLE OF GOOD HOPE Map pp200–2

☎ 787 1200; www.castleofgoodhope.co.za; Entrance on Buitenkant St, City Bowl; adult/child Mon-Sat R18/8, Sun R9/4; ◷ 9am-4pm; tours 11am, noon & 2pm Mon-Sat

Built between 1666 and 1679 to defend Cape Town, the stone-walled castle has never seen action in all its 350 years, unless you count the more recent stormings by hordes of school kids and tourists. It's worth coming for one of the tours (the noon tour on weekdays coincides with the changing of the guard, since the castle is still the headquarters for the Western Cape military command), although you can quite easily find your own way around. A key ceremony is held at 10am weekdays. There are extensive

City Centre Top Five

- Take the cable car up **Table Mountain** (p64)
- Learn about Cape Town's troubled history at the **District Six Museum** (p61)
- Tour the **Houses of Parliament** (p61)
- Go souvenir shopping in **Greenmarket Square** (p129)
- Discover the best of local contemporary art at the **South Africa National Gallery** (p64)

displays of militaria and some interesting information about the castle's archaeology and the reconstruction of the so-called Dolphin Pool. The highlight is the bulk of the **William Fehr Collection** (☺ 9.30am-4pm), including some fabulous bits of Cape Dutch furniture, such as a table seating 100, and paintings by John Thomas Baines.

COMPANY'S GARDENS Map pp200–2

The surviving six hectares of Jan van Riebeeck's original 18-hectare vegetable garden are found around Government Ave with main gates at the south end of Adderley St next to St George's Cathedral and on Annandale Rd in Gardens. They once provided fresh produce for the ships of the Dutch East India Company (Vereenigde Oost-Indische Compagnie; VOC), but, as sources of supply were diversified, the grounds became a superb pleasure garden, planted with a fine collection of botanical specimens from South Africa and the rest of the world. They are a lovely place to escape the bustle of the city, although there are occasional reports of muggings (security has apparently been beefed up in response).

You'll pass through the gardens on the way to the **South African Museum** (p64) and **South African National Gallery** (p64). Keep an eye out for statues designed by Sir Herbert Baker (p26). These include the Delville Wood Memorial, honouring South African soldiers who fell during WWI, and the statue of Cecil Rhodes, hand held high and pointing north in his vainglorious imperialist dream of an empire from the Cape to Cairo. It was he who imported the gardens' squirrels from North America.

DISTRICT SIX MUSEUM Map pp200–2

☎ 461 8745; www.districtsix.co.za; 25A Buitenkant St, City Bowl; adult/child R10/5; ☺ 9am-3pm Mon-Thu, 9am-4pm Fri

If you see only one museum in Cape Town, make it this one; note that almost all township tours stop here first to explain the history of the pass laws. The museum is as much *for* the people of the now vanished District Six as it is *about* them. The displays are moving and poignant: a floor covered with a large-scale map of District Six, former residents having labelled where their demolished homes and features of their neighbourhood were; reconstructions of home interiors; faded photographs and recordings. Most memorable of all are the staff, practically all displaced residents themselves, each with a heartbreaking story to tell (see the boxed text on p52). You can arrange **walking tours** (☎ 466 7208; R50; 10 people minimum) of the old **District Six**.

GOLD OF AFRICA MUSEUM Map pp200–2

☎ 405 1540; www.goldofafrica.com; 96 Strand St, City Bowl; adult/child R20/10; ☺ 9.30am-5pm Mon-Sat

Established by Anglogold, the biggest gold-mining company in the world, this glitzy museum in the Martin Melck House (dating from 1783) promotes African gold jewellery. There are some stunning pieces, mostly from West Africa, and it's all well displayed with lots of background. The shop is worth a browse for interesting gold souvenirs including copies of some of the pieces in the museum.

GROOTE KERK Map pp200–2

☎ 461 7044; Upper Adderley St, City Bowl; admission free; ☺ 10am-2pm Mon-Fri; services 10am, 7pm Sun

Nip inside the once-grand mother church of the Dutch Reformed Church (Nederduitse Gereformeerde Kerk, or NG Kerk) to admire the mammoth organ and ornate Burmese teak pulpit. The first church on the site was built in 1704, but only parts of it remain; most of the current building dates from 1841. A number of early notables have tombs inside.

HOUSES OF PARLIAMENT Map pp200–2

☎ 403 2537; www.parliament.gov.za; Parliament St, City Bowl; admission free; tours by appointment Mon-Fri

Visiting the houses of parliament is one of the most fascinating things you can do in Cape Town. If parliament is sitting, fix your tour for the afternoon so you can see the politicians in action. Opened in 1885, this is where British prime minister Harold Macmillan made his 'Wind of Change' speech in 1960. The articulate tour guides will fill you in on the mechanisms and political make up of their new democracy. You must present your passport to gain entry. Also contact the **Parliamentary Millennium Project** (☎ 403 8246; www.pmpsa.gov.za) about touring its mapping and cultural exhibitions. Look out for the massive four-panel mural celebrating the adoption of the Constitution opposite the public entrance on Plein St.

KOOPMANS-DE WET HOUSE Map pp200–2

☎ 464 3280; www.museums.org.za/iziko; 35 Strand St, City Bowl; adult/child R5/2; ☺ Mon by appointment only

This is a classic example of a Cape Dutch townhouse, furnished with 18th- and early-19th-century antiques. It's an atmospheric place with ancient vines growing in the courtyard and floorboards that squeak just as they probably did during the times of Marie Koopmans-de Wet, the socialite owner after whom the house is named.

Flower sellers on Trafalgar Place (p59)

LONG ST Map pp200–2

This most attractive of the City Bowl's streets, stacked with second-hand bookshops, is also getting a reputation for its streetwear boutiques, a good complement to the host of bars and clubs that crank up at night. It's difficult to believe, given its hedonistic and utterly commercial nature (it even has its own website: www.longstreet.co.za), that this was once part of the city's Islamic quarter. Several of the area's old mosques remain including the **Noor el Hamedia Mosque** (1884), on the corner of Dorp St, and the **Palm Tree Mosque** at 185 Long St, the last 18th-century house on the street.

LONG ST BATHS Map pp200–2

☎ 400 3302; cnr Long & Buitensingel Sts; adult/child R8/5; ☼ 7am-7pm Mon-Sat, 7am-6pm Sun

These nicely restored baths with painted murals of city centre life on the walls are heated and very popular with the local community. You'll also find here the separate **Turkish steam baths** (R45). Women are admitted 8.30am to 7.30pm Monday and Thursday, 8.30am to 1pm Tuesday, 9am to 6pm Saturday; men 1am to 7.30pm Tuesday, 8am to 7.30pm Wednesday and Friday, and 8am to noon Sunday. Massages are available for women (R60).

LUTHERAN CHURCH Map pp200–2

☎ 421 5854; 98 Strand St, City Bowl; admission free; ☼ 10am-2pm Mon-Fri

Converted from a barn in 1780, the first Lutheran church in the Cape has a striking pulpit,

perhaps the best created by the master German sculptor Anton Anreith, whose work can also be seen in **Groote Kerk** (p61) and at **Groot Constantia**. (p36). Go to the room behind the pulpit to see the collection of old Bibles.

MICHAELIS COLLECTION Map pp200–2

☎ 481 3933; www.museums.org.za/iziko; Greenmarket Square, City Bowl; admission by donation; ☼ 10am-5pm Mon-Fri

Donated by Sir Max Michaelis in 1914, this impressive art collection is in the Old Townhouse, which used to be the City Hall. The Dutch and Flemish paintings and etchings from the 16th and 17th centuries (including works by Rembrandt, Frans Hals and Anthony van Dyck) have benefited from the recent bright repainting of the once gloomy house. Consider dropping by for lunch or a drink in the relaxed **Ivy Garden Restaurant** (p88) in the courtyard behind.

RUST EN VREUGD Map pp200–2

☎ 464 3280; www.museums.org.za/iziko; 78 Buitenkant St, City Bowl; ☼ Mon by appointment only

This delightful, 18th-century mansion was once the home of the state prosecutor. It now houses part of the William Fehr collection of paintings and furniture (the major part is in the Castle of Good Hope). Paintings by John Thomas Baines show early scenes from colonial Cape Town, while the sketches of Cape Dutch architecture by Alys Fane Trotter are some of the best you'll see. There's also a pleasant garden.

SIGNAL HILL & NOON GUN Map pp203–5

Once also known as Lion's Rump, as it is attached to Lion's Head by a 'spine' of hills, Signal Hill separates Sea Point from the City Bowl. There are magnificent views from the 350m-high summit, especially at night. Head up Kloof Nek Rd from the city and take the first turn-off to the right at the top of the hill. At this intersection you also turn off for Clifton (also to the right) and the lower cableway station (left).

Signal Hill was the early settlement's lookout point, and it was from here that flags were hoisted when a ship was spotted, giving the citizens below time to prepare their goods for sale and dust off their tankards.

At noon, Monday to Saturday, a cannon known as the **Noon Gun** is fired from the lower slopes of Signal Hill. You can hear it all over town. Traditionally this allowed the burghers in the town below to check their watches. It's a stiff walk up here through the Bo-Kaap – take Longmarket St and keep going until it ends. The **Noon Gun Tearoom & Restaurant** (p88) is a good place to catch your breath.

SLAVE LODGE Map pp200–2

☎ 460 8240; www.museums.org.za/iziko; 49 Adderley St, City Bowl; adult/child R10/2; ☼ 8.30am-4.30pm Mon-Sat

Once the Cultural History Museum, the former Slave Lodge of the VOC is a museum in transition, the aim being to focus the displays directly on the history and experience of slaves and their descendants in the Cape. The bits and pieces in its collection from ancient Egypt, Greece and Rome and the Far East may stay here but, if so, are likely to be relegated to upper-floor galleries.

One of the oldest buildings in South Africa, dating back to 1660, the Slave Lodge has a fascinating history in itself. Until 1811 the building was home, if you could call it that, to as many as 1000 slaves, who lived in damp, insanitary, crowded conditions. Up to 20% died each year. The slaves were bought and sold just around the corner on Spin St.

From the late 18th century the lodge was used as a brothel, a jail for petty criminals and political exiles from Indonesia, and a mental asylum. In 1811 it became Cape Town's first post office. Later it became a library, and it was the Cape Supreme Court until 1914. The walls of the original Slave Lodge flank the interior courtyard, where you can find the tombstones of Cape Town's founder, Jan van Riebeeck, and his wife Maria de la Queillerie. The tombstones were moved here from Jakarta where Van Riebeeck is buried.

SOUTH AFRICAN MISSIONARY MEETING HOUSE MUSEUM Map pp200–2

☎ 423 6755; 40 Long St, City Bowl; adult/child R7.50/4; ☼ 9am-4pm Mon-Fri

Cape Town's first church for slaves is also known as the Sendinggestig Museum and dates from 1802. Its interior is plain but quite handsome; the focus, as always, is the wooden pulpit.

GARDENS, TAMBOERSKLOOF, ORANJEZICHT & VREDEHOEK

BERTRAM HOUSE

☎ 424 9381; www.museums.org.za/iziko; cnr Orange St & Government Ave, Gardens; ☼ Mon by appointment only

A minor diversion if you're at this end of the Company's Gardens to arrange a visit to this, the only surviving, Georgian-style, brick house in Cape Town, dating from the 1840s. Inside it's decorated appropriately to its era with Regency-style furnishings and 19th-century English porcelain.

CAPE TOWN HOLOCAUST CENTRE Map p206

☎ 462 5553; www.museums.org.za/ctholocaust; 88 Hatfield St, Gardens; admission free; ☼ 10am-5pm Sun-Thu, 10am-1pm Fri.

This admirable museum is in the same complex of buildings as the **South African Jewish Museum** (p64). It's small, but packs a lot in with a considerable emotional punch. The history of anti-Semitism is set in a South African context with parallels drawn to the local struggle for freedom. Stop to watch the video tales of Holocaust survivors at the end.

LION'S HEAD Map pp203–5

The 2.2km hike from Kloof Nek Rd to the peak of Lion's Head is one of the best you can do in Cape Town and is highly recommended on a full-moon night when many people gather at the summit to watch the sun go down. The moonlight aids the walk back down, but you should always bring a torch (flashlight) with you. The track's start is clearly marked at the top of Kloof Nek; it involves a little climbing but there are chains on the rocks.

PLANETARIUM Map p206

☎ 424 3330; www.museums.org.za/iziko; 25 Queen Victoria St, Gardens; adult/child R10/6; ☼ 10am-5pm

Attached to the South African Museum, the displays and star shows here unravel the mysteries of the southern hemisphere's night sky. Shows (adult/child R20/6) are given on Tuesday (2pm and 8pm, the latter includes a 3D star show), Thursday (2pm) and Saturday (2.30pm). There are more frequent shows during school holidays.

SOUTH AFRICAN JEWISH MUSEUM
Map p206

☎ 465 1546; www.sajewishmuseum.co.za; 88 Hatfield St, Gardens; adult/child R50/25; ☉ 10am-5pm Sun-Thu, 10am-2pm Fri

This is one of the most imaginatively designed and interesting of the city's museums. Entry is through the beautifully restored **Old Synagogue** (1862); from here a wooden gangplank leads to state-of-the-art galleries with displays on the vibrant history of the nation's Jewish community, which today numbers about 90,000. Downstairs you'll find a partial recreation of a Lithuanian *shtetl* (village); many of South Africa's Jews fled this part of Eastern Europe during the pogroms and persecution of the late 19th and early 20th centuries. There's also a computerised system where you can trace Jewish relations in South Africa, and good temporary exhibitions.

It's possible also to visit the beautifully decorated baroque **Great Synagogue** (guided tours ☉ 10am-2pm Mon-Thu, 10am-4pm Sun). The Gardens Shul, as it was known, was consecrated the same year that Cape Town elected its first Jewish mayor, Hyman Liberman.

SOUTH AFRICAN MUSEUM Map p206

☎ 424 3330; www.museums.org.za/iziko; 25 Queen Victoria St, Gardens; adult/child R8/2, free Sun; ☉ 10am-5pm

South Africa's oldest museum is currently undergoing a major reorganisation of its collection. The first stage has largely been completed with a new gallery showcasing the art and culture of the area's first peoples, the Khoikhoi and San, and including the famous Linton Panel, an amazing example of San rock art. There's an extraordinary delicacy to the paintings, particularly the ones of graceful eland.

Throughout the rest of the building there is a fascinating collection of objects. Look out for: the startlingly lifelike displays in the African Cultures Gallery of African people (cast from living subjects); the terracotta Lydenburg Heads, the earliest known examples of African sculpture (AD 500–700); the Whale Well, hung with giant skeletons of these mammals and sometimes used as a venue for concerts; a stuffed quagga foal (the very exhibit that

---

Table Mountain Dos & Don'ts

Do

- Tell someone the route you're planning to climb and take a map (or better still a guide)
- Take water and some food
- Take a weatherproof jacket – the weather can change for the worse with lightning speed
- Wear proper hiking boots or shoes and a sun hat
- Take a mobile phone, if you have one

Don't

- Climb alone
- Leave litter on the mountain
- Make a fire on the mountain – they're banned

---

provided the DNA to start the rebreeding of the thought-to-be-extinct quagga); the fascinating Wonders of Nature Gallery; and the 2m-wide nest of the sociable weaver bird, a veritable avian apartment block.

SA NATIONAL GALLERY Map p206

☎ 467 4660; www.museums.org.za/iziko; Government Ave, Gardens; adult/child R10/2, Sun free; ☉ 10am-5pm Tue-Sun

There are always fascinating exhibitions here at South Africa's premier art space, as well as permanent displays, including the wonderful sculpture the *Butcher Boys* by Jane Alexander, looking like a trio of *Lord of the Rings* orcs who have stumbled into the gallery. Also check out the remarkable carved teak door in the courtyard, and a dinosaur sculpture made of wire. There's a pleasant café and a good shop with some interesting books.

TABLE MOUNTAIN NATIONAL PARK

The renamed Table Mountain National Park (www.tmnp.co.za) covers some three quarters of the peninsula and stretches from flat-topped Table Mountain to Cape Point. Here we focus on the main attraction – the 1086m mountain itself.

CABLE CAR Map p206

☎ 424 8181, www.tablemountain.net; summer rates one way/return adult R55/105, child R28/55; ☉ 8.30am-7pm Feb-Nov, 8am-10pm Dec-Jan

It's easy to see why the revolving cable car up Table Mountain is such a popular attraction.

Hoerikwaggo Hiking Trail

At the time of research, details were still to be finalised for the planned Hoerikwaggo Hiking Trail through Table Mountain National Park. The official launch will be in 2005, but this is already shaping up to be the No 1 hike in South Africa. It will start just south of the City Bowl in Vredehoek and run for five days and roughly 80km across the unique *fynbos*-covered world of Table Mountain, down the Atlantic Coast to Kommetjie and across to Silvermine to culminate at the very tip of Cape Point.

Table Mountain National Park (opposite), which is constructing and will be managing the trail, named it Hoerikwaggo after the ancient Khoikhoi and San word for Table Mountain. The trail's development has provided work for people in the peninsula's townships of Masiphumelele, Imizamo Yethu, Westlake, Ocean View and Red Hill, and involved airlifting some 50 tonnes of local sandstone to bridge gaps in and shore up eroded parts of the planned trail. There will be basic accommodation in existing structures on the mountain as well as camping allowed around designated areas with eco-friendly water and ablution facilities.

For more details, including the fees and registration system, check the park's website www.tmnp.co.za.

The views from the car and the summit are phenomenal. Once you are at the top there are souvenir shops, a café and some easy walks to follow. The cable cars (departing every 10 minutes in high season and every 20 minutes in low season) don't operate when it's dangerously windy, and there's obviously not much point going up if you are simply going to be wrapped in the cloud known as 'the tablecloth'. Call in advance to see if they're operating. The best visibility and conditions are likely to be first thing in the morning or in the evening.

If you don't have your own transport, **Rikkis** (p169) will come up here for R10; a non-shared taxi will cost around R50.

CLIMBING TABLE MOUNTAIN

More than 300 routes up and down the mountain have been identified, perhaps indicating how easy it is to get lost. Bear in mind that the mountain is more than 1000m high and conditions can become treacherous quickly. Thick mists can make the paths invisible, and you'll just have to wait until they lift. Unprepared and foolhardy hikers die here every year; read our dos and don'ts (p64) before setting off. Also, see p112 if you're looking for a guide.

None of the routes is easy but the **Platteklip Gorge** walk on the City Bowl side is at least straightforward. Unless you're fit, try walking down before you attempt the walk up. It took us about 2½ hours from the upper cableway station to the lower, taking it fairly easy. Be warned that the route is exposed to the sun and for much of the way is a straight-up slog.

Another option is the **Indian Windows** route that starts from directly behind the lower cableway station and heads straight up. The hikers you see from the cable car, perched like mountain goats on apparently sheer cliffs, are taking this route, and it's the one you'll end up on if you do the abseil from the summit.

If you don't fancy either of these, consider the **Pipe Track**, a less-steep route that runs along the western side of the mountain towards the Twelve Apostles. For details of this and a couple of popular routes to (or from) the summit to **Kirstenbosch Botanical Gardens** (p72), search out copies of either Mike Lundy's *Best Walks in the Cape Peninsula* or Shirley Brossy's *Walking Guide to Table Mountain*, which details 34 walks.

Top Five Viewpoints

- **Bloubergstrand** (p67) – head to this beach north of the city for a postcard-perfect view of Table Mountain.
- **Camps Bay** (p68) – drive down Kloof Rd towards this ritzy beachside suburb for sweeping views of the magnificent mountain crags known as the Twelve Apostles.
- **Chapman's Peak Drive** (p69) – pause along this thrilling cliffside road to take in the perfect view of horseshoe-shaped Hout Bay.
- **Signal Hill** (p63) – attend the firing of the Noon Gun here and then take in the activity of the waterfront and docks spread beneath.
- **Table Mountain** (p64) – you've done the rest, now do the best. The flat expanse of the summit provides sweeping vistas across the city from the sea to the Cape Flats.

ATLANTIC COAST

Eating pp91–3; Shopping pp122–3; Sleeping pp138–41

The Atlantic coast of the Cape Peninsula has some of the most spectacular coastal scenery in the world. The beaches include the trendiest on the Cape, with the emphasis on sunbathing. Although it's possible to shelter from the summer southeasterlies, the water comes straight from the Antarctic and swimming is exhilarating (ie, freezing).

The bland suburban neighbourhoods of Bloubergstrand and Milnerton to the north of the city will not be top of anyone's sightseeing wish list, but they still have their attractions, namely a beach with a view and a gigantic shopping centre, respectively. In contrast, the **Victoria & Alfred Waterfront** (always just called the Waterfront) is likely to be one of the first places you head to. It's a shining example of how to best redevelop a declining dock area into a tourist hot spot. The atmosphere is always buzzing and there's plenty to do, including making a trip out to **Robben Island** (opposite), the infamous prison island that is now a fascinating museum.

The outcrop of land west of the Waterfront is **Green Point**, a largely undeveloped area of reclaimed land with a stadium, a golf course and a large Sunday market. As well as being the name of the actual point, Green Point is also the name of the surrounding suburb, which includes a couple of smaller residential neighbourhoods: rocky **Mouille Point**, right on the Atlantic coast and an atmospheric place for a stroll on a stormy day; and **Waterkant**, the focus of gay life in Cape Town and currently one of the most happening parts of the city.

Separated from the City Bowl by Signal Hill, densely populated **Sea Point** is a somewhat down-at-heel residential suburb, once popular with Cape Town's Jewish population, but now filling up with dubious bars and massage parlours. Still, the numerous multistorey apartment buildings fringing the coast have an Art Deco, almost Miami Beach elegance, while Main Rd and Regent St are lined with good, cheap restaurants, cafés and shops.

Moving south, the exclusive and wealthy residential neighbourhoods of Bantry Bay, Clifton and Camps Bay follow hard and fast on each other in a tumble of mansions with to-die-for sea views. **Camps Bay**, in particular, is a popular spot with visitors and locals; it has good accommodation, restaurants and bars for those all-important drinks at sunset.

There's a stretch of protected parkland at Ouderkraal before the even more exclusive village of Llandudno, clinging to steep slopes above a sheltered beach. It has no shops. The remains of the tanker *Romelia*, which was wrecked in 1977, lie off Sunset Rocks here and down a coastal path the nude bathing beach, **Sandy Bay**.

Over the pass beside Little Lions Head (436m), Victoria Rd drops to the decidedly less-ritzy fishing community of Hout Bay nestling behind the almost vertical Sentinel and the steep slopes of Chapman's Peak. Inland from the 1km stretch of white sand, there's a fast-growing satellite town that still manages to retain something of its village atmosphere. There's also the township of **Imizamo Yethu**, also known as Mandela Park, in which it's possible to do a walking tour (p58).

At the end of the spectacular Chapman's Peak Drive lies the rustic community of **Noordhoek**, principally famous for is wide sandy beach. Further south is the surfing mecca of **Kommetjie** (pronounced komickey, but also known as just 'Kom'), an equally small, quiet and isolated crayfishing village.

Orientation

Bloubergstrand lies 25km north of the city on Table Bay; take the R27 off the N1 to get there. The N1 also goes right past Canal Walk in Milnerton.

The increased development at the Waterfront and Foreshore makes it slightly safer to walk from City Bowl: stick to Dock Rd and only do it during daylight hours. Otherwise, shuttle buses run frequently from Adderley St in front of the main train station up Strand St to the centre of the Waterfront. They also leave from near the Sea Point Pavilion in Sea Point. If you're driving, there are lots of free parking spaces around the Waterfront and, if they're full, there's plenty of paid parking at fairly inexpensive rates.

BLOUBERGSTRAND

BLOUBERGSTRAND BEACH Map pp196–7
This was where the British won their 1806 battle for the Cape. It is also the spot with the oft-photographed view of Table Mountain – you know, the one with wildflowers and sand dunes in the foreground, surf and, across the bay, the cloud-capped mountain ramparts looming over the city. The village of Bloubergstrand itself is attractive enough, with picnic areas, some long, uncrowded, windy stretches of sand, and a good pub, the Blue Peter (p102). This is windsurfer territory (p114), but there are also opportunities for some surfing, best with a moderate northeasterly wind, a small swell and an incoming tide.

GREEN POINT, WATERFRONT & ROBBEN ISLAND

Much of the Waterfront's charm derives from the fact that it remains a working harbour. Most of the redevelopment has been undertaken around the historic Alfred and Victoria Basins (constructed from 1860 and named after Queen Victoria and her son Alfred). Although these wharves are too small for modern container vessels and tankers, the Victoria Basin is still used by tugs, harbour vessels of various kinds, and fishing boats.

The Waterfront has tons of strict security and, although it is safe to walk around at all hours, there are plenty of merry men, so lone women should be a little cautious. See the Eating (p85) and Entertainment (p97) chapters for our pick of the numerous restaurants and bars.

CAPE MEDICAL MUSEUM Map pp203–5
☎ 418 5663; Portswood Rd, Green Point; admission by donation; ☽ 9am-4pm Tue-Fri
This museum is perhaps worth a few minutes on your way to the Waterfront. Its most fascinating display is on Dr James Barrie, a woman who disguised herself as a man for years so she could practise as a doctor; she performed the Cape Colony's first successful Caesarean operation in 1818.

ROBBEN ISLAND Map pp203–5
☎ 419 4200; www.robben-island.org.za; adult/child R150/75; hourly ferries 8am-3pm, sunset tours 5pm & 6pm Dec-Jan
Proclaimed a UN World Heritage Site in 1999, Robben Island is unmissable. Most likely you will have to endure crowds and being hustled around on a guided tour that at 2½ hours is

Transport

Shared taxis run regularly along Main Rd through Green Point to the end of Regent Rd in Sea Point. Golden Arrow buses (p166) follow the same route, then continue to Victoria Rd and down to Hout Bay. After that, it's private transport only along Chapman's Peak Drive to Noordhoek and all points further south. Be warned that parking at Clifton and Camps Bay in summer can be a nightmare, especially on the weekend.

woefully short – such is the price of the island's infamy. Still, you should go to see this shrine to the struggle against apartheid.

Used as a prison from the early days of the VOC right up until the first years of majority rule, Robben Island's most famous involuntary resident was Nelson Mandela. You will learn much of what happened to Mandela and other inmates, since one of those former inmates will be leading your tour. The guides are happy to answer any questions you may have, and although some understandably remain bitter, as a whole this is the best demonstration of reconciliation you could hope to see in Cape Town.

Booking a tour is essential as they are extremely popular; otherwise be prepared for a long wait. Tickets can be booked at the **Nelson Mandela Gateway** departure point beside the Clock Tower or at **Cape Town Tourism** (☎ 426 4260) in the city.

The standard tour includes being guided through the old prison, as well as a 45-minute bus ride around the island with commentary on the various places of note, such as the prison house of Pan-African Congress (PAC) leader Robert Sobuke, the lime quarry in which Mandela and many others slaved, and the church used during the island's stint as a leper colony. There will also be a little time for you to wander around on your own; you could check out the penguin colony near the landing jetty.

All tours have a set departure and return time but, when you book, consider asking to extend your time on the island so you have

Atlantic Coast Top Five

- Dig into South Africa's troubled past on **Robben Island** (p67)
- Dive with sharks at **Two Oceans Aquarium** (p68)
- Strip off on beautiful **Sandy Bay Beach** (p68)
- Motor along spectacular **Chapman's Peak Drive** (p69)
- Swim at **Sea Point Pavilion** (p68)

time to see **Cell Stories**, a remarkable exhibition in the prison's A Section (not part of the regular tour). Here in each of 40 isolation cells is an artefact and story from a former political prisoner: chess pieces drawn on scraps of paper; a Christmas card from a forgotten wife; an intricately patterned belt made from fishing nets and old shoe leather; a soccer trophy. It's all unbelievably moving.

SA MARITIME MUSEUM Map pp203–5
☎ 405 2880; www.museums.org.za/iziko; Dock Rd, Waterfront; adult/child R10/3; ⏱ 10am-5pm

There are lots of model ships and some full-sized ones at this marginally interesting museum, which is a bit of a poor relation at the Waterfront. Admission includes entry to SAS *Somerset*, a wartime vessel now permanently docked beside the museum.

TWO OCEANS AQUARIUM Map pp203–5
☎ 418 3823; www.aquarium.co.za; Dock Rd, Waterfront; adult/child R55/25; ⏱ 9.30am-6pm

As aquariums go, this an excellent one. It features denizens of the deep from the cold and the warm oceans that border the Cape Peninsula, including ragged-tooth sharks. There are seals, penguins, turtles, an astounding kelp forest open to the sky, and pools in which kids can touch sea creatures; these things alone are worth the entry fee.

Qualified divers can get in the water for a closer look. Sharing the tank with five sharks, a 150kg, short-tailed stingray, other predatory fish and a delightful turtle wouldn't be everyone's idea of fun, but for experienced divers (certificate required) this is a great way to get really close to the ocean action. The cost is R400 including hire of diving gear.

Get your hand stamped on entry and you can return any time during the same day for free.

SEA POINT
SEA POINT PAVILION Map p207
☎ 434 3341; Beach Rd, Sea Point; adult/child R10/5; open 7am-6.50pm Oct-Apr, 8.30am-5pm May-Sep

A Sea Point institution, this huge outdoor-pool complex with some lovely Art Deco decoration gets very busy on hot summer days, not surprisingly, since the pools are always at least 10ºC warmer than the ocean. Sea Point's coast is rocky and swimming is dangerous, although there are a couple of rock pools. At the north end, **Graaff's Pool** is for men only and is generally favoured by nudists. Just south of here is **Milton's Pool** which also has a stretch of beach.

CLIFTON
CLIFTON BEACHES Map pp198–9
There are four linked beaches at Clifton, accessible by steps from Victoria Rd. They might be the trendiest beaches on the Cape, almost always sheltered from the wind, but the water is cold. If you care about these things, No 1 and No 2 beaches are for models and confirmed narcissists, No 3 is the gay beach, and No 4 is for families. Although vendors hawk drinks and ice creams along the beach, there are no shops down here, so bring your own food if you're out for a day of sunbathing.

CAMPS BAY
CAMPS BAY BEACH Map p208
With the spectacular Twelve Apostles of Table Mountain as a backdrop, and soft white sand, Camps Bay has one of the most beautiful beaches in the world. That it is within 15 minutes of the city centre also makes it very popular, particularly on weekends. The beach is often windy, and again the water is decidedly on the cool side. There are no lifeguards and the surf is strong, so take care if you do swim.

SANDY BAY
LLANDUDNO & SANDY BAY BEACHES Map pp198–9
At Llandudno there's surfing on the beach breaks (mostly rights), best at high tide with a small swell and a southeasterly wind. You'll also need to head here if you want to get to Sandy Bay, Cape Town's nudist beach and gay stamping ground. It's a particularly beautiful stretch of sand and there's no pressure to take your clothes off if you don't want to. Like many such beaches, Sandy Bay has no direct access roads. From the M6, turn towards Llandudno, keep to the left at forks, and head towards the sea until you reach the Sunset Rocks parking area. The beach is roughly a 15-minute walk to the south. Waves here are best at low tide with a southeasterly wind.

Cape Town's Top Five Beaches
- **Muizenberg** – for families and fun surfing (p75)
- **Clifton** – to see and be seen (p68)
- **Cape Point** – for isolation and wildness try Diaz beach at the Point (p76)
- **Bloubergstrand** – for photos of Table Mountain and windsurfing (p68)
- **Boulders** – for penguins try Foxy Beach (p75)

Clifton beaches (p68)

HOUT BAY

CHAPMAN'S PEAK DRIVE Map p210
After R150 million of safety work, Chapman's Peak Drive reopened to mixed reviews in 2003. Environmentalists were up in arms about what had been done to ensure that the dangerous rock slides that had closed the road in the first place wouldn't be a problem in the future. Plus there was the issue of the toll booths and the R20 toll that everyone now needs to pay to travel along this 5km road linking Hout Bay with Noordhoek. It remains, however, one of the most spectacular stretches of coastal road in the world and a thrilling drive. Perched on a rock near the Hout Bay end of the drive is a bronze **leopard statue**. It has been sitting there since 1963 and is a reminder of the wildlife that once roamed the area's forests (which have also largely vanished).

DUIKER ISLAND CRUISES Map p210
Although increasingly given over to tourism, Hout Bay's harbour still functions and the southern arm of the bay is an important fishing port and processing centre. From here you can catch regular daily cruises to Duiker Island, also known as Seal Island because of its colony of Cape fur seals. Three companies run these cruises daily, usually with guaranteed sailings in the mornings. The cheapest, with a none-too-spectacular, glass-bottomed boat, is **Circe Launches** (☎ 790 1040; www.circelaunches .co.za; adult/child R30/10); the others are **Drumbeat Charters** (☎ 791 4441; adult/child R45/20)

and **Nauticat Charters** (☎ 790 7278; www.nauticat charters.co.za; adult/child R50/20).

HOUT BAY MUSEUM Map p210
☎ 790 3270; 4 Andrews Rd, Hout Bay; adult/child R2/1; ⊗ 8.30am-4.30pm Tue-Fri, 9am-2pm Sat
This is a one-room museum next to the tourist office, with minor-league displays on local history. Contact them about the guided walks they sometimes run on the weekends.

WORLD OF BIRDS Map p210
☎ 790 2730; www.worldofbirds.org.za; Valley Rd, Hout Bay; adult/child R40/28; ⊗ 9am-5pm
South Africa's largest aviary, with more than 330 species of birds. A real effort has been made to make the aviaries large and natural with lots of tropical landscaping.

NOORDHOEK

NOORDHOEK BEACH Map pp196–7
A magnificent 5km stretch of beach, favoured by surfers and horse riders. It tends to be windy, and dangerous for swimmers. The Hoek, as it is known to surfers, is an excellent right beach break at the northern end that can hold large waves (only at low tide); it's best with a southeasterly wind.

KOMMETJIE

KOMMETJIE BEACH Map pp196–7
The focal point for surfing on the Cape, offering an assortment of reefs that hold a very big swell. Outer Kommetjie is a left point out from the lighthouse. Inner Kommetjie is a more protected smaller left with lots of kelp (only at high tide). They both work best with a southeasterly or southwesterly wind.

TWO OCEANS CRAFTS & CULTURE CENTRE Map pp196–7
☎ 785 3495; cnr Kommetjie & Chasmay Rds, Sun Valley
On the road towards Kommetjie from Fish Hoek, beside the township of Masiphumelele, is this cheerful and creative cultural centre where you can buy excellent crafts made at a local training centre, such as the Bambanani bowls circled by figures holding hands. There's also the Sonwabile restaurant serving Xhosa food, and the Chakalaka jazz performances on the first Sunday of the month. See p58 for details of a walking tour starting from here.

SOUTHERN SUBURBS

Eating pp94–5; Shopping pp131–2; Sleeping pp141–2

Heading south around the bulk of Devil's Peak will take you into the expensive residential areas clinging to the eastern slopes of Table Mountain and collectively known as the Southern Suburbs.

Woodstock, Observatory and Rondebosch have a laid-back, bohemian air, and a mixed racial profile. This is the territory of the University of Cape Town (UCT), the buildings of which can be seen up on the side of Table Mountain. **Observatory** ('Obs' for short) is the centre of holistic practices in the Mother City, hosting a monthly lifestyle fair along its main drag (Lower Main Rd).

By the time you reach leafy Newlands and Bishopscourt you'll be in no doubt that this is a rich and mainly white place to live. This said, the area around **Claremont** station is a fascinating study in contrasts, with black and coloured traders crowding the streets around the ritzy Cavendish Square mall (p131); Mandela has a home in Bishopscourt; and we've seen white beggars on Newlands' streets. Times are certainly changing.

Wyberg, the next major suburb south, is another place where the haves rub shoulders with the have-nots. The most likely reason you'll head here is to attend a performance at the **Maynard-ville Open Air Theatre** (p106). Old wealth leads the way immediately to the west in **Constantia**, home to South Africa's oldest wineries (p36) as well as many huge, salubrious and well-protected mansions. It's a verdant area that culminates in **Tokai** with its shady forest reserve.

Orientation

If you're driving, take the N2 from the city centre or the M3 from Orange St in Gardens. These freeways merge near the Groote Schuur Hospital in Observatory, then run around Devil's Peak. The M3 sheers off to the right soon after (it can be a dangerous manoeuvre getting into the right lanes!) and then runs parallel to the east side of the mountain with clearly indicated turn-offs for UCT, the Rhodes Memorial, Newlands and the Kirstenbosch Botanical Gardens. Stick on the M3 to get to Constantia and Tokai.

> ### Transport
> The Simon's Town railway line is a useful way to get to most of the Southern Suburbs, with stops at Observatory, Rondebosch, Newlands and Claremont.

Main Rd beginning in Observatory and running parallel to the M3 goes through Rondebosch, and past the Irma Stern Museum and the Baxter Theatre on its way to Newlands and Claremont where it becomes Newlands Rd. If you're heading to the cricket ground, Newlands train station is next to the east exit. For the rugby stadium and Newlands Brewery you'll need to exit on the west side of the station and walk north for about five minutes along Sport Pienaar Rd to Boundary Rd.

OBSERVATORY

TRANSPLANT MUSEUM Map p208

☎ 404 5232; www.gsh.co.za; Groote Schuur Hospital, Observatory; adult/child R5/3; ☼ 9am-1.45pm Mon-Fri

Drop by the quirky Transplant Museum detailing the history of the world's first heart transplant, in the very theatre in which it all happened in 1967. The displays have a fascinating Dr Kildare quality to them, especially given the heart-throb status of Dr Christiaan Barnard at the time. To reach the hospital from Observatory station, walk west along Station Rd for about 10 minutes. If you're driving from the city, take the Eastern Blvd (N2), turn off at Browning Rd, and then turn right on Main Rd.

RONDEBOSCH

GROOTE SCHUUR Map pp198–9

☎ 686 9100; Groote Schuur Estate, Klipper Rd; admission R50; tours by appointment only

One of SA's seminal buildings, a symbol of the country's past and its future. Since Rhodes bequeathed it to the nation, it has been the home of a succession of prime ministers, culminating with FW de Klerk. The recently restored interior, all teak panels and heavy colonial furniture, antiques and tapestries of the finest calibre, is suitably imposing. But its most beautiful feature is the colonnaded veranda overlooking the formal gardens, sloping uphill towards an avenue of pine trees and sweeping views of Devil's Peak. The tour includes tea on the veranda. You must bring your passport to gain entry to this high-security area; the entrance is unmarked but easily spotted on the left as you take the Princess Anne Ave exit off the M3.

IRMA STERN MUSEUM Map pp198–9

☎ 685 5686; www.irmastern.co.za; Cecil Rd, Rosebank; adult/child R8/4; ☾ 10am-5pm Tue-Sat

Based in the charming home of this pioneering 20th-century artist, this is the best museum to visit in the Southern Suburbs. Irma Stern (1894–1966) lived in this house for 38 years and her studio has been left intact, as if she'd just stepped out into the verdant garden for some fresh air. Her ethnographic art-and-craft collection from around the world is as fascinating as her own expressionism art, which has been compared to her Gauguin's.

To reach the museum from Rosebank station, walk a few minutes west to Main Rd, cross over and walk up Chapel St.

OUDE MOLEN FARM VILLAGE

Map pp198–9

☎ 448 6419; Alexandra Rd, Pinelands

In a once abandoned section of the buildings and grounds of the Valkenberg mental hospital is the Oude Molen Farm Village, the only organic farm within Cape Town's city limits. You can volunteer to work here through the Workers on Organic Farms scheme (www .wwoof.org) as well as stay at a backpackers lodge (p142). A horse trail leads from here, through the mental hospital grounds and Observatory up to Devil's Peak; for details of how to arrange rides see p113.

Southern Suburbs Top Five

- Enjoy afternoon tea on the terrace at **Groote Schuur** (p70)
- Pack a picnic for the Sunday open-air concerts in **Kirstenbosch Botanical Gardens** (p72)
- Get acquainted with a singular Capetonian artist at the **Irma Stern Museum** (p71)
- Spend a lazy day watching cricket at **Newlands** (p115)
- Go wine tasting around the vineyards of **Constantia** (p36)

RHODES MEMORIAL Map pp198–9

In 1895 Cecil Rhodes purchased the eastern slopes of Table Mountain for £9000 as part of a plan to preserve a relatively untouched section. After his death an impressive granite memorial to Rhodes was constructed here, commanding a view of the Cape Flats and the mountain ranges beyond – and, by implication, right into the heart of Africa. Despite the classical proportions of the memorial and the eight large bronze lions, Rhodes looks rather grumpy. Behind the memorial there's a pleasant tearoom (p95) in an old stone cottage. The exit for the memorial is at the Princess Anne Interchange on the M3.

UNIVERSITY OF CAPE TOWN

Map pp198–9

For the nonacademic there is no real reason to visit UCT, but it is an impressive place to walk around. Unlike most universities, it presents a fairly cohesive architectural front, with ivy-covered neoclassical façades, and a fine set of stone steps leading up to the temple-like

Cecil Rhodes: Empire Builder

The sickly son of an English vicar, Cecil John Rhodes (1853–1902) was sent to South Africa in 1870 to improve his health. He not only recovered, but went on to found the De Beers mining company (which in 1891 owned 90% of the world's diamond mines) and become prime minister of the Cape in 1890 at the age of 37.

Famous for wanting to build a railway from the Cape to Cairo (running through British territory all the way) Rhodes pushed north to establish mines and develop trade. He was successful in establishing British control in Bechuanaland (later Botswana) and the area that was to become Rhodesia (later Zimbabwe).

His grand ideas of Empire went too far though when he became involved in a failed uprising in the Boer-run Transvaal Republic in 1895. An embarrassed British government forced Rhodes to resign as prime minister in 1896. He then took control of Rhodesia and Bechuanaland, his personal fiefdoms.

As his health deteriorated, the unmarried Rhodes became entangled in the schemes of the glamorous and ruthless Princess Randziwill. She was later jailed for her swindles. A year after the end of the Boer War he returned to Cape Town, only to die from his ailments, at the age of 49, at his home in Muizenberg. Rhodes' reputation was largely rehabilitated by his will. He devoted most of his fortune to the Rhodes scholarship, which sends recipients to Oxford University, and his land and many properties in Cape Town now belong to the nation.

Jameson building. Check out Smuts and Fuller Halls halfway up the steps. Visitors can usually get parking permits at the university – call at the information office on the entry road, near the bottom of the steps.

As you're following the M3 from the city, just after the open paddocks on Devil's Peak, you'll pass the old **Mostert's Mill**, a real Dutch windmill dating from 1796, on the left. Just past the old windmill, also on the left, is the exit for the university. To get there, turn right at the T-intersection after you've taken the exit.

Alternatively, if you approach UCT from Woolsack Dr, you'll pass the **Woolsack,** a cottage designed in 1900 by Sir Herbert Baker for Cecil Rhodes, who once owned the entire area. The cottage was the winter residence of Rudyard Kipling from 1900 to 1907 and it's said he wrote the poem *If* here.

NEWLANDS & BISHOPSCOURT
KIRSTENBOSCH BOTANICAL GARDENS
Map pp196–7

☎ 762 9120; www.nbi.ac.za; Rhodes Dr, Bishopscourt; adult/child R20/5; ☻ 8am-7pm Sep-Mar, 8am-6pm Apr-Aug

Among the most beautiful gardens in the world, Kirstenbosch has an incomparable site on the eastern side of Table Mountain, overlooking False Bay and the Cape Flats. The 36-hectare landscaped section merges almost imperceptibly with the 492 hectares of *fynbos* (fine bush) vegetation cloaking the mountain slopes.

The gardens were established by Jan van Riebeeck, who appointed a forester in 1657. A group of shipwrecked French refugees on their way to Madagascar was employed during 1660 to plant the famous wild almond hedge as the boundary of the Dutch outpost (it's still there). Van Riebeeck called his private farm Boschheuwel, and most likely it wasn't until the 1700s, when the gardens were managed by JF Kirsten, that they got the name Kirstenbosch.

The main entrance at the Newlands end of the gardens is where you'll find plenty of parking, the information centre, an excellent souvenir shop and the **conservatory** (☻ 9am-5pm). Further along Rhodes Dr is the Ryecroft Gate entrance, the first you'll come to if you approach the gardens from Constantia. Call to find out about free guided walks, or hire the My Guide electronic gizmo (R25) to receive recorded information about the various plants you'll pass on the three signposted circular walks.

Apart from the almond hedge, some magnificent oaks, and the Moreton Bay fig and camphor trees planted by Cecil Rhodes, the gardens are devoted almost exclusively to indigenous plants. About 9000 of Southern Africa's 22,000 plant species are grown here. You'll find a fragrance garden that has been elevated so you can more easily sample the scents of the plants; a Braille Trail; a *kopje* (hill) that has been planted with pelargoniums; a sculpture garden; and a section for plants used for *muti* (medicine) by *sangomas* (traditional African healers).

Aloes in Kirstenbosch Botanical Gardens (see above)

The atmosphere-controlled conservatory displays plant communities from a variety of terrains, the most interesting of which is the Namaqualand and Kalahari section, with baobabs and quiver trees, among others. There is always something flowering but the gardens are at their best between mid-August and mid-October. The **Sunday afternoon concerts** (adult/child including entry to the gardens R30/10; ☼ 5.30-6.30pm end Nov-Apr) are a Cape Town institution.

If you're driving from the city centre, the turn-off to the gardens is on the right at the intersection of Union Ave (the M3) and Rhodes Ave (the M63). Alternatively, walk down from the top of Table Mountain along either **Skeleton Gorge** (which involves negotiating some sections with chains) or **Nursery Ravine**. This could be done in three hours by someone of moderate fitness. The trails are steep and well marked, but the way to the gardens from the cableway, and vice versa, is not signposted. Also take note of our tips for climbing Table Mountain (p64).

NEWLANDS BREWERIES Map pp198–9
☎ 658 7386; 3 Main Rd, Newlands; free; tours by appointment only
Complementing the sporting theme of the area nicely is the South African Brewery, around which free guided tours are available (minimum eight people). Parts of the brewery

date back to the mid-1800s and have been granted National Monument status. Tours last about two hours, finishing up with a tasting session in the Letterstedt underground pub.

RUGBY MUSEUM Map pp198–9
☎ 686 2151; Sports Science Institute, Boundary Rd, Newlands; admission free; ☼ 9am-5pm Mon-Fri
Die-hard rugby fans only will want to take a look around this tiny museum which contains a predictable collection of boots, ties, balls and other paraphernalia.

TOKAI
TOKAI ARBORETUM Map pp196–7
If you're wine tasting in the Constantia area, or driving down to False Bay, you may want to swing by this pleasant wooded area, a favourite spot for picnics and walks. The Tokai Arboretum is a historic planting of some 150 different trees begun in 1885 by Joseph Storr Lister, the conservator of forests for the Cape Colony. There's a pleasant café here where you can pick up a map for the walk to **Elephant's Eye Cave**, the forest's best walk. The 6km zigzag path is fairly steep and offers little shade as you climb higher up Constantiaberg, so bring a hat and water.

To reach the forest from the city centre, follow the M3 towards Muizenberg and take the Retreat and Tokai exit.

FALSE BAY

Eating pp95–6; Shopping p132; Sleeping pp142–3
The beaches on False Bay, to the southeast of the city, are not quite as scenically spectacular (or as trendy) as those on the Atlantic side, but the water is often 5°C or more warmer, and can reach 20°C in summer. This makes swimming far more pleasant. Suburban development along the coast is more intense, presumably because of the train line, which runs all the way through to Simon's Town, the most interesting single destination on the Cape Peninsula besides the Cape of Good Hope.

On the eastern side of False Bay you'll need a car to reach **Strand** and **Gordon's Bay**, each a cross between a satellite suburb and a beach resort. They're nothing particularly special, but do have great views back to the Cape and are themselves in the shadow of the spectacular Hottentots Hollandberge range. The R44 to Cape Hangklip is a superb stretch of coastal road that rivals Chapman's Peak Drive (p156).

Heading back west along the R310 you'll skirt the southern edge of the estuarine lake **Zeekoevlei**, attached by a slim channel to the smaller lake that is part of the **Rondevlei Nature Reserve**. Stick on the R310 and you'll arrive in **Muizenberg**, one of the Cape's oldest settlements, established by the Dutch as a staging post for horse-drawn traffic in 1743. Muizenberg's heyday was the early 20th century when it was a prestigious seaside resort favoured by Cape Town's wealthy elite. By the turn of the millennium it had fallen on hard times and had become an area synonymous with poor whites, black immigrants from neighbouring countries, and crime. In the last few years, though – on the back of Cape Town's property boom – it has undergone something of a renaissance with derelict buildings being renovated and trendy new café's and shops opening up.

Transport

The train is a good way to get to many False Bay destinations; the line hugs the coast from Muizenberg to the terminus at Simon's Town and offers spectacular views. It's reasonably safe as long as you travel first class and during the peak times.

Continuing west along the bay brings you to the genteel suburb of **St James** (famous for the last-remaining, primary colour-painted, Victorian bathing huts) and then the charming fishing village of **Kalk Bay**. Named after the kilns that produced lime from seashells for painting buildings in the 17th century, this is one of the most appealing destinations on the bay with its many antique and craft shops, good café's and a lively daily fish market. Sadly, the fishing community is suffering hard times in the wake of the government's decision to slash the number of fishing licences issued.

The next suburbs along, Fish Hoek and Clovelly, have wide, safe beaches but are less attractive than their neighbours. Best to press on to **Simon's Town**, the nation's third-oldest European settlement. Named after governor Simon van der Stel, this was the VOC's winter anchorage from 1741 and became a naval base for the British in 1814. It has remained one ever since, the frigates now joined by pleasure boats that depart for thrilling cruises to Cape Point. St George's St, the main thoroughfare, is lined with preserved Victorian buildings and there's an intriguing Muslim side to the town that is slowly being revived. At the southern end of town is Boulders – the reason for the name becomes evident once you hit the beach, dotted with massive boulders; it's here that you'll also see the area's famous colony of penguins.

The possibility of spotting more exotic wildlife is one of the many temptations that should entice you all the way to **Cape Point**, part of the Table Mountain National Park. Chances are that you'll see the Cape's infamous baboons (see the boxed text on p76), but the pleasures of the rugged coastline, magnificent stretches of pristine, *fynbos*-covered land, and deserted beaches will more than make up for this.

Orientation

You'll need a car to explore the east side of False Bay and to get to Grassy Park for the Rondevlei Nature Reserve: from the city centre the easiest way here is to take the M5 and down to Prince George Drive. The train to Simon's Town is a slightly more limiting option.

By car, False Bay is reached most quickly along the M3. Main Rd is the coastal thoroughfare linking Muizenberg, St James, Kalk Bay and Fish Hoek, although a prettier alternative route between Muizenberg and Kalk Bay is mountainside Boyes Rd which provides fantastic views down the peninsula. From Fish Hoek, you can either head west across the peninsula to Kommetjie (p69) or continue down coastal Simonstown Rd to Simon's Town. In the centre of Simon's Town this road becomes St George's St and then later the M4 as it heads inexorably towards the entrance to Cape Point.

ZEEKOEVLEI

RONDEVLEI NATURE RESERVE

Map pp196–7

☎ 706 2404; Fisherman's Walk Rd, Zeekoevlei; adult/child R10/5; ⏰ 7.30am-5pm Mar-Nov, 7.30am-7pm Mon-Fri Dec-Feb, 7.30am-7pm Sat & Sun Dec-Feb

This small nature reserve encompasses picturesque wetlands that protect native marsh and dune vegetation. Hippos lived in this area 300 years ago and were reintroduced to the reserve in 1981. There are now six of them, but it's very unlikely that you'll spot them unless you stay overnight – for details of how to do this, contact **Imvubu Nature Tours** (p59) based

False Bay Top Five

- The fine grub and atmosphere at Kalk Bay's **Olympia Café** (p95)
- Surfing at **Muizenberg Beach** (p75)
- Hiking at **Cape Point** (p76)
- Visiting the penguins at **Boulders** (p75)
- Kayaking along the coast from **Simon's Town** (p113)

at the reserve. Guided walks are available and you can spot some 231 species of birds from the waterside trail, as well as from two viewing towers and hides.

MUIZENBERG

JOAN ST LEGER LINDBERGH ARTS CENTRE Map p209

☎ 788 2795; 18 Beach Rd, Muizenberg;
🕑 9am-5pm Mon-Fri

The great granddaughter of the founder of the *Cape Times*, Joan St Leger was an artist and poet. She bequeathed her Sir Herbert Baker–designed home plus the adjoining properties to make this arts centre, which is the cultural hub of Muizenberg. It comprises four houses – Sandhills, where Baker lived for a short while, Swanbourne, Rokeby and Crawford-Lea. In front is a bronze sculpture of an athlete saluting the sea by Stella Shawzin. Apart from the changing art displays, a wonderful reference library and a gallery of evocative photos of how Muizenberg once looked, there is also a good café and guest-house (p142) here. Concerts are held on the first Thursday morning of the month (R35) and the last Wednesday evening of the month (R85) in the conservatory.

MUIZENBERG BEACH Map p209

The iconic, Victorian bathing chalets may have been removed, but Muizenberg's broad, white beach remains highly popular with surfers – you can hire boards or get lessons from **Gary's Surf Shop** (p114) and there are free lockers in the pavilions on the promenade. Families love it here too because the beach shelves gently and the sea is generally safer (not to mention warmer) than elsewhere along the peninsula. There's plenty of parking, too.

NATALE LABIA MUSEUM Map p209

☎ 464 3280; www.museums.org.za/iziko; 192 Main Rd, Muizenberg; 🕑 Mon by appointment only

At the time of research this charming Venetian-style mansion, a satellite of the South African National Gallery, was undergoing renovation. The house still belongs to the family of the Italian Count Natale Labia who had it built in 1930. When it opens once again it promises to be a lovely house museum.

ST JAMES

RHODES COTTAGE MUSEUM Map p209

☎ 788 1816; 246 Main Rd, St James; admission by donation; 🕑 9.30am-4.30pm

Cecil Rhodes' pretty cottage, Rust-en-Vrede, is now an engaging museum where you can find out all about Rhodes, who was the founder of De Beers and who died in a neighbouring cottage in 1902 (p71). Yet another of Sir Herbert Baker's designs, the cottage has particularly

Whale Watching in False Bay

From late May to early December, False Bay is a favourite haunt of whales and their calves, with the peak viewing season being October and November. Southern right whales, humpback whales and bryde (pronounced bree-dah) whales are the most commonly sighted, and they often come quite close to the shore. Good viewing spots include the coastal walk from Muizenberg to St James (p83); Boyes Drive; the Brass Bell at Kalk Bay (p95); and Jager's Walk at Fish Hoek. You can also take whale-watching cruises from Simon's Town's harbour (p75).

pleasant gardens, which are a lovely spot to rest and spot whales during the season (p75).

ST JAMES TIDAL POOL Map p209

The tidal pool is safe for children to swim in and is thus popular with local schools and families. It's also where you'll see the last of the much-photographed, colourfully painted Victorian bathing huts. You can hire one for the day for R20 during the summer season.

KALK BAY

KALK BAY HARBOUR Map p209

Kalk Bay's attractive fishing harbour is at its most picturesque in the late morning when the community's few remaining fishing boats pitch up with their daily catch and a lively quayside market ensues. This is an excellent place to buy fresh fish for a *braai* (barbecue).

FISH HOEK

JAGER'S WALK Map pp196–7

At the southern end of the beach at Fish Hoek, this paved walk provides a pleasant stroll to Sunny Cove (which is on the train line). If you're feeling energetic, you could walk the remaining 5km from here along an unpaved road to Simon's Town.

SIMON'S TOWN & BOULDERS

BOULDERS BEACH PENGUIN COLONY Map p210

☎ 701 8692; www.tmnp.co.za; adult/child R10/5; 🕑 8am-5pm

Some 3km south of Simon's Town is Boulders, an area with a number of large boulders and small sandy coves, within which you'll find Boulders Beach, part of **Table Mountain National Park** (p64) and famous for being home to a colony of 3000 African penguins. Delightful as they are, the penguins are also pretty stinky, which may put you off.

There are two entrances to the penguins' protected area. The first, as you come along Queens Rd (the continuation of St George's St) from Simon's Town, is at the end of Seaforth Rd; the second is at Bellevue Rd, where you'll also find accommodation and places to eat. You can observe the penguins from the boardwalk at Foxy Beach and at Boulders Beach. The penguin colony has only been here since the mid-1980s; nobody knows why the birds came and they may just as easily take off again. They look pretty healthy, but the African penguin (formerly called the jackass penguin) is an endangered species susceptible to avian malaria and pollution. The sea is calm and shallow in the coves, so Boulders is popular with families and can get extremely crowded, especially on holidays and weekends.

Rikkis (p161) meets all trains to Simon's Town and goes to Boulders.

HARBOUR CRUISES Map p210

☎ 083 257 7760, 786 2136; Simon's Town Harbour Jetty; harbour cruise R25

Among the several boat tour operators in Simon's Town is **Southern Right**, which runs the popular Spirit of Just Nuisance cruise around the harbour. Speedboat trips to Cape Point and Seal Island are R250, and during the whale-spotting season (p75) it also offers cruises to get up close to these magnificent animals.

HERITAGE MUSEUM Map p210

☎ 786 2302; Almay House, King George Way, Simon's Town; adult/child R3/2; ☉ 11am-4pm Tue-Fri, Sat & Sun by appointment only

Simon's Town's most interesting museum, the Heritage includes displays on the Cape Muslim community of more than 7000 people, forcibly removed during apartheid. It's enthusiastically curated by Zainab Davidson, whose family was kicked out in 1975. Nearby Alfred Lane leads to the handsome mosque and attached school built in 1926.

SIMON'S TOWN MUSEUM Map p210

☎ 786 3046; Court Rd, Simon's Town; suggested donation R5 ; ☉ 9am-4pm Mon-Fri, 10am-1pm Sat, 11am-3pm Sun

This rambling museum is about 600m south of the train station. Based in the old governor's residence (1777), its extensive exhibits trace the history of the town and port, and include a display on Just Nuisance, the Great Dane that was adopted as a navy mascot in WWII, and whose grave above the town makes for a healthy walk.

There's also a statue of Just Nuisance in Jubilee Square by the harbour.

SOUTH AFRICAN NAVAL MUSEUM
Map p210

☎ 787 4635; St George's St, Simon's Town; admission free; ☉ 10am-4pm

Definitely one for naval nuts, it nonetheless has plenty of interesting exhibits, including a mock submarine to play out boyish adventure fantasies.

CAPE OF GOOD HOPE

CAPE POINT Map pp196–7

☎ 780 9010; www.capepoint.co.za; admission R35; ☉ 7am-6pm Sep-Apr, 7am-5pm May-Aug

Truly awesome scenery, some fantastic walks and deserted beaches, plus the chance to spot wildlife including bonteboks, elands and zebras, are what a visit to this nature reserve is all about. Go on one of the many tours that whip into the reserve, now part of Table Mountain National Park; pause at the tourist centre; walk to Cape Point and back and even then you'll not have seen the half of it. Take your time to explore the reserve the way it should be – on foot. Pick up a map at the entrance gate if you intend to go walking, but bear in mind that there is minimal shade in the park and that the weather can change quickly.

If the weather is good – or even if it isn't – you can easily spend at least a day here. It's particularly beautiful in spring, when the wildflowers are in bloom. There are a number of picnic spots; there's also a restaurant but it's generally packed with tour-bus crowds.

It's not a difficult walk, but if you're feeling lazy a **funicular railway** (adult/child one way R20/10, return R29/15; ☉ 10am-5pm) runs up from the restaurant to the kiosk next to the lighthouse (1860). The old lighthouse was too often obscured by mist and fog, so a new lighthouse was built at Diaz Point in 1919, reached

---

Don't Feed the Baboons!

There are signs all over Cape Point warning you not to feed the baboons. This isn't just some mean-spirited official stricture designed to keep baboons from developing a taste for potato chips and chocolate. The baboons are highly aggressive and will quiet happily grab food from your hands or climb in the open doors and windows of your car to get at it. The damage inflicted might end up being more serious than baboon crap on your car seats, so keep an eye out and your food carefully hidden away.

by a walkway along the rocks; if the winds are howling, as they often are, the old lighthouse is likely to be as far as you'll feel safe in going.

There are some excellent beaches, usually deserted. This can make them dangerous if you get into difficulties in the water, so take care. One of the best beaches for swimming or walking is **Platboom Beach**. **Maclear Beach,** near the main car park, is good for walks or diving but is too rocky for enjoyable swimming. Further down towards Cape Point is beautiful **Diaz Beach**. Access is on foot from the car park. On the False Bay side, the small but pretty beach

at **Buffels Bay** offers safe swimming; there's a great 3.5km walk from here to the spectacular Paulsberg peak which plunges in a sheer cliff of 369m into the sea.

Numerous tour companies include Cape Point on their itineraries; both **Day Trippers** (p57) and **Downhill Adventures** (p110) are recommended because they offer the chance to cycle within the park. The only public transport to the Cape is with **Rikkis** (p169), which runs from Simon's Town train station. The best option is to hire a car for the day, so you can explore the rest of the peninsula.

CAPE FLATS

Eating p96; Sleeping pp143–4

For the majority of Capetonians, home is in one of the townships sprawling across the shifting sands of the Cape Flats. Stricken with crime, poverty and AIDS, the inhabitants fill the dusty, litter-strewn streets; most white locals, and many coloureds too, wouldn't dream of visiting here and will advise you not to either. Don't listen.

Taking a tour – the only way of safely travelling here besides making friends with and being accompanied by a resident – is one of the most illuminating and life-affirming things you can do while in Cape Town. You'll learn a lot about South African history and the cultures of black South Africans. Better still is to stay overnight at one of several B&Bs (p143) in Langa ('sun' in Xhosa), founded in 1927 and the oldest planned township in South Africa, or in Khayelitsha, one of the nation's largest townships with an estimated population of more than 1.8 million.

If you've toured any other Third-World hellhole, what you'll see here will come as little surprise. What is shocking is that it can exist in close proximity to such wealth and apparent indifference, and that the vast majority of residents show visitors such courtesy and friendliness.

The infrastructure has certainly improved since 1994, with the rows of concrete Reconstruction and Development Program (RDP) houses being the most visible example. However, vast squatter camps with a communal standpipe for water and a toilet shared among scores of people still remain and are expanding all the time.

Orientation

The half-day itineraries of most townships tours (p58) are similar. After starting in the Bo-Kaap for a brief discussion of Cape Town's colonial history, you'll move on to the District Six Museum, then be driven to the Cape Flats to visit some or all of the following townships: Langa, Guguletu, Crossroads and Khayelitsha. Tour guides are generally flexible in where they go, and respond to the wishes of the group. The listings below detail possible stops.

Transport

One of the best ways to see the Cape Flats townships is on an organised half-day tour. See p58 for more details.

Small church, Langa, Cape Flats (p78)

LANGA

GUGA S'THEBE ARTS & CULTURAL CENTRE Map pp196–7

☎ 695 3493, 082 746 0246; cnr Washington & Church Sts, Langa; ☽ 10am-5pm Mon-Fri, 10am-1pm Sat

Brilliantly decorated with gorgeous ceramic murals, this is one of the most impressive buildings in the townships if not all of Cape Town. Classes for bead-work and the making of traditional garments and curios are organised by Nombuyiselo Ngxizele.

TSOGA ENVIRONMENTAL RESOURCE CENTRE Map pp196–7

☎ 694 0004; Washington St, Langa; ☽ 8am-5pm Mon-Fri

On a patch of barren wasteland is this centre where respect for the environment and people is taught. Prince Charles planted a tree here in 1997 – it's not doing too well by the looks of it. The centre has a recycling depot and a market garden; it also runs various workshops. The restaurant **Eziko** (p96) is across the road.

GUGULETU

SIVUYILE TOURISM CENTRE Map pp196–7

☎ 637 8449; ☽ 8am-5pm Mon-Fri, 8am-2pm Sat

Inside a local technical college, this tourism centre has an interesting photographic display on the townships, artists at work, an Internet café and a good gift shop. You'll also find the creative **Uncedo Pottery Project** here.

CROSSROADS

PHILANI NUTRITION CENTRE

Map pp196–7

☎ 387 5124; www.philani.org.za

This long-running, community-based, health and nutrition organisation has six projects

Cape Town's Top Five for Children

- Get to know the Cape's sea life at the **Two Oceans Aquarium** (p68)
- Meet the Penguins at **Boulders Beach** (p75)
- Experience the thrill rides at **Ratanga Junction** (p108)
- Check out the air power at **Thundercity** (p108)
- Splash around in the tidal pool at **St James** (p75)

Cape Town Top Five Freebies

- Enjoying the musical performances and buskers at the **Waterfront** (p67)
- Hiking up **Table Mountain** (p64)
- Watching the sun set at **Clifton** or **Camps Bay** (p68)
- Wandering through the **Company's Gardens** and visiting the **South African Museum** on Sunday (p63)
- Wine tasting at **Klein Constantia** (p36)

running in the townships, including a weaving factory in Khayelitsha's Site C and the printing project here. Women are taught how to feed their families adequately on a low budget, and the crèche and various projects enable them to earn an income through weaving rugs and wall hangings, making paper, printing and other crafts. Philani goods are available from many shops around the Cape.

KHAYELITSHA

Also worth checking out is the **Khayelitsha Craft Market** (p129).

GOLDEN'S FLOWERS Map pp196–7

Golden Sonwabo Nonquase is a talented bloke who together with his family makes beautiful flowers from scrap tins. The idea of making the flowers came to him in a recurring dream and has become one of Khayelitsha's most successful home businesses.

ROSIE'S SOUP KITCHEN Map pp196–7

☎ 362 6131

From Monday to Saturday the wonderful Rosie serves some 600 meals a day to the poor at 60 cents a plate. A wooden shed outside her home has been built as a canteen.

TYGERBERG TOURISM FACILITY

Map pp196–7

If you want to climb what locals refer to as Khayelitsha's Table Mountain, then head here. An impressive wooden staircase leads to the top of this sand hill, which is the highest point in the townships, and provides a sweeping view of the surroundings, particularly at sunset. The cultural and tourism centre at the foot remains empty for the time being.

Walking Tours

Walking Tours

Central Cape Town is an ambler's delight. A wander down Long St and across Greenmarket Square to St George's Mall will provide enough colour and interest for most casual strollers, but if you want a more focused point to your perambulations try out the first couple of walks detailed here. If it's the sea breeze you hanker for, journey down to False Bay and enjoy the sweeping coastal views around Muizenberg. Organised walking tours are listed at the start of the Neighbourhoods chapter (p57).

CENTRAL CAPE TOWN: ART & ART DECO WALK

Cape Town experienced a building boom in the 1930s. This walk takes you past prime examples of the grand Art Deco architecture from this era, while introducing pieces of contemporary public art. There are plenty of opportunities to shop, eat, drink and rest along the way.

Starting from **Cape Town Train Station** 1 look across to the corner of Adderley and Riebeeck Sts to view the **Colosseum Building** 2. Designed by WH Grant, one of Cape Town's foremost Art Deco architects, this orange-and-cream-painted building has striking 'Aztec-style' mouldings. Turn right onto the pedestrianised St George's Mall; here, opposite Waterkant St, is Brett Murray's controversial statue **Africa** 3, (see the boxed text on

> ### Walk Facts
>
> **Start** Cape Town Train Station
> **End** General Post Office
> **Distance** 2km
> **Duration** 2 hours minimum

p29). This African curio bronze statue, sprouting bright yellow Bart Simpson heads, is typical of Murray's quirky, satirical style and caused much public debate on its unveiling in 2000.

Continue to the junction with Strand St, turn right and look out for pink-and-blue-painted **Boston House** 4, at No 44, and the neighbouring **Delene's** 5. Turn left on to Burg St. At No 24 you'll see the blue-and-cream **New Zealand House** 6, designed by WH Grant in a style known as Cape Mediterranean. Next door at No 26 the elegant symmetry of **Hardware House** 7 leads you onto the more elaborate pink, grey and cream **Namaqua House** 8, on the corner of Shortmarket St.

You're now in cobbled **Greenmarket Square** 9, created as a farmers' market in the early 18th century and filled from Monday to Saturday with one of the city's best crafts and souvenir markets (p129). Three quarters of the buildings surrounding the square hail from the 1930s, the main exception being the **Old Town House** 10, completed in 1761, and now home to the Michaelis Collection (p62) of Dutch and Flemish masterworks.

Walking in a clockwise direction around the square, check out **Kimberley House** 11 at 34 Shortmarket St, which is built of sandstone with teak window frames and an attractive diamond theme design. **Market House** 12, fronting on to the square, is the most elaborately decorated building of all and has majestic stone carved eagles and flowers on its façade. Nip into the building's entrance on Shortmarket St and climb up to the hair clinic on the first floor to see the equally impressive original Art Deco interior.

As you come out of Market House, before returning to Greenmarket Square, spend a moment to admire a piece of modern art that is easily overlooked. Set into the pavement at the junction of Shortmarket St and St George's Mall is **Come to Pass** 13 by Fritha Langerman and Katherine Bull, winners in 2002 of the Cape Town Public Sculpture Competition. If you're feeling peckish, there are several good options in the area including **Crush** 14 (p89) on St George's Mall and **Cin-full** 15 on Shortmarket St (p89).

Back on the square the dazzling-white **Protea Insurance Building** 16 was built in 1928 and renovated in 1990. Opposite is **Shell House** 17, once the South African headquarters of Shell, now housing a hotel and restaurants. Exit the square on Burg St and take the next right on to the pedestrianised portion of **Church St** 18. There's a flea market here from Monday to Saturday and you'll find Cape Town's best collection of galleries and crafts shops.

On the corner of Burg and Wale Sts is the **Waalburg Building** 19. Take a moment to admire the bronze and Table Mountain stone panels decorating the building's façade and depicting scenes of South African life. Opposite is the **Western Cape Legislature** 20, its grey bulk enlivened by the fun stone-carved detail of animal heads.

Just past **St George's Cathedral** 21 (p61) on Wale St is the entrance to **Company's Gardens** 22 (p61). It's a lovely place to rest and if you have time you should explore the country's best collection of contemporary art at the **South African National Gallery** 23 (p64).

Returning to Wale St, turn into St George's Mall and continue to Longmarket St, passing **Newspaper House** 24 at No 122, another Cape Mediterranean–style building by Grant. Turn right down Longmarket St and keep on it until you get to the corner of Parliament St where you won't miss the glossy black, chrome-and-glass façade of **Mullers Opticians** 25, one of the best preserved Art Deco shopfronts in the city.

On the corner of Parliament and Darling Sts stands **Old Mutual** 26, the most impressive Art Deco building in all of Cape Town. This 18-storey building, built in 1939, was once the tallest structure in Africa bar the Pyramids. On its façade you'll find one of the longest continuous stone friezes in the world, while the side of the building on Parliament St is adorned with noble carvings of African races.

Next to Old Mutual, on the corner of Darling and Plein Sts is grey and blue **Scotts Building** 27 displaying yet again Grant's elegant designs. Finish up by taking a look inside the **General Post Office** 28 across the road. Here you'll discover colourful painted panels of Cape Town scenes by GW Pilkington and Sydney Carter.

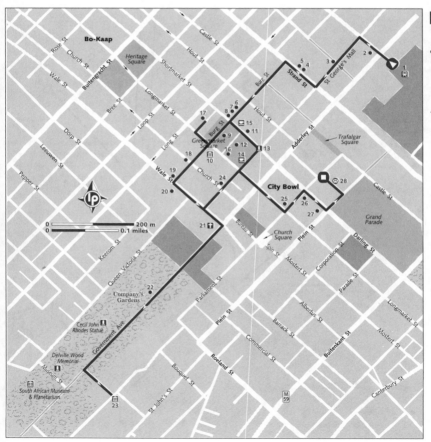

CENTRAL CAPE TOWN: HISTORY WALK

Cape Town's turbulent history is revealed in the many buildings, statues and street names that grace the City Bowl and Bo-Kaap. This walk will give you an insight into the forces and personalities that shaped the Cape Town you see today.

South Africa's oldest European fortification, the star-shaped **Castle of Good Hope 1** (p60) is an appropriate place to start. Immediately west is **Grand Parade 2**, the former military-parade and public-execution ground, which is now home to a lively market every Wednesday and Saturday. Jan van Riebeeck's original, mud-walled fort was here, too, and you can see its position outlined in red at the Plein St end of the Parade. The balcony of the impressive **Old Town Hall 3** on the southwest side of the parade, is where Nelson Mandela gave his first public speech in 27 years following his release from prison in February 1990.

Walk up Buitenkant St to the **District Six Museum 4** (p61) to learn about the history of this demolished inner-city area, a victim of apartheid's laws. From the museum turn right onto Albertus St, then turn right again

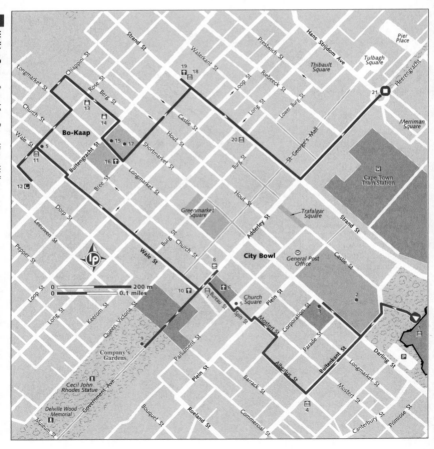

at Corporation St to reach Mostert St and its continuation, Spin St. On the traffic island beside pretty Church Square, look down to see a circular plaque marking the location of the old **slave tree 5** under which slaves were sold, until emancipation in 1834. In front of you is the **Groote Kerk 6** (p60), mother church for the Dutch Reformed Church. Across the road is the old **Slave Lodge 7**, now a history museum (p63), and in the middle of the square the Colonel Blimpish statue of 19th-century statesman Jan Hendrik Hofmeyr.

Spin St leads into Adderley St, named after the politician Charles Adderley who barracked successfully in London for Cape Town not to be turned into a penal colony. On Adderley St you'll find the **Off Moroka Café 8** (p89), one of the city's best African cafés, as good a place as any to drop by for a drink or bite to eat.

Prior to the mid-19th century, Adderley St was called the Heerengracht (Gentleman's Canal) after the waterway that once ran from the **Company's Gardens 9** (p61) down here to the sea. Explore the gardens by all means if you have the time, but otherwise continue northwest up Wale St, past **St George's Cathedral 10** (p61), for several blocks until you cross Buitengracht (another canal filled over and made into a road) and the start of the area known as the **Bo-Kaap**.

To discover something on the history of this strongly Muslim area of the city, drop by the **Bo-Kaap Museum 11** (p60), on Wale St. The Bo-Kaap's steep streets, some of which are still cobbled, are lined with 18th-century, flat-roofed houses and mosques; you'll hear the call to prayer from the **Auwal Mosque 12**, on Dorp St, the oldest such place of worship in Cape Town. Chiappini and Rose Sts contain the prettiest houses, many of which sport bright paint jobs.

Return to Buitengracht St via Shortmarket St along which you'll find both **Monkeybiz 13** (p128) and **Streetwires 14** (p128), two businesses doing their bit to empower the disadvantaged and alleviate some of the city's social problems. You'll most likely find more crafts on sale in the large car park that now covers **Van Riebeeck Square 15**, sandwiched between Buitengracht and Bree Sts. Here also is **St Stephen's Church 16** built in 1799, originally the African Theatre and later a school for freed slaves before it became a church in 1839.

Adjacent to Van Riebeeck Square is **Heritage Square 17**, a beautiful collection of Cape Georgian and Victorian buildings saved from the wrecking ball in 1996. It's since been transformed into one of the city's trendiest dining and drinking enclaves as well as the Cape Heritage Hotel (p134).

Continue down Bree St to the junction with Strand St. To the left lies the **Gold of Africa Museum 18** (p61) in the beautifully restored Martin Melck House, dating from 1781. The house was named after the German merchant who built the Cape's first **Lutheran Church 19** (p62), located next door.

Heading southeast down Strand St take note of the elegant façade of the 18-century **Koopmans-de Wet House 20** (p61), now a museum only open by appointment. At Adderley St turn left and continue past the station, to where the street takes up its old name of Heerengracht. Here you'll find the statues of **Jan van Riebeeck** and his wife **Maria de la Queillerie 21**. They are located on the spot where Van Riebeeck is thought to have first landed in 1652. Cross the road to reach the train station and the end of the walk.

MUIZENBERG–ST JAMES ROUND WALK

Muizenberg (p75) is currently undergoing something of a renaissance. This invigorating coastal walk allows you to discover the new cafés and shops opening up in the area as well as the wealth of notable architecture and spectacular views of False Bay that these grand properties command.

Starting at **Muizenberg Station 1**, exit onto Main Rd heading north past Muizenberg Park. Turn left on the corner of this small park up Camp Rd, passing the old red and white **synagogue 2**; Muizenberg had a large Jewish population in the 1920s and 30s. A flight of concrete steps leads up to Boyes Dr. From here the road gently climbs the slope until you have a commanding view across Muizenberg and its broad, flat beach. You'll pass a wrought-iron gate leading down to

Walk Facts

Start Train, Muizenberg Station
End Muizenberg Station
Distance 3km
Duration 1 hour

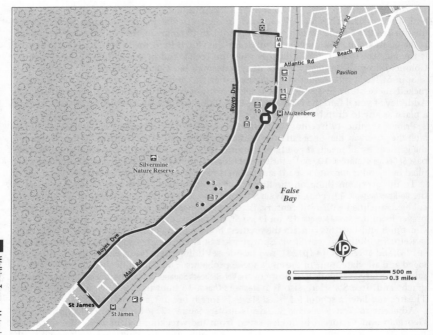

the **grave 3** of the mining magnate Sir Abe Bailey (1864–1940) whose house **Rust-en-Vrede 4**, with its red tiles and high gables, can be glimpsed on Main Rd below. Rust-en-Vrede was commissioned by Cecil Rhodes, but he never lived in it; Rhodes died in a nearby cottage before the house could be completed.

As you round the corner, panoramic views open up across False Bay towards Simon's Town (p75) and Cape Point (p76). This is also a prime location for whale watching from the end of September to early November. On the right is the Silvermine Nature Reserve; there are several marked tracks up the mountain here should you wish to gain a higher vantage point. If not, keep walking until you see the primary-colour-painted Victorian-style **bathing huts 5** at St James (p75). The Jacob's Ladder steps lead steeply down from Boyes Dr to Main Rd and the underpass at St James' Station, which leads through to the coastal walking path. Take a dip in the tidal pool to cool down and then continue along the coastal path back towards Muizenberg.

As you approach the grand Spanish-style **mansion 6** with green-glazed roof tiles (called Gracelands after Elvis' pad) you'll see another underpass that will allow you to nip across busy Main Rd and visit **Rhodes' Cottage 7** (p75). Back on the coastal path, on the right hand side is the thatched **Bailey's Cottage 8**, once Sir Abe Bailey's guest cottage and now reserved for use by members of parliament. Closer to Muizenberg, on Main Rd, you'll also pass the Italianate **Natale Labia Museum 9** (p75) and the white-washed **Posthuys 10**. Dating from around 1740 and one of Cape Town's oldest European-style buildings, the Posthuys, is now a small museum of limited appeal. It's only a minute's walk from here back to Muizenberg Station. Recommended places for refreshments are either the **Olive Station 11** (p96) or the **Empire Café 12** (p95).

Eating

Eating

Top Five Dining Locations

- **Kloof St, Gardens** (pp89-92) – the road up Table Mountain is paved with dining treasures.
- **Lower Main Rd, Observatory** (pp94-5) – join the bohos and student set at Cape Town's best range of cheap and colourful ethnic eateries.
- **Main Rd, Kalk Bay** (pp95-6) – fuel up on the culinary goodies available along the False Bay coast.
- **V&A Waterfront** (pp92-3) – there are more restaurants and cafés here than you'll have days to eat.
- **Victoria Rd, Camps Bay** (pp92-3) – where the beautiful people gather for cocktails, seafood and nibbles at sundown.

Cosmopolitan, inventive and – a few exceptions aside – amazingly good value: this sums up Cape Town's impressive dining scene, where you can sample everything from traditional African and Cape Malay dishes (see p15) to Thai noodles or Indian samosas.

Not everything works – quantity is often confused with quality, and there's an unfortunate predilection for stodge and viscous sauces. But there's a sufficient variety of restaurants and cafés to suit practically everyone's taste and budget. And with both the sea and fruitful farmlands on hand, you can be pretty much assured of fresh, top-quality ingredients.

Capetonians seem to have an insatiable appetite for new restaurants. The same place can be a hit one season, and dead the next, patrons having moved on to the latest hot spot. This said, there are some honourable, longstanding troupers and plenty of reliable areas, such as the Waterfront or Camps Bay, for finding a good feed.

Most restaurants are licensed but some allow you to bring your own wine for little or no corkage. Call ahead to check the restaurant's policy. For more information on wine, see p33. Also check the Bars & Pubs listings in the Entertainment chapter (p98), as many of these places serve great food.

Self Catering

Cape Town's main supermarkets are Pick 'n' Pay, Checkers and Woolworths (modelled on Marks & Spencers in the UK), which has sprouted food-only outlets across the city. You'll find branches of all three operations at **Victoria Wharf** (Map pp203–5), **Gardens Centre** (Map p206) and **Cavendish Square** (Map pp198–9) shopping malls. Delis such as Melissa's (p90) and Gionvanni's Deli World (p92) are ideal places to stock up on picnic items.

Tipping

Waiters in Cape Town earn a pittance and rely heavily on tips. The standard tip for good service is 10% to 15%, but leave more if you think the staff have earned it. A few places include a service charge on the bill.

Opening Hours

Cafés and restaurants generally open seven days a week, the former serving food from 7.30am to about 5pm. A few places (more usually in the City Bowl) will be closed on Sunday or occasionally Monday. If a restaurant opens for lunch it will generally be from 11.30am to 3pm; dinner usually kicks off around 7pm with last orders at 10pm.

Meal Times

Capetonians start the day early, particularly in the summer months; join them for breakfast between 7am and 9am. Lunch runs anywhere from noon to 3pm while dinner starts around 7pm and finishes at 10pm. Note that at weekends dining later in the evening is more common, so if you're finding it difficult to get a reservation, ask for an early dinner and promise you'll be done by 9pm.

Booking Tables

Most restaurants take reservations for lunch and dinner so call ahead if you want to ensure a seat. We've included reservation recommendations for restaurants that are especially popular.

How Much?

Recently there's been a lot of controversy about overcharging in restaurants. The danger sign is 'sq' on the menu where the price should be. This usually applies to premium seafood items such as crayfish and Mozambique prawns and means that you'll pay whatever the establishment considers is the market price that day. Check what the price is for the dish (not just per kg) before you finally order if you want to avoid a nasty shock in the bill.

This said, eating in Cape Town is generally a good-value affair and in many cases a downright bargain. Typically, for breakfast or a quick alcohol-free lunch you're looking at around R50 to R70 (see the Cheap Eats listing in each neighbourhood section). The cost of dinner including a couple of glasses of wine is more typically in the range of R150 to R200 although you can easily pay much more.

Perfect Picnic Spots

If ever a city was made for picnics it's Cape Town. Fill up your basket and head to one of these choice spots:
- **Clifton** (p68) – sunset supper on the beach. Remember to bring candles for the ultimate romantic experience.
- **Lion's Head** (p63) – another sunset spectacular. Hike up this hill with your picnic on a full-moon night to enjoy the spectacular view.
- **Kirstenbosch Botanical Gardens** (p72) – a Sunday afternoon institution, particularly during the summer months when you can enjoy a concert on those verdant rolling lawns.
- **Buitenverwachting** (p36) – the Constantia estate on which to enjoy a prepacked picnic (R85); book on ☎ 794 1012.
- **Tokai Forest** (p73) – tranquil and soulful, this shady forest is close by the arboretum, which has a good café, and is handy for walks up the mountain.
- **Bloubergstrand** (p67) – enjoy the postcard-perfect views of Table Mountain from this northern beach strip.

CITY CENTRE

Inner-city hot dining spots include Heritage Square, which has no fewer than five restaurants and cafés to choose from, and that eternal favourite, Long St. There are plenty of cafés to be found around Greenmarket Square and St George's Mall, too. The Bo-Kaap, a good location for Cape Malay food, is best visited during the day; in the evenings it can be dead.

CITY BOWL & BO-KAAP

AFRICA CAFÉ Map pp200–2 _African_
☎ 422 0221; 108 Shortmarket St, City Bowl; meals R125; ⏱ 6.30-11pm Mon-Sat
With fantastic décor, this is the best place in Cape Town to sample a range of African food. No fewer than 15 different dishes make up the pan-continental feast and you can have as much as you like of each.

BIESMIELLAH Map pp200–2 _Cape Malay_
☎ 423 0850; Wale St, Bo-Kaap; mains R50; ⏱ noon-11pm Mon-Sat
Authentic Cape Malay and Indian food is served at this Bo-Kaap institution decorated with tapestries of the Taj. It's all halal and no alcohol is served.

BUKHARA Map pp200–2 _Indian_
☎ 424 0000; 33 Church St, City Bowl; mains R70
Considered by many to be Cape Town's best Indian restaurant. Enjoy the spicy, tasty food in a stylish setting.

CARA LAZULI Map pp200–2 _Moroccan_
☎ 426 2351; 11 Buiten St, City Bowl; mains R70; ⏱ 7.15-11pm Mon-Sat
Adjoining Richard Griffin's other fun restaurant Madame Zingara, the Moroccan-themed Cara Lazuli offers up a similar party atmosphere with tarot card readers and belly dancers to supplement the inventive menu of tagines and couscous. The fresh-mint, iced granitas are delicious and you can finish your meal off with a hookah.

COL' CACCHIO Map pp203–5 _Italian_
☎ 419 4848; Seeff House, 42 Hans Strijdom Ave, City Bowl; mains R50
The high ceilings and hard surfaces of this old building make for a noisy dining experience, but with thin-crust pizzas this delicious you'll be prepared to make allowances.

FIVE FLIES Map pp200–2 *Mod South African*
☎ 424 4442; 14–16 Keerom St, City Bowl; 2/3/4 courses R110/135/155
In the wood-panelled Dutch Club building (1752), this is a wonderfully atmospheric place with a central cobbled courtyard. It offers menus of inventive contemporary cooking.

GINJA & SHOGA
Map pp200–2 *Mod South African/Asian*
☎ 426 2368, 426 2369; 121 Castle St, Bo-Kaap; mains R70; 7.30-10pm Mon-Sat
An old warehouse on the edge of the Bo-Kaap has been transformed into this duo of hip restaurants. Ginja downstairs offers up modern fusion food while Shoga upstairs has more of an Asian slant to its menu, including tandoori and stir-fry dishes.

IVY GARDEN RESTAURANT
Map pp200–2 *Cape Malay/Western*
☎ 423 2360; Old Town House, Greenmarket Square, City Bowl; mains R70
Delightful courtyard restaurant behind the Old Town House, serving snacks and full meals. Try the platter of four Cape specialities for R69 and, for something sinfully delicious, the brandy pudding (R24).

KENNEDY'S
Map pp200–2 *Mod South African*
☎ 424 1212; 251 Long St, City Bowl; mains R80
A stylish restaurant, with a hint of 1930s glamour, serving some interesting dishes using local produce such as springbok, ostrich and crocodile. There's a cigar lounge and bar, and good live jazz from around 9.30pm.

MADAME ZINGARA
Map pp200–2 *Mod South African*
☎ 426 2458; 192 Loop St, City Bowl; mains R70; 7-11pm Mon-Sat
Known for its rose-petal-scattered surfaces and wild bohemian atmosphere, Madame Zingara is a confirmed crowd pleaser. Unless you're a committed carnivore we'd advise against the whopper stack of beef fillets doused in chilli-chocolate sauce, but otherwise don't miss out on a fun night here or at its sister establishment Cara Lazuli.

MARCO'S AFRICAN PLACE
Map pp200–2 *African*
☎ 423 5412; 15 Rose Lane, Bo-Kaap; mains R60-70; noon-11pm
Marco Radebe's African restaurant strikes all the right notes, with a good range of local dishes and drinks. Try Themba's meatballs, Zwelethu's chicken or Mqomboh beer. At night when the band starts (cover charge R10) expect to start dancing with the waiters.

MARIMBA Map pp203–5 *African*
☎ 418 3366; Cape Town Convention Centre, City Bowl; mains R80; 9am-11pm
Glam African dining is on offer as the new convention centre sets out its culinary stall at this sleek operator on the city side of the huge complex. The outdoor terrace is a pleasant place to sit once the day's traffic has died down and there's live music nightly.

MESOPOTAMIA
Map pp200–2 *Middle Eastern*
☎ 424 4664; cnr Long & Church Sts, City Bowl; mains R60; noon-11pm Mon-Sat
With kilims on the wall and floor cushions around low, copper, salver tables, Mesopotamia conjures up an Ottoman atmosphere in which to serve excellent meze. There's belly dancing from around 9pm Friday and Saturday.

MINATO Map pp200–2 *Japanese*
☎ 423 4712; 4 Buiten St, City Bowl; mains R70
Knocking the socks off trendier sushi joints around town is this Japanese-run, hole-in-the-wall-style place which is open from 7pm until whenever the owner feels like it. Very relaxed and authentic.

NOON GUN TEAROOM & RESTAURANT
Map pp203–5 *Cape Malay*
☎ 424 0529; 273 Longmarket St, Bo-Kaap; set menu R90; 10am-10pm Mon-Sat
After witnessing the noon blast of the cannon, slip into this homely, family-run restaurant on Signal Hill to enjoy the view and Cape Malay dishes such as *bobotie* (beef pie). It can get busy with tour groups.

Eating – City Centre

ROBERTSON'S

Map pp200–2   *Mod South African*
☎ 422 2465; 125 Buitengracht St, City Bowl; Mains R55; ⏲ 6.30am-11pm

Take your pick from the restaurant or more casual bar/bistro areas at this modern operation serving a good range of dishes. The oxtail stew is delicious. There's free parking and a shaded balcony at the back with views of Table Mountain.

ROYAL EATERY

Map pp200–2   *Gourmet Burgers*
☎ 422 4536; 279 Long St, City Bowl; mains R60; ⏲ noon-midnight Mon-Sat

We love the retro style of this gourmet burger bar that also serves good salads and pasta dishes. It serves late into the night.

SAVOY CABBAGE

Map pp200–2   *Mod South African*
☎ 424 2626; 101 Hout St, City Bowl; mains R70-90

This long-running star performer on the city's contemporary dining scene is keeping up standards. The food (a terrine of local foie gras with citrus salad, the signature minced-beef-stuffed cabbage rolls) doesn't clobber you with its flavours, and the staff are equally soothing and professional.

VERANDA Map pp200–2   *Mod South African*
☎ 423 6363; Metropole Hotel, 38 Long St, City Bowl; mains R55-70

The City Bowl's latest boutique hotel sports a smart, relaxed restaurant on the 1st floor overlooking Long St. Traditional dishes such as *bobotie* get a twist and are made with duck and raisin-studded rice. The Moroccan chicken pie is fantastic.

Cheap Eats

CAFE MOZART Map pp200–2   *Café*
☎ 424 3774; 37 Church St, City Bowl; mains R30-50

Watch the world go by from the outdoor tables at this deservedly popular café serving good bistro-style food.

CIN-FULL Map pp200–2   *Café*
☎ 424 5249; 38 Shortmarket St, City Bowl; mains R20-30

Having conquered the mega shopping mall Canal Walk (Map pp196–7), Cin-full brings its baked goods to the city. The cinnamon buns, made on the premises and drenched in cream cheese icing, are a sticky delight. It does a good range of inexpensive sandwiches, too.

CRUSH Map pp200–2   *Café*
☎ 422 5533; 100 St George's Mall, City Bowl; mains R20-30

Proving healthy eating need not be boring, Crush brings a splash of contemporary style and colour to St George's Mall with its freshly squeezed juices, smoothies and tasty wraps.

LOLA'S Map pp200–2   *Café*
☎ 423 0885; 228 Long St, City Bowl; mains R20-30

This long-established funky vegetarian café is the most chilled place to hang out on Long St. It has street tables and a gay-friendly vibe.

MEXICAN KITCHEN Map pp200–2   *Mexican*
☎ 423 1541; 13 Bloem St, City Bowl; buffet lunch R45

This riotously colourful eatery offers authentic Mexican dishes, a relaxed vibe, and a great-value buffet lunch.

MR PICKWICK'S Map pp200–2   *Café*
☎ 424 2696; 158 Long St, City Bowl; mains R20-30; ⏲ 8am-1am Mon-Thu, 8am-4am Fri

The place to recuperate after a night out clubbing. This licensed, deli-style café stays open very late for good snacks and meals. Try the foot-long rolls.

OFF MOROKA CAFE AFRICAINE

Map pp200–2   *African*
☎ 422 1129; 120 Adderley St, City Bowl; mains R25-30, cover during performances R1; ⏲ 6.30am-9pm Mon-Thu, 6.30am-midnight Fri, 8.30am-midnight Sat

The ultimate, inner-city, cultural melting pot, Off Moroka serves a fab range of African dishes and hosts live music and experimental DJs in the evenings. Always potentially interesting are the off-the-wall poetry and literary sessions at 8pm on Monday.

GARDENS & VREDEHOEK

Too cool for school Kloof St is the focus of dining in this part of the city, but you'll also uncover a few other gems around Dunkley Square east of the Company's Gardens and further up the hill in Vredehoek.

ARNOLD'S Map p206   *Mod South African*
☎ 424 4344; 60 Kloof St, Gardens; mains R40-60; ⏲ 9am-late

We've had some good reviews for this casual bistro-style place and it really deserves them. The food is tasty and good value and the atmosphere is very welcoming. Try the biltong salad or unique 'bushman's' game burger.

AUBERGINE Map p206   *Mod South African*
☎ 465 4909; 39 Barnet St, Gardens; 3-course menu R210
Set in the convivial 19th-century home of the first chief justice of the Cape, Aubergine is one of Cape Town's outstanding restaurants. Chef Harald Bresselschmidt creates many memor-able dishes such as a puff pastry tart of aubergine and tomato or sesame-coated quail cutlets.

CAPE COLONY Map p206   *Mod South African*
☎ 483 1850; Mount Nelson Hotel, 76 Orange St, Gardens; 3-course menu R225; 🕑 6.30-10.30pm
With a trompe l'oeil scene of Table Mountain dominating one wall and sumptuous furnishings and place settings, the Cape Colony does glamour to the nines. The cooking doesn't disappoint either with many local ingredients, such as ostrich, crocodile and springbok, brought into imaginative play. There's live jazz and a dinner dance on Saturday night. For sheer indulgence, also visit the Nellie for a delicious afternoon tea (R95) from 2.30pm to 5.30pm.

MANOLO Map p206   *Mod South African*
☎ 422 4747; 30 Kloof St, Gardens; mains R82
The trendy renovation of this traditional bungalow includes Philippe Starck chairs on the veranda and a glowing cocktail bar inside. There's trendy food to match, such as *fynbos*-crusted salmon and lemongrass-infused *naartjie*. The free parking is a boon in this area.

MARIA'S Map p206   *Greek*
☎ 461 8887; 31 Barnet St, Gardens; mains R60
This small, friendly taverna facing Dunkley Square has been around forever, offering a decent range of Greek dishes.

NELSON'S EYE Map p206   *Steak*
☎ 423 2601; 9 Hof St, Gardens; mains R80-100
This darkly atmospheric steak house, serving prime meat with some delicious sauces, gets most people's thumbs up as Cape Town's best steak house. Also a good place to try local game and ostrich.

Top Five Gardens & Vredehoek

- Aubergine (p90)
- Cape Colony (p90)
- Melissa's (pp90-1)
- Nelson's Eye (p90)
- Yindee's (p90)

OCEAN BASKET Map p206   *Seafood*
☎ 422 0322; 75 Kloof St, Gardens; mains R60
The main branch of a chain restaurant that is beloved by families for its jolly decoration, good-value meals and fresh, simple approach to seafood. Eat in the patio garden at the back.

YINDEE'S Map p206   *Thai*
☎ 422 1012; 22 Camp St, Gardens; mains R50-60; 🕑 6.30-10.30pm Mon-Sat
Book ahead if you want to savour the fine Thai cuisine at this red-painted mansion on the corner of Kloof and Camp Sts. Inside you can either dine Western style in an elegant, deep-blue dining room, or sit on cushions at low tables in the red room.

YUM Map p206   *Café*
☎ 461 7607; 2 Deer Park Dr West, Vredehoek; mains R60; 🕑 8.30am-3pm Mon, 8.30am-10pm Tue-Fri, 9am-10pm Sat, 9am-3pm Sun
It's well worth dragging yourself up the hill for this casual café with a relaxed vibe and interesting food such as coconut and lime pancakes for breakfast. If you like the preserves and pasta sauces, they're on sale.

Cheap Eats

CAFÉ GAINSBOURG Map p206   *Café*
☎ 422 1780; 64 Kloof St, Gardens; mains R40-50
Minimalist decorated café that's proving a popular spot for breakfast, lunch or just a coffee.

CAFÉ RITEVE Map p206   *Jewish*
☎ 465 1594; 88 Hatfield St, Gardens; mains R30; 🕑 9.30am-5pm Mon-Wed, 9.30am-10pm Thu & Sun, 9.30am-3pm Fri
Sample good Jewish cuisine from chopped liver to crumbed hake at this contemporary bistro in the South African Jewish Museum. All the food is kosher, and the café sometimes hosts live music, plays and comedy shows in the evenings (from R65 for meal and show).

NAKED ON KLOOF Map p206   *Café*
☎ 424 4748; 51 Kloof St, Gardens; mains R25; 🕑 8am-midnight
This breezy deli-café specialises in wraps (a variety of fillings rolled up in lavash bread) and fresh fruit juices. It's not as hot as it once was, but still worth considering for a snack.

MELISSA'S Map p206   *Deli/Café*
☎ 424 5540; 94 Kloof St, Gardens; mains R30; 🕑 7.30am-8pm Mon-Fri, 8am-8pm Sat & Sun

Pay by the kilogram for the delicious lunch buffets at this super-popular place, then browse the shelves for goodies – such as handmade fudge, fig nougat, potato chips and muesli rusks – for a picnic or gourmet gifts. There's another branch on the corner of Kildare and Main Rds in Newlands (Map pp198–9).

VIDA E CAFFÉ Map p206 Café
☎ 426 0627; 34 Kloof St, Gardens; mains R20; ☿ 7.30am-5pm Mon-Fri
Shaping up to be the Starbucks of Cape Town, Vida e Caffé does coffee, freshly squeezed orange juice, Portuguese-style pastries and beefy filled rolls with considerable panache, making it ideal for breakfast or a fast lunch. There are also branches in Victoria Wharf at the Waterfront (Map pp203–5) and off Tulbagh Square in the City Bowl (Map pp200–2).

ATLANTIC COAST

It's natural that you'll want to dine with an ocean view while in Cape Town, so the following Atlantic Coast suburbs are the ones to head for.

GREEN POINT, WATERFRONT & WATERKANT

Green Point and the Waterkant are riding high as the hot dining locations; the Cape Quarter in particular is the place to see and be seen. The Waterfront's plethora of restaurants and cafés offers unrivalled variety, convenience and a lively atmosphere, but keep an eye on prices at what is essentially a giant tourist trap.

ANATOLI Map pp203–5 Turkish
☎ 419 2501; 24 Napier St, Green Point; meals R60; ☿ 7-11pm Tue-Sun
Wall-carpeted Anatoli has been here for years and with good reason: the delicious meze (cold/hot R18/26) brought around on enormous wooden trays make a great meal.

ANDIAMO Map pp203–5 Italian
☎ 421 3687; Shop C2, Cape Quarter, Waterkant; mains R60; ☿ 8am-11pm
This deli, restaurant and bar is one of the most popular spots in this hip shopping and dining centre. Lounge in one of the seagrass sofas while nibbling at antipasto, or cruise Cape Town's widest selection of olive oils in the deli.

BELUGA Map pp203–5 Mod South African
☎ 418 2948; The Foundry, Prestwich St, Green Point; mains R80
The smart set dines in this chic warehouse. There's Beluga caviar on the menu, but also cheaper dishes and a pleasant café, too.

DEN ANKER Map pp203–5 Belgian/Seafood
☎ 419 0249; Pierhead, Waterfront; mains R80; ☿ 11am-11pm
One of the more charming of the Waterfront's dining options offers a great range of authentic Belgian beers with which to wash down a menu heavy on mussels and other seafood.

EMILY'S Map pp203–5 Mod South African
☎ 421 1133; Shop 202 Clock Tower Centre, Waterfront; mains R80
Emily's is justly renowned for its eclectic and artistic approach to modern South African cooking – imagine a marinated crocodile and avocado pizza and you'll get the brightly coloured picture. You're also sure to find something to your taste on the epic wine list.

JEWEL TAVERN Map pp198–9 Chinese
☎ 448 1977; off Vanguard Dr, Duncan Dock, Foreshore; mains R55-70; ☿ 11am-2.30pm, 6-10pm Mon-Sat, 6-9pm Sun
Cape Town's best Chinese restaurant lies hidden away in the docks. Don't even think about walking here, but certainly drop by if you have a craving for dim sum or the succulently sizzling platters of beef, chicken or seafood.

MARIO'S Map pp203–5 Italian
☎ 439 6644; 89 Main Rd, Green Point; mains R40-70; ☿ noon-2.30pm Tue-Fri & Sun, 6.45-10.30pm Tue-Sun
Customer praise is scribbled all over the walls and ceiling at this long-running restaurant. It serves perfectly al dente pasta and an extensive list of specials.

ONE.WATERFRONT
Map pp203–5 Mod South African
☎ 418 0520; Cape Grace, West Quay, Waterfront; R70-100
The fishcakes are a winner at the Cape Grace's smart yet casual restaurant, as are many more of chef Bruce Robertson's inventive, not-to-be-tried-at-home dishes. Some exciting options for vegetarians here, too.

PIGALLE Map pp203–5 Seafood
☎ 421 434; 57A Somerset Rd, Green Point; mains R80-100; ☿ noon-3pm Mon-Sat, 7pm-midnight
With its entrance off Highfield Rd, Pigalle brings the glamour of the dinner-dance back

to Cape Town, in possibly the city's most dramatic interior. Huge silver chandeliers, Elvis on the wallpaper – it's like dining on an Andy Warhol cruise ship. The menu features retro favourites such as shrimp cocktail, with the seafood platter (R250) offering outstanding value. The hard-sell on bottled water, rolls and other extras should be turned down though.

THE RESTAURANT

Map pp203–5   *Mod South African*

☎ 419 2921; 51A Somerset Rd, Green Point; mains R90; ☽ 11am-3pm Mon-Fri, 7-10pm Mon-Sat

Chef Graeme Shapiro avoided conscription by cooking at the famed Darley St Thai and Bathers' Pavilion in Sydney before returning to Cape Town to open this great little restaurant. The décor is jumble-sale chic, while the food is paired back to essentials and all the better for it. A lunch dish of line fish, string fries and salsa (R50) is a bargain.

WAKAME Map pp203–5   *Seafood*

☎ 433 2377; cnr of Beach Rd & Surrey Place, Moullie Point; mains R70; ☽ noon-10pm

Come here more for the glorious coastal view, trendy décor (love that dinosaur-style fish skeleton above the sushi bar) and relaxed vibe rather than for the food which can be patchy. It's an ideal spot for sunset drinks, away from the crowds at Camp's Bay. Downstairs is the **Newport Market & Deli**, another of Cape Town's cool grocery stores-cum-cafés.

WILLOUGHBY & CO

Map pp203–5   *Seafood*

☎ 418 6115; Shop 6132 Victoria Wharf, Waterfront; mains R60-70; ☽ restaurant 11.30am-10.45pm, deli 9am-8.30pm

Huge servings of sushi are the standout from a good-value, fish-based menu at this casual eatery and deli on the ground floor of Victoria Wharf. It's commonly acknowledged as one of the better places to eat at the Waterfront.

ZERO932 Map pp203–5   *Belgian*

☎ 439 6306; 79 Main Rd, Green Point; mains R70; ☽ 9am-11pm

The main attraction at this trendy Belgian-beer restaurant is Saldanha rope-grown mussels served in 1kg pots or open faced on platters, but there are plenty of other dishes too. Or you could just sample some of the 26 different bottled beers plus three more on tap.

Cheap Eats

DUTCH Map pp203–5   *Café*

☎ 425 0157; 34 Napier St, Waterkant; mains R30

This very orange corner café in the heart of the Waterkant provides a prime scoping spot for the passing parade. Don those Ray Bans and tuck into a toasted ciabatta with smoked trout.

GIONVANNI'S DELI WORLD

Map pp203–5   *Deli/Café*

☎ 434 6983; 103 Main Rd, Green Point; mains R20-30; ☽ 8.30am-9pm

It's not as big as rival delis, but bursts with energy and flavoursome products. The staff will make up any sandwich you fancy. If you can't wait to eat, there's a small café.

LA PETITE TARTE Map pp203–5   *Café*

☎ 425 9077; Shop A11 Cape Quarter, 72 Waterkant St, Waterkant; mains R30-40; ☽ 8am-4pm Mon-Fri, 8am-2pm Sat

Home-made, savoury and sweet French-style tarts lead the way at this adorable café on the Dixon St side of the Cape Quarter, where you can also savour Mariage Frères teas.

NEWS CAFÉ Map pp203–5   *Café/Bar*

☎ 434 6196; 83 Main Rd, Green Point; mains R40; ☽ 7.30am-2am

A buzzy café-bar that's a good spot for anything from breakfast or a bistro-type meal to late-night drinks.

VIE EN SCENE Map pp203–5   *French*

☎ 418 3671; Unit 12A Cape Quarter, 72 Waterkant St, Waterkant; mains R30; ☽ 10am-midnight

This French crêperie and piano bar is a pleasant spot if you're in the mood for dessert; it also offers substantial meals and has tango dancing on Wednesday nights, jazz on Sunday.

SEA POINT TO NOORDHOEK

There's no shortage of places to eat along Sea Point's Main Rd and Regent St, many of them at the budget end of the scale, which reflects the suburb's less than hip credentials. In contrast, Camps Bay, a playground of the rich and beautiful, couldn't be hotter – and you'd be well advised to book ahead anywhere here if you wish to get a prime spot for sunset drinks and nibbles.

BLUES Map p208 *Mod South African*
☎ 438 2040; The Promenade, Victoria Rd, Camps Bay; mains R85; ⏱ noon-midnight
Overlooking the beach, Blues is a smart casual restaurant in the 'Californian tradition', which means the menu has something to please practically everyone.

BUZBEY GRILL Map p207 *Steak & Seafood*
☎ 439 5900; 14 Three Anchor Bay Rd, Sea Point; mains R60-70; ⏱ 6-11pm Tue-Sat
A retro institution that attracts an older crowd who value a well-done steak or plate of seafood; the calamari is legendary.

LA PERLA Map p207 *Italian*
☎ 439 9538; Beach Rd; mains R60-70; ⏱ noon-11.30pm
This stylish operator has terrace seating and a comfy bar that is one of the few decent seaside options in this area. It serves some 30-plus pastas.

MARINER'S WHARF Map p210 *Seafood*
☎ 790 1100; Harbour Rd, Hout Bay; mains R70-100; ⏱ 9am-10pm
A contrived, harbour-side complex with several options. In the upmarket Wharfside Grill, the waiters are dressed as sailors to match the sea-salt décor. The cheaper deal is at the takeaway downstairs.

PARANGA Map p208 *Mod South African*
☎ 438 0404; Shop 1 The Promenade, Victoria Rd, Camps Bay; main R90
Soft, cream-coloured furnishings and a palm tree add tropical luxury to this upmarket seafood restaurant best known for being owned by the son of heart transplant surgeon Christian Barnard.

SUIKERBOSSIE Map p210 *European*
☎ 790 1450; 1 Victoria Ave, Hout Bay; mains R70; ⏱ 9am-4.30pm Tue-Sun
There's a lovely tea garden at this large 1930s house, perched at the top of the hill before you descend to Hout Bay. It's often used for functions, so call ahead. The Sunday carvery (R108) is very popular.

Top Five Sea Point to Noordhoek
- Blues (p93)
- Buzbey Grill (p93)
- Cedar (p93)
- La Perla (p93)
- Fish on the Rocks (p93)

Cheap Eats

ARI'S SOUVLAKI Map p207 *Greek*
☎ 439 6683; 83A Regent St, Sea Point; mains R25; ⏱ 10am-midnight
Meze, shwarma and felafel are on offer at this Greek institution. It's nothing fancy but it's honest.

CEDAR Map p207 *Middle Eastern*
☎ 433 2546; 104 Main Rd, Sea Point; mains R40; ⏱ 11.30am-9.30pm
Unpretentious, family-run the Cedar serves a tasty range of meze and Lebanese dishes. It has many flavoured tobaccos for its hookah pipes.

FISH ON THE ROCKS Map p210 *Seafood*
☎ 790 0001; Harbour Rd, Hout Bay; mains R25; ⏱ 10.30am-8.15pm
Enjoy eating some of Cape Town's best fish and chips at a prime spot right at the end of Hout Bay Harbour Rd.

KAUAI Map p207 *Hawaiian*
☎ 434 7645; cnr Regent St & Clarens Rd, Sea Point; mains R20-30
A slick Hawaiian-franchise operation, Kauai offers a wide range of smoothies, juices and healthy sandwiches. There are several other branches around the city, including at Lifestyles on Kloof (p129).

NEW YORK BAGELS Map p207 *Deli/Café*
☎ 439 7523; 51 Regent Rd, Sea Point; mains R30; ⏱ 7am-11pm
As well as the deli there's the airy multilevel café next door where you wander around various stalls to choose a mix 'n' match meal of, say, a hot-beef-on-rye sarnie followed by a spicy stir-fry.

SANDBAR Map p208 *Café*
☎ 438 8336; 31 Victoria Rd, Camps Bay; mains R30
One of Camps Bay's better value options is this less self-consciously fashionable café with street tables serving good sandwiches and light meals.

Eating – Atlantic Coast

SOUTHERN SUBURBS

Along Lower Main Rd in Observatory it's wall-to-wall restaurants, cafés and bars, most with menus that are slanted towards the tastes and budgets of the resident student population. More upmarket restaurants can be found in and around Constantia's wineries. Kirstenbosch has several decent dining options in case you forget your picnic basket.

BARRISTERS Map pp198–9
☎ 674 1792; cnr Kildare Rd & Main St, Newlands; mains R70; ☼ 8am-10.30pm Mon-Sat, 5-10pm Sun
Long-time favourite of the rugger bugger set, Barristers offers up quality steaks in a dark and sophisticated setting.

BUITENVERWACHTING
Map pp198–9   *Mod South African*
☎ 794 3522; Klein Constantia Rd, Constantia; mains R100; ☼ noon-1.30pm Tue-Fri, 7-9pm Tue-Sat
Elegant furnishing and blissful views across the vines to the mountain add to the epicurean delights at this recently revamped winery restaurant. Try its plate of tuna prepared in a variety of ways or the venison with rösti of artichoke and leek.

DIVA Map p208   *Italian*
☎ 448 0282; 88 Lower Main Rd; mains R50
Best known for its tasty pizzas (the Mediterranean with wine-soaked aubergine is a favourite), Diva offers up plenty of other Italian goodies in a faded Venetian-style atmosphere.

FAT CACTUS Map pp198–9   *Mexican*
☎ 685 1920; 47 Durban Rd, Mowbray; mains R50; ☼ 11am-11pm
At this casual, fun Mexican café-bar, the combo platter is big enough for two people to share. There's a good kids' menu too. Across the road is the owner's wife's good and lively Greek restaurant, called simply **Greek!** (☎ 686 4314).

JONKERHUIS Map pp196–7   *Cape Malay*
☎ 794 4255; Groot Constantia, Constantia; mains R80; ☼ 9am-11pm Tue-Sat, 9am-5pm Sun & Mon
Waiters dressed in 17th-century slave costumes serve up traditional Cape dishes such as *bobotie* and *bredies* (pot stews of meat or fish, and vegetables) at this pretty, atmospheric restaurant. Its Cape brandy tart is a tea-time treat.

LA COLOMBE Map pp196–7   *French*
☎ 794 2390; Constantia Uitsig, Spaanschemat River Rd; mains R90
The menu – all written in French – changes daily at this light and relaxed Provençal-style restaurant with a poolside setting.

PEDDLARS ON THE BEND
Map pp196–7   *Traditional European*
☎ 794 7747; Spaanschemat River Rd; mains R50-60
If you don't fancy all that highfalutin' wine-estate fodder, the hearty dishes such as chicken pie and *eisbein* (pork knuckle) served at this lively pub should suit you fine.

SIMON'S Map pp196–7   *Mod European*
☎ 794 1143; Groot Constantia, Constantia; mains R50-90; ☼ noon-10.30pm
The new restaurant at Groot Constantia is a sophisticated affair seating over 200 with an open kitchen, mezzanine level and open terrace. The range of the menu, from jalapeno burgers to Nambian seafood curry, is wide.

SPAANSCHEMAT RIVER CAFÉ
Map pp196–7   *Mod South African*
☎ 794 3010; Constantia Uitsig, Spaanschemat River Rd; mains R60
This relaxed restaurant at the entrance to the estate is good value and serves huge portions, often made with organic and free-range products. The desserts are divine.

SILVER TREE Map pp196–7 *Mod South African*
☎ 762 9585; Kirstenbosch Botanical Gardens, Rhodes Dr, Bishopscourt; mains R40-65; ☼ 8am-10pm
Kirstenbosch's main restaurant is a smart affair, with crisp white tablecloths and a central fireplace. Call about the monthly food and wine evenings.

Cheap Eats
CAFÉ GANESH Map p208   *Indian/African*
☎ 448 3435; 38B Trill Rd, Observatory; mains R30-40
Junkyard décor and matchbox label wallpaper create the chic-shack atmosphere at this funky student hang-out, dishing up tasty felafel, roti, curries and the like. Call to find out about its monthly dance parties.

GARDENER'S COTTAGE Map pp198–9   *Café*
☎ 689 3158; Montebello Craft Studios, 31 Newlands Ave, Newlands; mains R40
This cute café and tea garden in the grounds of the craft studios is worth visiting for its relaxed atmosphere and simple, hearty meals.

KIRSTENBOSCH TEA ROOM

Map pp196–7 *Café*

☎ 797 4883; Kirstenbosch Botanical Gardens, Rhodes Dr, Bishopscourt; mains R20-30

This new café in the gardens is proving popular with its high-roofed design and general menu of sandwiches, quiches and light meals such as fish and chips. If you want some food to eat in the gardens, drop by the **Fynbos Food Court** which also sells beer and wine.

MILLER'S PLATE Map pp198–9 *Café*

☎ 685 6233; Josephine Mill, Boundary Rd, Newlands; mains R30-40; ☻ 8.30am-4pm Sun-Fri

Set amid bamboo, palms and Japanese maple trees, this very pleasant café is in the Josephine Mill next to the rugby ground. It does a three-course roast lunch on Sunday for R60.

RHODES MEMORIAL RESTAURANT

Map pp198–9 *Traditional European*

☎ 689 9151; Groote Schuur Estate, Rondebosch; mains R40-60

This thatched, stone cottage is a fantastic spot for lunch or afternoon tea. The scones are just enormous. It's on the side of Devil's Peak and right behind the memorial.

FALSE BAY

Kalk Bay's Main Rd has long runneth over with appealing cafés, but Muizenberg is beginning to give it a run for its money as a convivial place to dine on False Bay. Simon's Town has a few fine options too, all of which could convince you to linger longer around False Bay than planned.

MUIZENBERG, KALK BAY & SIMON'S TOWN

BALTAZAR Map p209 *German*

☎ 788 4912; 33 Palmer Rd, Muizenberg; mains R50-60; ☻ noon-3.30pm, 6-11pm Tue-Sun

Part of the Muizenberg Village shopping arcade, this appealingly rustic place has a quiet courtyard serving Germanic and continental-style cuisine such as Eisbein, sauerkraut and goulash. Lunch specials run at R20.

BON APPETIT Map p210 *French*

☎ 786 2412; 90 St George's St, Simon's Town; mains R80-90; ☻ noon-2pm & 6.30-10pm Tue-Sun

A quaint and intimate French bistro serving classic dishes such as twice-cooked cheese soufflé and tarte tatin. There's a set menu for R140 or R160.

BRASS BELL Map p209 *Seafood*

☎ 788 5455; Kalk Bay Station, Main Rd, Kalk Bay; mains R60-70

There are several options at this Cape Town institution between the train station and the sea. The formal restaurant serves everything from breakfast to dinner. There's an alfresco pizzeria and, of course, the bar. Fish *braais* (barbecues) are held on the terrace from 6.30pm on Sunday.

CAPE TO CUBA

Map p209 *Mod South African/Cuban*

☎ 788 1566; Main Rd, Kalk Bay; mains R60-80

It's really the wonderful décor rather than the food at this beach shack that's the homage to Havana. *Everything* you see is for sale (save the peasant-costumed waitresses dishing out daiquiris). At night flickering candles replace the sea views, both of which add a sparkle to the restaurant's already considerable charms.

EMPIRE CAFÉ Map p209 *Café*

☎ 788 1250; 11 York Rd, Muizenberg; mains R50; ☻ 7am-4pm Tue-Sun, 6.30-10.30pm Thu & Sat

One of the original owners of Olympia Café in Kalk Bay is behind this superb operation which has fast become the surfies favourite hang-out. It's on two levels and has local art exhibitions as well as excellent light meals.

OLYMPIA CAFÉ & DELI Map p209 *Café*

☎ 788 6396; 134 Main Rd, Kalk Bay; mains R40-75; ☻ 7am-9pm

A Cape Town institution that sets the standard for relaxed rustic cafés by the sea. It's renown

Eating – False Bay

for its breakfasts and breads and pastries made on the premises, but Mediterranean-influenced main dishes are generally delicious, too.

Cheap Eats
BALMORAL ON THE BEACH
Map p209 *Café*
☎ 788 6441; Unit 2, 52 Beach Rd, Muizenberg; mains R30; 9am-5pm Wed-Mon
Smartest of the several new cafés in the area, Balmoral's menu includes a few interesting choices: try butternut risotto cakes with shaved pecarrino and spinach, or the chocolate cake.

CAFÉ MATISSE Map p209 *Mediterranean*
☎ 788 1123, 76 Main Rd, Kalk Bay; mains R30-40; 8.30am-11pm
The eclectic décor and candles at night enhance the atmosphere at this bistro, which serves pizzas and a good meze plate for R56.

MEETING PLACE Map p209 *Café*
☎ 786 1986; 98 St George's St, Simon's Town; mains R40; 9am-4pm Mon, 9am-9pm Tue-Sun
Relax on the balcony overlooking the Simon's Town main street at this trendy deli-café, a foodie's delight.

MONEY TREE CAFÉ Map p209 *Café*
☎ 788 2242 ; Main Rd, Kalk Bay; mains R20-30; 9am-4pm Tue-Sun
The wives of the many unemployed fishermen cook for and run this delightful café across the road from the harbour. Drop by for a slice of milk tart or lemon meringue if nothing else.

OLIVE STATION Map p209 *Deli/Café*
☎ 788 3264; 165 Main Rd, Muizenberg; mains R30; 8am-5pm Mon, 8am-9pm Wed-Sat, 9am-9pm Sun
The olives sold here are grown locally and cured in wooden barrels. Try the ones with roasted garlic and the Middle Eastern–style *throubs* (dry cured olives). In the attached espresso bar overlooking the sea, dine on Lebanese dishes such as *kibbeh* (emulsified paste of lamb and bulgur) and filo pastry pies.

CAPE FLATS
If you want to try traditional Xhosa cuisine such as *samp* (pounded dried bean kernels), *pap* (maize porridge) and tripe, arrange with a tour company (see p57) or private guide to visit these places. Bookings are essential.

EZIKO Map pp196–7 *African*
☎ 694 0434; cnr Washington St & Jungle Walk, Langa; mains R30-40; 9am-6pm Mon-Fri, 9am-10pm Sat
Getting good reviews and much support (including sponsorship from the likes of Woolworths and the British High Commission), Eziko is one the best places to eat in Langa; try the chef's special fried chicken or the traditional breakfast.

GUGU LE AFRIKA Map pp196–7 *African*
☎ 361 1975; 8 Lwandle Rd, Khayelitsha; mains R30
This catering training centre is a professional operation, with a menu of reasonably priced Western and African dishes. Check out the adjacent fabric-printing and design workshop.

LELAPA Map pp196–7 *African*
☎ 694 2681; 49 Harlem Ave, Langa; buffet R75
Sheila serves up delicious buffets in her well-appointed home. She's well travelled and loves to chat with guests about life in the townships and elsewhere.

MASANDE RESTAURANT
Map pp196–7 *African*
☎ 371 7173; Philani Flagship Printing Project, Crossroads; mains R30
The name means 'let us prosper' and you can try dishes such as *samp* and beans with stew; *pap* and tripe; and *umvubo* (sour milk and mealie meal), as well as home-brewed beer.

Entertainment

Entertainment

From drumming your hands numb at the Drum Café (p105) to dancing the night away at a Long St club, Cape Town certainly knows how to throw a party (or a 'jol' as they say in South Africa). The city has such a lively atmosphere (especially in summer) that many people put in some very long nights; most bars and clubs don't get going until after 11pm anyway.

Wednesday, Friday and Saturday are the biggest nights for drinking and clubbing. As well as the more commercial venues there's a range of informal places that come and go. Some started out as private parties that were just too good to stop. Among the hottest tickets in town are those for the monthly Vortex trance parties (p103), while *everyone* wants to dress to impress at the Mother City Queer Project bash each December (p103).

It's not all about drinking and dancing. Cape Town has a decent range of cinemas and theatres, while music spans the gamut from classical to rock via jazz and marimba. Free live music is a feature of the Waterfront, in particular.

Although it's improving, examples of entertainment integration remain rare in Cape Town; bars and clubs where blacks, coloureds and whites happily rub shoulders are few and far between. And practically the only way you're going to safely explore the nightlife of the Cape Flats is on a tour (see p57).

The weekly arts guide in the *Mail & Guardian* is the best place to find out what's going on, and the daily *Cape Argus* has an entertainment section, too. The monthly magazine *Cape etc* is also good for listings; it's available at Cape Town Tourism offices, CNA shops and other bookstores.

Tickets & Reservations

COMPUTICKET
☎ 083 915 8000; www.computicket.co.za
Cape Town's computerised booking agency handles ticketing for all major sporting events. There are outlets in the Golden Acre Centre (Map pp200–2), at the Waterfront (Map pp203–5), in the Gardens Centre (Map p206) and in Sea Point's Adelphi Centre (Map p207) as well as other places.

BARS & PUBS

Long and Kloof Sts and the gay Waterkant district are incredibly lively all night long on summer weekends, as is the Waterfront. Most bars open around 3pm and close after midnight but much later from Friday to Sunday. Alternative opening times are listed in the following reviews.

CITY BOWL

COOL RUNNINGS Map pp200–2
☎ 426 6584; 227 Long St, City Bowl
This reggae theme bar has shifted down to the heart of Long St, above Adventure Village, bringing with it the laid-back Caribbean atmos-

phere. There's another popular branch in Observatory (p101).

FIREMAN'S ARMS Map pp200–2
☎ 419 1513; 25 Mechau St, City Bowl
Dating from 1906, this is one of the few old-style pubs left in town – so old in fact that it still has the Rhodesian and old South African flags pinned up alongside a collection of fireman's helmets. It's a place to come to watch rugby on the big-screen TV, grab some seriously tasty pizza or just down a lazy pint or two.

M BAR Map pp200–2
☎ 423 7247; www.metropolehotel.co.za; 38 Long St, City Bowl
Like stepping into the sexiest tomato in town, this overwhelmingly red bar hides its charms

Top Five Bars & Pubs
- **Eclipse** (p100) Sundowners at Camps Bay
- **Fireman's Arms** (p98) Beer, pizza and testosterone
- **Jo'burg** (p99) Grooving with the hip crowd
- **The Nose Wine Bar** (p100) Wine tasters
- **Planet** (p99) Champagne cocktails and glamour

at the back of the revamped Metropole Hotel. Versace-clad sofas just add to the glamour.

MARVEL Map pp200–2
☎ 426 5880; 236 Long St, City Bowl; 🕙 8pm-4am Mon-Sat

A groovy, understated bar that's currently one of the best on Long St. There are cosy booths at the front, a pool table at the back and a selection of hot DJs throughout the week.

PA NA NA SOUK BAR Map pp200–2
☎ 423 4889; Heritage Square complex, 100 Short-market St, City Bowl; 🕙 11am-1am Mon-Sat

Welcome to the style kazbah at this sybaritic bar with balconies overlooking the Heritage Square's restored courtyard.

PURPLE TURTLE Map pp200–2
☎ 423 6194; cnr Long & Shortmarket Sts, City Bowl

The antithesis of hip is this grunge and Goth centre. Dress down or in black with purple make-up to feel at home. It's worth checking out for its alternative-music gigs too.

JO'BURG Map pp200–2
☎ 422 0142; 218 Long St, City Bowl

Long St's most crowded hang-out has live music on Sundays and a pool table at the back. Check out the Brett Murray (p29) light sculptures decorating the walls, including a highly aroused Bart Simpson.

VELVET LOUNGE Map pp200–2
☎ 083 709 0419; 136 Bree St, City Bowl; 🕙 7pm-2am Mon-Sat

The entrance to this spacious gay- and lesbian-friendly bar is on Dorp St. There are two levels, with pool tables and a fish tank upstairs and a lot less pumped-up crowd than in the Waterkant.

GARDENS & ZONNEBLOEM

ASHOKA, SON OF DHARMA Map p206
☎ 422 0909; 68 Kloof St, Gardens

Not quite so trendy as it once was, Dharma has restyled itself as Ashoka. The Café del Mar set can breath easy; it's still the same old chill-bar and fusion bistro.

CAFE BARDELI/COHIBAR Map p206
☎ 423 4444; Darter's Rd, Gardens; 🕙 9am-1am Mon-Sat

In the Longkloof Studios building just off Kloof St, Bardeli is still a reliable place to sink

a chardonnay or beer, grab something to eat and be seen with trendy media types. Adjoining is **Cohibar** which hosts the Habit, a lesbian/woman's night on the last Saturday of the month.

PERSEVERANCE TAVERN Map p206
☎ 461 2440; 83 Buitenkant St, Zonnebloem

Cecil Rhodes called this pioneering pub his local. The flickering candles in the dim interior still give it plenty of atmosphere.

PLANET Map p206
☎ 483 1864; Mount Nelson Hotel, 76 Orange St, Gardens

A fabulous mobile of the planets hangs above this delectable, silver-coated champagne and cocktail bar, serving some 250 different bubblies and 50-odd alcoholic concoctions. The old Nellie has never looked so groovy.

STAG'S HEAD HOTEL Map p206
☎ 465 4918; 71 Hope St, Gardens; 🕙 11am-1am

Traditional bar where a motley assortment of locals stare morosely into their beers. Head to the rear to find the younger crowd. Upstairs is the alternative and new wave dance club Hectic on Hope (p102).

SHACK Map p206
☎ 461 5892; 43-45 De Villiers St, Zonnebloem

This happening bar on several levels has a pool hall and table football, and packs an interesting, studenty crowd. It's part of the complex of venues, including the **Jam**, (☎ 4652106; 43 De Villiers St, Zonnebloem) on the edge of District Six.

WATERFRONT & GREEN POINT

BAR CODE Map pp203–5
☎ 421 5305; www.leatherbar.co.za; 18 Cobern St, Green Point; 🕙 8pm-2am Sun-Thu, 10pm-4am Fri & Sat

Dress in denim, leather and latex for the Mother City's only down 'n' dirty leather bar, otherwise you won't be let in. Check the Web site for details of weekly events.

BARAZA Map p208
☎ 438 1758; Victoria Rd, Camps Bay
This comfy seaside cocktail bar has a totally killer view – and you may have to kill to be able to admire it from one of the hotly contested cane chairs.

BASCULE BAR Map pp203–5
☎ 410 7100; Cape Grace, West Quay, Waterfront
The Grace's sophisticated, earth-toned lounge bar specialises in whisky – more than 400 varieties of it! If you're feeling flush go for the 50-year-old Glenfiddich, just R15,200 a tot. It also has an all-female string quartet fiddling away every Wednesday.

BRONX Map pp203–5
☎ 419 9219; 35 Somerset Rd, Waterkant
The city's premier gay bar attracts a mixed crowd. It's a lively place with buff barmen and DJs that keep patrons dancing until dawn. Monday nights are for karaoke enthusiasts.

BUENA VISTA SOCIAL CAFÉ
Map pp203–5
☎ 433 0611; Exhibition Bldg, 81 Main Rd, Green Point
Taking its inspiration from the famous CD of Cuban music, Buena Vista is *mucho simpatico*. A tapas menu supplements the mix of cigars, Bacardi and coke, and bronzed babes.

CAFE MANHATTAN Map pp203–5
☎ 421 6666; 74 Waterkant St, Waterkant
Russell Shapiro's convivial and long-running restaurant-bar pretty much got the Waterkant's gay scene up and running. The restaurant's not much cop, but the bar has outdoor tables in just the right spot to catch the crowds, many of whom are heading to the Cape Quarter.

CASTRO'S POOL LOUNGE Map pp203–5
☎ 425 3857; 10 Dixon St, Waterkant; ☷ noon-late
Twelve pool tables and a full-sized snooker table (R3 a game) are available at this atmospheric basement bar in the heart of the Waterkant.

CHILLI 'N' LIME Map pp203–5
☎ 498 4668; 23 Somerset Rd, Green Point
It's been around for ages, which says something. A younger, straighter crowd usually hangs out at this bar and club in the heart of the gay district.

FERRYMAN'S FREEHOUSE Map pp203–5
☎ 419 7748; East Pier Rd, Waterfront
Adjoining Mitchell's Waterfront Brewery, this traditional, wood-clad pub-restaurant serves a variety of freshly brewed beers and good-value meals.

THE NOSE WINE BAR Map pp203–5
☎ 425 2200; www.thenose.co.za; Cape Quarter, Dixon St, Waterkant
It took a British and Australian couple to realise what Cape Town was missing: a first-class wine bar. Sip your way around some 35 of the Cape's best wines with 12 changing on a monthly basis. They also serve good food and run wine-tasting courses (p33).

OPIUM Map pp203–5
☎ 425 4010; 6 Dixon St, Waterkant
Another cutting-edge, cool cocktail lounge for the *Wallpaper** magazine generation, with a long, long bar and boasting 'smoky sleazy sounds' – which makes it sound a whole lot more interesting than it actually is.

ROSIE'S Map pp203–5
☎ 072 250 7621; 125A Vos St, Waterkant
Russel Shapiro's bar for the rather less fashion-conscious gay. Tends to attract an older crowd and those looking for sugar daddies as they idle around the green baize pool tables.

TANK Map pp203–5
☎ 419 0007; Shop B15, Cape Quarter, Waterkant St, Waterkant
Pacific rim cuisine for the style set is offered at this uber-chic lounge bar and restaurant. Most patrons seem to just hang by the luminous bar and fish tank practising their poses and pouts, though.

VASCO DA GAMA TAVERN Map pp203–5
☎ 425 2157; 3 Alfred St, Green Point
Sink a pint and munch on excellent, good-value seafood, including Mozambique prawns and Portuguese sardines, while old blokes argue the toss at the other end of the laminated bar.

ATLANTIC COAST
CAFÉ CAPRICE Map p208
☎ 438 8315; Victoria Rd, Camps Bay; ☷ 9am-2am
Owned by a star Springbok rugby player, and steps away from the beach, the Caprice is as popular for breakfast as it is for sundowner

The Nose Wine Bar, Waterkant (see opposite)

drinks. Grab a pavement table for the best view, or sink into a sofa if you're in a more relaxed mood.

ECLIPSE Map p208
☎ 438 0882; The Promenade, Victoria Rd, Camps Bay
The chic London chain of cocktail bars touches down on the top floor of the Promenade complex, providing a postcard-perfect view of the beach. Let wafer-thin, tattooed waitresses bring you something tall and chilled to enjoy on a chocolate-leather ottoman as the sun slips beneath the horizon.

LA MED Map p208
☎ 438 5600; Glen Country Club, Victoria Rd, Clifton
A favourite spot for sunset drinks, although essentially it's just a bar with lots of outdoor tables and a good view. The entrance, on the way to Clifton from Camps Bay, is easily passed.

LEOPARD LOUNGE Map p208
☎ 437 9000; Twelve Apostles Hotel, Victoria Rd, Camps Bay
There's no mistaking the theme of this bar, with the leopard print and out-of-gay-Africa theme worked overtime. It's worth dropping by for the view, kitsch atmosphere and choice of 50-plus martinis and top-class nibbles.

RED HERRING Map pp196–7
☎ 789 1783; cnr Beach & Pine Rds, Noordhoek
If you're down this way, say after a drive along Chapman's Peak Drive, it's a pleasant place to drop by for a drink or a bite to eat. There's a good view of the beach from the roof terrace.

SOUTHERN SUBURBS

BILLY THE B.U.M.'S Map pp198–9
☎ 683 5541; Letterstead House, cnr Main & Campground Rds, Newlands
This smart bar, owned by Springbok rugby player Bobby Skinstad, is one of the most happening options in this neck of the woods.

CAFÉ CARTE BLANCHE Map p208
☎ 447 8717; 42 Trill Rd, Observatory
With bags of boho-chic, this tiny café-bar plastered with art on two cosy floors is *the* place for a secret assignation or late-night canoodlings.

COOL RUNNINGS Map p208
☎ 448 7656; 96 Station St, Observatory
Sand has been dumped outside this chain reggae bar to create that beach-side feel, carried through in the island-hut décor.

CURVE BAR AT THE BIJOUX Map p208
☎ 448 0183; 178 Lower Main Rd, Observatory

It's at the dodgy end of Observatory, but safe enough to venture to when there's a club night on (for which you'll pay around R20 admission). The décor comprises cool industrial style in an abandoned cinema space.

DON PEDRO'S Map pp198–9
☎ 447 4493; 113 Roodebloem Rd, Woodstock

It's a long-time favourite with white liberals for a boozy late night out, and is now popular with the yuppies moving into the area. They've also recently opened a branch at Muizenberg (Map p209).

FORESTERS' ARMS Map pp198–9
☎ 689 5949; 52 Newlands Ave, Newlands;
☾ 10am-11pm Mon-Sat, 9am-4pm Sun

Affectionately known as Forries, this big mock-Tudor pub has been around for over a century. It offers a convivial atmosphere and good pub meals.

ROLLING STONES Map p208
☎ 448 9461; 94 Lower Main Rd, Observatory

Otherwise known as Stones, this giant pool bar has a long balcony – a great spot from which to observe the comings and goings of Lower Main Rd. There are other branches around town including one at 166A Long St and on Regents Rd, Sea Point.

A TOUCH OF MADNESS Map p208
☎ 448 2266; 12 Nuttal Rd, Observatory

Now installed in roomier premises, this café-bar keeps its eclectic art-house atmosphere, dressed up in purple with lace trimmings. Yet another hang-out for the wannabe bohemian.

ELSEWHERE

BLUE PETER Map pp196–7
☎ 554 1956; Popham St, Bloubergstrand;
☾ 11am-11pm

As good a reason as any for heading up to Bloubergstrand. Grab a beer, order a pizza and plonk yourself on the grass outside to enjoy the classic views of Table Mountain and Robben Island.

POLANA Map p209
☎ 788 7162; Kalk Bay Harbour, Kalk Bay

Tempting Portuguese-style food – sardines, langoustines and *lulas* (baby calamari) – is

served at this great bar overlooking the rocks. It's so comfy and convivial you'll find it hard to leave.

CLUBS

With top overseas DJs such as Paul Oakenfield, Sister Bliss and Paul van Dyk jetting in to play alongside local hotshots such as Krushed 'n' Sorted, Ryan Dent and Dino Morran, Cape Town's club scene is firmly plugged into the global dance network. There are clubs to suit practically everyone's musical taste and fashion look and lots of special one-off events, some held in spectacular locations. Cover charges range from R10 to R50 and most places don't really get going until after midnight with a notional 4am closing time. The clubbing column in Tuesday's *Cape Argus* and music listings in Friday's *Mail & Guardian* are the first places to check out what events are coming up.

CITY BOWL, GARDENS & ZONNEBLOEM

Long St and its immediate surroundings are the epicentre of the city's club scene, but there are also a couple of options over in nearby Gardens and Zonnebloem.

DELUXE Map pp200–2
☎ 422 4832; Unity House, cnr Long & Longmarket Sts, City Bowl; cover R30

With a leaning towards the latest grooves in French house and tribal trance, Deluxe attracts a slightly older and more musically sophisticated mixed–gay crowd.

FEZ Map pp200–2
☎ 423 1456; 38 Hout St, City Bowl; cover R40

The funky Moroccan theme is carried on at this sister venue to Pa Na Na Souk Bar (p99). Expect queues out the door at weekends and a lively, young crowd.

HECTIC ON HOPE Map pp200–2
No phone; 69 Hope St, Gardens; cover R10

New wave, electronica and alternative dance hits from recent decades are what draw the studenty, screw-fashion crowd to this school hall–style venue above an old boozer.

THE LOUNGE Map pp200–2

☎ 424 7636; 194 Long St, City Bowl; cover R15

Thumping drum-and-bass, breakbeats and hip-hop provide the soundtrack for that cool drink on the long, iron-lace balcony at this grungy old club that keeps going and going.

MERCURY LOUNGE Map pp200–2

☎ 465 2106; www.mercuryl.co.za; 43 De Villiers St, Zonnebloem; cover R10

Upstairs in this very groovy, unpretentious club is the excellent Mercury Live (p105). You can get down to everything from classic Duran Duran to Motown hits at 'Shaken not Stirred' and 'Straight no Chaser' DJ events on Friday and Saturday.

169 ON LONG Map pp200–2

☎ 426 1107; 169 Long St, City Bowl

One of the best Long St venues, where funky R&B music, sometimes live, and a long cool balcony are large parts of the attraction.

RHODES HOUSE Map pp200–2

☎ 424 8844; www.rhodeshouse.com; 60 Queen Victoria St, City Bowl; cover R50

Shimmy and pout with the glam set at this luxurious venue spread over a grand old house. The long queues and cooler-than-thou attitude can be a pain, but with the right party crowd it can be an awesome night out.

SNAP Map pp200–2

No phone; 6 Pepper St, City Bowl; cover R20

The Cape Flats comes to the city at this urban African club with a welcoming, predominantly black audience. Dance to music from across Africa including *kwaito*, *kwassa-kwassa*, *kizamba* and *makossa*.

SUTRA Map pp200–2

☎ 422 4218; www.sutragroovebar.co.za; 86 Loop St, City Bowl; cover R40

R&B, cutting-edge electronic house and tribal house are on the eclectic dance menu at this lush Oriental-themed club.

THE VALVE Map pp200–2

☎ 084 361 3321; Groote Kerk Arcade, Parliament St, City Bowl

This atmospheric venue hosts a dance party for lesbian and lesbian-friendly folk on the first and third Friday of the month.

GREEN POINT & WATERKANT

SLIVER & CONFESSION Map pp203–5

☎ 421 4798; 27 Somerset Rd, Waterkant; cover R20

The two clubs here add up to one of the best dance experiences in Cape Town. It's a predominantly gay crowd, particularly upstairs at the luminously painted Confession where hard house and bare chests are the go. Sliver gives it up to a more mixed crowd with happy clappy house. Chill out in the fairy-light festooned courtyard.

PURGATORY Map pp203–5

☎ 421 7464; 8B Dixon St, Waterkant; cover R50

This is what you get if you spend R2 million on your venue. Terraces overlook the dance floor and giant nude paintings hang in the VIP bar downstairs at this ultra-stylish place with a mainly straight crowd.

ELSEWHERE

CLUB GALAXY Map pp196–7

☎ 637 9132; College Rd, Ryelands Estate, Athlone; cover R30

You can get down to R&B, hip-hop and live bands at this long-time Cape Flats dance venue with a black and coloured crowd. The equally legendary West End jazz venue (p104) is next door.

MCQP

The Mother City Queer Project (MCQP) costume party is the closest Cape Town comes to a no-holds-barred Mardi Gras event. It's been held each December since 1994 when 2000 people turned up for the first theme party, the Locker Room Project.

Organised as a tribute to a deceased lover by 'party architect' André Vorster (who really is an architect), the bash followed in the tradition of Mexico's Festival of the Dead and was such a raging hit that it has become a firm fixture on the city's events calendar. You have to come in a costume (if you don't you won't be let in) which leads everyone – both gay and straight – to join in the fun with abandon.

Each year the party gets bigger and bigger. The 2003 10th anniversary extravaganza, Kitsch Kitchen, took over the massive Cape Town Convention Centre with its 10 dance floors. Tickets (around R160) can be bought, usually from the start of December, at Computicket (p98) outlets and a couple of other venues around the city. For full details see the MCQP website (www.mcqp.co.za).

NEW DOCKSIDE Map pp196–7

☎ 552 2030; www.docksidesuperclub.com; Century City, Century City Blvd, Milnerton; cover R50

A mega club on four floors with state-of-the-art everything beside the mammoth Canal Walk shopping centre. International DJs such as Paul van Dyk occasionally grace the decks.

VORTEX

☎ 794 4032; vortex@mweb.co.za

This trance party organiser got the whole scene up and running in Cape Town. Wonderful outdoor events are usually staged an hour's drive or so outside the city in some picturesque field. For the full trance party calendar (including events other than Vortex) check out www.psykicks.net. The main backpacker hostels should know when these monthly out-of-town overnight raves are happening and can often arrange transport.

LIVE MUSIC

At times it seems as if Cape Town is pounding to a perpetual beat. The opportunities to catch musical performances are wide and varied, spanning everything from acapella buskers at the Waterfront or in Greenmarket Square to thumping African funk at Mama Africa. Apart from the places listed here, good live music is also on offer at the restaurants Kennedy's (p88), Marco's African Place (p88) and Marimba (p88). And don't forget the Sunday afternoon concerts at Kirstenbosch (p72).

JAZZ

Jazz offered (and still offers) one of the few opportunities for South Africans of all races to interact as equals. Some excellent jazz is played in Cape Town and, while there are few permanent venues, many places occasionally have jazz – check the papers for details.

A night at a township jazz club is an unforgettable experience, but you are strongly advised not to go alone. Contact companies organising township tours (p58) to enquire about visiting the famous Duma's Falling Leaves (☎ 426 4260) in Guguletu. Also check out the Chakalaka jazz performances at the Two Oceans Crafts and Culture Centre in

Kommetjie (p69) on the first Sunday of the month.

The highlight of the jazz calendar is the two-day North Sea Jazz Festival (www.nsjfcapetown.com) held at the end of March at the Cape Town Convention Centre. Past performing artists have included the likes of Hugh Masakela, Yousou N'dour and Herbie Hancock with a strong showing of local acts.

DIZZY JAZZ Map p208

☎ 438 2686; 41 The Drive, Camps Bay; cover R20

Just off Victoria Rd in Camps Bay, this convivial restaurant (specialising in seafood platters) and music venue has live jazz on Friday and Saturday and other types of music the rest of the week.

GREEN DOLPHIN Map pp203–5

☎ 421 7471; www.greendolphin.co.za; Waterfront; cover R20

A consistently good line-up of artists performs at this upmarket jazz venue and restaurant, which serves decent food. Shows kick off at 8pm. If you don't mind an obstructed view, the cover charge is a little lower. The nearby Quay 4 sometimes has local bands and musos performing, too.

HANOVER STREET Map pp196–7

☎ 418 8966; www.grandwest.co.za; GrandWest Casino, 1 Vanguard Dr, Goodwood; cover R30; ☽ 9pm-late Wed, Fri & Sat

A well-stocked bar and top acts are the draw at this classy venue at the new casino.

MANNENBURG'S JAZZ CAFÉ
Map pp203–5

☎ 421 5639; Clock Tower Centre, Waterfront; cover R30-80

Jazz and African jive is on the menu every night at this famed jazz club and restaurant newly relocated to the Waterfront. It's free to see the bands playing the sundowner set from 5pm to 7pm, but a cover charge kicks in later.

WEST END Map pp196–7

☎ 637 9132; Cine 400 Bldg, College Rd, Ryelands; cover R30; ☽ 8pm-late Fri & Sat

One of Cape Town's top jazz venues, West End attracts international stars. You'll need to drive here but there's plenty of security.

Abdullah Ibrahim

Arguably Cape Town's greatest musical export, Abdullah Ibrahim was born Adolph Johannes Brand in Cape Town in 1934. His has been a lifelong obsession with jazz: he began piano lessons at the age of seven and as a boy was said to always carry a dollar to ensure that he could snap up any jazz albums that he might discover on his wanderings. This earned him the moniker Dollar Brand, under which he began performing at the age of fifteen. His music marries intrinsically African sounds with the idioms of jazz – rippling drum beats, gospel harmonies, incisive brass motifs and angular piano lines.

Brand formed the Jazz Epistles with the legendary Hugh Masekela and recorded South Africa's first jazz album in 1960. Two years later, after moving to Zurich, he was spotted by Duke Ellington, who arranged recording sessions for him at Reprise Records and sponsored his appearance at the Newport Jazz Festival in 1965. A string of acclaimed albums and festival appearances followed.

Converting to Islam in 1968 Brand took the name Abdullah Ibrahim. He returned briefly to South Africa in the mid-1970s and in 1974 recorded the seminal album *Manenberg* with saxophonist Basil Coetzee. Acknowledged as one of South Africa's most influential jazz artists, he returned to live in South Africa in 1990 and maintains a recording and performing presence to this day. For more information, see the Web site: www.abdullahibrahim.com/indexf.html.

BANDS

DRUM CAFÉ Map p206

☎ 461 1305; www.drumcafe.co.za; 32 Glynn St, Gardens; admission plus drum hire Mon, Wed & Fri R60/80

It's a curious scene: a killer bunch of black brothers teaching whites to beat out a rhythm on *djembes*. But you'd be mad to miss out on the facilitated drum circles held every Monday, Wednesday and Friday from 9pm at this warehousey, hang-out. Huge fun and a breath of truly African entertainment. Check the website for details of events and kids workshops.

HARBOUR MUSIC CLUB Map p209

☎ 082 853 4088; www.kalkbay.co.za/harbourmusic; Acoustic Music Café, cnr Main & Camp Rd, Muizenberg; cover R20

Catch aspiring and well-established musos such as Robyn Auld at this largely folk and rock music club. There are generally performances every Sunday.

MAMA AFRICA Map pp200–2

☎ 426 1017; 178 Long St, City Bowl; mains R70; cover R15, R10 if dining

The buzzing atmosphere here, fuelled by the swinging African bands playing nightly, outpaces the variable food, which includes a tourist-pleasing range of game and African dishes. Bookings are essential at weekends unless you want to perch at the bar.

MERCURY LIVE Map pp200–2

☎ 465 2106; www.mercuryl.co.za; 43 De Villiers St, Zonnebloem; cover up to R40

Top SA bands and overseas visitors belt their stuff out at this flexible venue with great sound quality and a laid-back student union atmosphere.

RIVER CLUB Map p208

☎ 448 6117; Observatory Rd, Observatory

This is a good place to catch local bands and performers, although it's become more up-market and mainstream.

CLASSICAL

The incredibly active **Cape Town Philharmonic** (www.ctpo.co.za) is at the forefront of the Mother City's classical music scene, performing concerts mainly at City Hall as well as at Artscape, the Waterfront and a few other locations around the Cape. The Philharmonic also teams up with **Cape Town Opera** (www.capetownopera.co.za) which has performed at the Waterfront's Aqua Opera season (on a floating stage in the harbour) and on Robben Island. There are a couple of monthly classical music concerts at the Joan St Leger Lindbergh Arts Foundation in Muizenberg (p75).

ARTSCAPE Map pp200–2

☎ 421 7695; www.artscape.co.za; 1-10 DF Malan St, Foreshore

Consisting of three different sized auditoria, the old Nico performing arts complex is the hub of classical and theatrical performances in Cape Town. You can catch regular classical concerts as well as ballet, opera and theatre. Walking around this area at night is not recommended; book ahead for a non-shared taxi since there are none to be found on the streets. There's plenty of secure parking.

CITY HALL Map pp200–2

☎ 410 9809; Darling St, City Bowl

The grand 1905 former City Hall is now home to the Cape Philharmonic Orchestra. There are good acoustics, but a total lack of air conditioning so expect to sweat it out. Even if the main seats are sold out (and they often are) it's usually possible to get a space on the choir benches behind the orchestra at the last minute.

ST GEORGE'S CATHEDRAL Map pp200–2

☎ 424 7360; www.stgeorgescathedral.com; Wale St, City Bowl

A good programme of classical music is performed at the people's cathedral throughout the year, including orchestral works by the greats, usually on the last Sunday of the month. It's worth coming to hear the cathedral's magnificent organ.

THEATRE, CABARET & COMEDY

The Cape Town theatre scene isn't huge, but it's growing and there's often something interesting to catch beyond the blockbusters that check into **Artscape** (p105), as well as the **Cape Town Convention Centre** (p60). The comedy scene is particularly lively: make a note to catch up star performers such as TV star Marc Lottering, founder of the Cape Comedy Collective Mark Sampson and international sensation Pieter-Dirk Uys (opposite). For details of the theatre festivals at Spier and Oude Libertas in Stellenbosch see p148.

BAXTER THEATRE Map pp198–9

☎ 685 7880; www.baxter.co.za; Main Rd, Rondebosch

Three venues at this landmark spot in the southern suburbs cover everything from kids' shows to Zulu dance spectaculars.

CAPE COMEDY COLLECTIVE

Map pp198–9

☎ 689 3000; Grouse, Main Rd, Rondebosch

Every Thursday join the heckling student pub crowd at the Grouse for an evening of comedy from host Sean Wilson and some of the Cape's best wise crackers. For details of other comedy shows around town see www.samp.co.za and www.comedyclub.co.za.

EVITA SE PERRON

☎ 022-492 2851; www.evita.co.za; Evita's Platform, Darling; tickets R75; performances 2pm & 8pm Sat, 2pm Sun

The shows, featuring satirist Pieter-Dirk Uys' cast of characters, touch on everything from South African politics and history to ecology. Nothing is off limits, including the country's struggle with racism. Frequently hilarious and often thought-provoking. See boxed text opposite for more information.

INDEPENDENT ARMCHAIR THEATRE

Map p208

☎ 447 1514; 135 Lower Main Rd, Observatory

This bar and casual theatre-cum-lounge has an eclectic range of other events, including comedy, Japanese animated and quirky movie nights, and band gigs.

LITTLE THEATRE & ARENA THEATRE

Map p206

☎ 480 7129; www.uct.ac.za/depts/drama; UCT Hiddingh Campus, Orange St, Gardens

Wait for good reviews before going to see the productions of widely varying quality and content from students at the University of Cape Town's drama department staged in these two small venues.

MAYNARDVILLE OPEN-AIR THEATRE

Map pp196–7

☎ 421 7695; www.artscape.co.za; cnr Church & Wolf Sts, Wyberg

From mid-January to the end of February it's a bit of a (chilly) ritual to attend the Shakespeare productions staged at this charming outdoor venue in the park. Take a blanket and pillow for the hard seats. At other times of the year, dance, jazz and additional theatre performances also take place here.

ON BROADWAY Map pp203–5

☎ 418 8338; www.onbroadway.co.za; 21 Somerset Rd, Waterkant; tickets R50/60

This is a hugely popular cabaret-supper venue, so book ahead. The dynamic drag and comedy duo, Mince, do their stuff every Tuesday and Sunday; there are shows nightly except Monday.

THEATRE ON THE BAY Map p208

☎ 438 3301; 1 Link St, Camps Bay

As you'd expect of a venue in this well-heeled suburb, the programme is far from adventur-

South Africa's Gay Icon

The uncrowned queen of Cape Town is without doubt actor and writer Pieter-Dirk Uys, whose alter ego Evita Bezuidenhout is the republic's very own Dame Edna Everage – she likes to be known as 'the most famous white woman in Africa'. Evita holds forth in the long-running show *Tannie Evita Praat Kaktus (Aunty Evita Talks Cactus)*, a readily understandable and very funny mixture of English and Afrikaans covering a variety of pertinent topics, not least her own role in the end of apartheid and the process of reconciliation.

Evita, who has had her own TV chat show and has perfume and wine named after her, is not the only character in Uys's repertoire. Bambi Kellerman is Evita's rather disreputable younger sister; Ouma Ossewanie Kakebenia Poggenpoel her outspoken 100-year-old mother; and Ms Nowell Fine a liberal, loud-mouthed *kugel* (Jewish woman). It's not all role-playing as Uys steps out as himself to front shows on racism (*Dekaffirnated*) and AIDS (*For Facts Sake*).

Having been embraced by the establishment, and even introduced to the real queen, Elizabeth II, on her visit to Cape Town, Uys performs these shows regularly at his wonderfully kitsch theatre in Darling (p153). For more details, see www.evita.co.za.

ous, but worth a look if you fancy a conventional play or a one-person show.

CINEMAS

Cape Town has plenty of cinemas (including several specialising in art-house movies) showing all the latest international releases. The big multiplexes can be found at the Waterfront (Map pp203–5), Cavendish Square (Map pp198–9) and Canal City (Map pp196–7).

There are several film festivals each year, including the SA International Gay & Lesbian Film Festival (usually in February or March) and the Encounters documentary festival in July. See the local press for listings of films and where they are showing.

CAVENDISH NOUVEAU Map pp198–9
☎ 082 167 89; Cavendish Square, Claremont; Tickets R35, Tue R18

With its sibling Cinema Nouveau Waterfront (Map pp203–5) this classy multiplex showcases the best of independent and art-house movies. It's worth booking seats in advance since it's very popular.

CINE 12 Map p208
☎ 437 9000; www.12apostleshotel.com; Victoria Rd, Camps Bay

Imagine you're a Hollywood mogul as you get comfy in the luxurious red-leather-upholstered seats of the Twelve Apostles Hotel's private cinema. There are just 16 seats in all and if you want, you and your friends can hire the whole

place out to watch any movies from the hotel library's choice of 250-plus DVDs. Otherwise, come to the hotel's restaurant for dinner and check out what's screening afterwards.

IMAX THEATRE Map pp203–5
☎ 419 7365; BMW Pavilion, Waterfront

Offering the biggest screen entertainment in Cape Town, you might want to take the kids along here to see one of the eye-popping documentaries.

LABIA Map p206
☎ 424 5927; www.labia.co.za; 68 Orange St, Gardens; Tickets R25

Together with its two-screen **Labia on Kloof** (☎ 424 5727; Map p206) in the Lifestyles on Kloof centre around the corner, this is the best cinema for 'mainstream alternative' films. It is named after the old Italian ambassador and local philanthropist Count Labia and is something of a local movie mecca.

CASINO

GRANDWEST CASINO Map pp196–7
☎ 505 7174; www.grandwest.co.za; Old Goodwood showgrounds, Milnerton

This overblown Disneyland of gambling was inspired by Cape Town's architectural heritage, the old post office serving as the model for the florid façade. There's plenty to keep you entertained even if you're not into gambling, including a state-of-the-art cinema complex, food court, Olympic-sized ice rink (p113), kids theme park and music shows.

AMUSEMENT PARKS

RATANGA JUNCTION Map pp196–7

☎ 550 8504; www.ratanga.co.za; Century City, Milnerton; adult/child including rides R90/45; ☺ 10am-5pm Wed-Fri, 10am-6pm Sat, 10am-5pm Sun

This African-themed amusement park is next to Canal Walk shopping centre. It's open from the end of November to the beginning of May. For a 90-second adrenaline rush the 100km/h Cobra rollercoaster is recommended.

THUNDERCITY Map pp196–7

☎ 934 8007; www.thundercity.com; Tower Rd, Cape Town International Airport; admission R30; ☺ 10am-5pm

Your kids (and many a dad) will love you for taking them to the world's largest privately owned collection of ex-military aircraft. If you've got plenty of spare rand you can arrange to fly in one, otherwise it's fun to climb in and out of the cockpits and imagine yourself as Tom Cruise.

Activities & Sport

Activities & Sport

Cape Town offers a raft of activities that together constitute an outdoor–thrill seeker's charter. Whether you're up for a heart-pumping abseil off Table Mountain, sand boarding or skydiving, you won't have to look very far for an operator who'll be quick to take your money. With wind-whipped waves and Table Mountain on hand, surfing, walking and rock climbing are hugely popular and can easily be organised. For some more extreme adventures such as shark-cage diving, rafting, kloofing (canyoning) or paragliding, you're going to have to be prepared to travel out of the city and wait for the ideal weather conditions or time of year. It's not all about adrenaline, either. Cape Town is a fine place for a leisurely game of golf or just kicking back and watching sport in a luscious setting.

ACTIVITIES

ABSEILING

The main event is the operation at the top of Table Mountain, but abseiling is also part of kloofing trips (p113) as well as some mountain-climbing expeditions (p112).

ABSEIL AFRICA
☎ 424 4760; www.abseilafrica.co.za; R295
These guys offer what they claim is the 'world's highest abseil': a 112m drop off the top of Table Mountain. Don't even think of tackling this unless you've got a head (and a stomach) for heights, but we guarantee this shimmy down a rope will give you a huge adrenaline rush. Take your time, because the views are breathtaking. Bookings can also be made through the parent company **Adventure Village** (Map pp200–2; ☎ 424 1580; 229B Long St, City Bowl).

CANOEING & WHITE-WATER RAFTING

A dearth of fast-flowing rivers in the immediate vicinity of Cape Town means that your only option for this adventure is a day trip to the Breede River, 100km east of the city. The season runs from June to September.

FELIX UNITE RIVER ADVENTURES
☎ 683 6433; www.felixunite.com
In business since 1986 organising river-based adventures, this operator runs three-day/two-night trips to the Breede River for R995.

CYCLING

Since 1977, the **Pick 'n' Pay Cape Argus Cycle Tour** (☎ 083 910 6551; www.cycletour.co.za) around the peninsula has been held in the second week of March. With more than 30,000 entrants each year, it is the largest bicycle race in the world. Also see the listing for **Day Trippers** (p57); some of its tours include cycling, such as trips to Cape Point.

DOWNHILL ADVENTURES Map p206
☎ 422 0388; www.downhilladventures.com; cnr Orange & Kloof Sts, Gardens
A variety of cycling trips and adventures are available from this long-established outfit. Try a thrilling mountain-bike ride down from the lower cable-car station on Table Mountain (R350), or ride through the Constantia winelands and the Cape of Good Hope (R500). You can also rent bikes.

PEDAL POWER ASSOCIATION
☎ 689 8420; www.pedalpower.org.za
Check its website for details of races and cycle tours around the Cape.

Cape Town's Top Five Adrenaline Rushes

- Abseiling off **Table Mountain** (above)
- Mountain biking in **Tokai** forest (above)
- Paragliding down to **La Med** (p114)
- Diving with sharks at the **Two Oceans Aquarium** (opposite)
- Surfing at **Kommetjie** (p114)

DIVING & SHARK-CAGE DIVING

Cape Town offers a number of excellent shore- and boat dives. Corals, kelp beds, wrecks, caves, drop-offs, seals and a wide variety of fish are some of the attractions. The best time is from June to November, when the water on the False Bay side is warmer and visibility is greater. Diving any time of the year off the Atlantic coast will require a 5mm wetsuit.

Shark-cage diving is heavily promoted in Cape Town, despite the fact that the action is at Gansbaii, some 150km southeast of the city. The closest town to Gansbaii is Hermanus (p156), where there are no less than eight operators vying for trade. It's a popular but controversial activity. Operators use bait to attract the sharks to the cage, which means that these killer fish are being trained to associate humans with food. It's not a pleasant scenario, especially if you're a surfer, several of whom have been attacked by sharks.

Day trips from Cape Town cost about R1100; in Hermanus you'll pay roughly R300 less and you won't have to get up at the crack of dawn. With most of the operators you must have an internationally recognised diving qualification to take part, although some allow snorkellers into the cage. Be warned: your chances of spotting sharks is much lower in the warmer summer months.

If all this sounds like too much trouble, but you still want to get up close and personal with a shark, visit the **Two Oceans Aquarium** (p68) at the Waterfront.

BRIAN MCFARLANE

☎ 028-312 2766; www.hermanusinfo.co.za /greatwhite; trips R800

The most highly recommended operator in Hermanus. He's often booked solid.

PRO DIVERS Map p207

☎ 433 0472; www.prodiverssa.co.za; 88B Main Rd, Sea Point

Opposite the Adelphi Centre in Sea Point, this recommended operator is conveniently located to hostels and guesthouses in the area.

SHARK LADY ADVENTURES Map p157

☎ 028-313 3287; www.sharklady.co.za; 61 Marine Dr, Hermanus; trips R850

Another popular choice; the shark lady herself, Kim Maclean, has been running trips for over 10 years. These include breakfast, lunch and diving gear.

TABLE BAY DIVING Map pp203–5

☎ 419 8822; Shop 7, Quay 5, Waterfront

Reputable operator based at the Waterfront. It charges R150 per dive plus R20 for travel and R150 for equipment hire. Its PADI, open-water course is R2350 and it can also arrange shark-cage diving trips to Gansbaai.

Shark tank at the Two Oceans Aquarium (p68)

FLYING & MICROLIGHTING

The are several legal ways to get high in Cape Town and all are guaranteed to give you a fantastic buzz.

AQUILA MICROLIGHT SAFARIS

☎ 712 1913, 083 580 7250; http://home.mweb.co.za/ts/tskorge

An enthusiastic chap offers tours in his motor-powered mircrolight at Wintervogel Farm, about 40km north of the city. Flights start at R600 and you'll get great views of the country-side with Table Mountain and Robben Island in the distance.

CIVAIR

☎ 934 4488; www.civair.com

National charter operator offering both helicopter and small-plane tours of the Cape. Scenic flights kick off at R1800 for two people for 20 minutes up to R5400 for an hour-long tour covering the whole of the Cape. Or fly out to the winelands for lunch from R9000.

LIFE OUT THERE

☎ 556 6396; www.lifeoutthere.co.za

Charter a seaplane to fly up to Langebaan or down to Hermanus. The company can arrange several other light-aircraft flights and adrenaline-pumping adventures on the ground or in the sea.

SKY'S THE LIMIT

☎ 856 4962, 082 959 7062; www.skysthelimit.co.za

Fly in practically anything with Aggie Dent, who holds about 40 different types of pilot licence – everything from military jets to balloons and biplanes.

GOLF

Golf is a big deal on the Cape with some 55 courses dotted around the city. Some are superb and many welcome visitors (but you should book). For details of fees etc, contact the **Western Province Golf Union** (☎ 686 1668; wpga@global.co.za).

ERINVALE GOLF ESTATE

☎ 847 1906; Lourensford Rd, Somerset West

Sheltered, beautiful course (designed by Gary Player) that hosts the South African Open. Located in the lee of the Helderberg mountains,

around 35km east of the city centre; take the N2 and turn off at Somerset West to get here.

MILNERTON GOLF CLUB Map pp196–7

☎ 434 7808; Tanglewood Cresent, Milnerton

About 12km north of the City Bowl along the R27, Milnerton has a magnificent position over-looking Table Bay with great views of Table Mountain. Wind can be a problem, though.

RIVER CLUB Map p208

☎ 448 6117; Observatory Rd, Observatory

The place to come if you just want to practise your swing. The River Club (p105) has a driving range and offers lessons.

MOWBRAY GOLF CLUB Map pp196–7

☎ 685 3018; Raapenberg Rd, Mowbray

Considered by some as the best in-town course for its rural setting and lots of birdlife.

HIKING & CLIMBING

The mountainous spine of the Cape Peninsula is a hiking and rock-climbing paradise, but it's not without its dangers, chief of which are the capricious weather conditions (see the boxed text on p64). Numerous books and maps give details, including Mike Lundy's *Best Walks in the Cape Peninsula*, but to get the best out of the mountains it's recommended to take a guide.

CITY ROCK Map p208

☎ 447 1326; www.cityrock.co.za; cnr Collingwood & Anson Sts, Observatory

Popular new indoor climbing gym offering climbing courses. It also rents and sells climbing gear.

MOUNTAIN CLUB OF SOUTH AFRICA
Map p206

☎ 465 3412; www.mcsa.org.za; 97 Hatfield St, Gardens

Serious climbers can contact the club, which can recommend guides. It has a climbing wall (R5; ☷ 10am-2pm Mon-Fri, 6-9pm Tue & Wed).

VENTURE FORTH

☎ 447 4672; www.ventureforth.co.za

Excellent guided hikes and rock climbs with enthusiastic, savvy guides. Outings are tailored to your requirements and aim to get you off the beaten track. The basic fee of R400 includes all refreshments and city-centre trans-fers; longer or more complex trips cost more.

HORSE RIDING

The cost of horse riding is around R80 to R100 per hour and there are a variety of locations for it including the beach, mountains and winelands.

SLEEPY HOLLOW HORSE RIDING

☎ 789 2341, 083 261 0104; Noordhoek

This operation can arrange horse riding along the wide and sandy Noordhoek beach as well as in the mountainous hinterland.

MONT ROCHELLE EQUESTRIAN CENTRE Map p40

☎ 083 300 4368; fax 876 2363; Franschhoek

Offers horseback tours of the wineries around Franschhoek for R80 per hour.

LIGHTHOUSE FARM LODGE Map p208

☎ /fax 447 9177; msm@mweb.co.za; Violet Bldg, Oude Molen Village, Alexandria Rd, Mowbray

Horse riding is R100 per hour at this eco-village where you'll also find a number of other interesting operations (see p71). There's a trail running up to the Rhodes Memorial through the neighbouring Valkenberg Hospital.

OLIPHANTSKOP FARM INN

☎ 022-772 2326; Langebaan

For about R90 per hour you can ride along the beach on the horses stationed at this inn, about 3km north of Langebaan (Map p146) on the main road.

WINDSTONE BACKPACKERS

☎ 022-772 2326; on R45, 16km from Langebaan

This operation caters for beginners through to advanced riders. For R85 per hour you have a chance to catch your own horse, groom it and then ride through the countryside.

ICE SKATING

ICE STATION Map pp196–7

☎ 535 2260; www.icerink.co.za; Grand West Casino, 1 Vanguard Dr, Goodwood; admission R18-28 depending on day & size of rink

One of the few good reasons to head out to the casino is to take advantage of its Olympic-sized ice rink. Call up for the opening hours since they change frequently. Weekends are the best time to visit if you want to skate around to the latest hit tunes.

HOT-AIR BALLOONING

WINELAND BALLOONING Map p155

☎ 863 3192; 64 Main St, Paarl; per person R1550

You'll need to get up very early in the morning, but a hot-air balloon trip over the winelands will be unforgettable. Contact Carmen or Udo who run trips between November and April, but only when the weather conditions are right.

KAYAKING

REAL CAPE ADVENTURES

☎ 790 5611, 082 556 2520; www.seakayak.co.za

This company runs a variety of kayaking trips around the Cape and further afield for paddlers of all levels. Simon's Town and Kalk Bay are good spots and tend to be less buffeted by wind than the Atlantic coast.

WALKER BAY ADVENTURES

☎ 028-314 0925; Prawn Flats, Hermanus

A Hermanus-based operation running sea-kayaking tours (R150) that give you the opportunity to see whales up close and personal. It also does lagoon cruises and rents kayaks and boats.

SEA KAYAK SIMON'S TOWN

☎ 082 501 8930; www.noordhoek.co.za; Wharf Rd, Simon's Town

You'll get a discount on trips with this operator if you're staying at Simon's Town Backpackers which it also runs. Paddles out to the penguins at Boulders are R200. It also offers a variety of other tours including to Zandvlei estuary at Muizenberg, whale watching from kayaks off Glencairne and overnight kayaking safaris.

KLOOFING

Kamikaze Canyon is just one of the kloofs (cliffs or gorges) near Cape Town in which you can go kloofing (called canyoning elsewhere). This sport, which entails climbing, hiking, swimming and jumping, is great fun, but can be dangerous (so check out operators' credentials carefully before signing up). Two long-running operators are Abseil Africa/Adventure Village (see p110) and Day Trippers (see p57). On the Abseil Africa tour, the high jumps into pools are optional, but on the Day Trippers tour there's one 5m jump that you cannot avoid. The cost for a day trip is around R550.

180° ADVENTURES

☎ 462 0992; www.180.co.za

Mainly involved in arranging corporate training exercises, this outfit is experienced at running kloofing trips and also offers an interesting Cape Town–based variation: a 2.3km walk from Deer Park to the Castle through the stormwater canals running under the city. The cost is R300 and you need a minimum of two people.

PARAGLIDING

On a day when the winds aren't too strong, look up while you're lounging at Camps Bay beach, or having a beer at La Med at the Glen Country Club in Clifton, and you might see a paraglider heading towards you. It's possible for the total novice to arrange a tandem flight (but be prepared to lug your paraglider up the mountain). Make an enquiry on your first day in Cape Town – the weather conditions have to be just right.

SOUTH AFRICAN HANG-GLIDING & PARAGLIDING ASSOCIATION

☎ 012-668 1219; www.paragliding.co.za

This is a Pretoria-based organisation which can provide names of operators, and plenty of schools offer courses for beginners.

PARAGLIDING CAPE TOWN

☎ 082 727 6584; flights from R750

The telephone number above puts you through to Ian Willis, who is part of a collective of paragliding instructors and enthusiasts offering tandem flights in and around Cape Town. As well as launches off Lion's Head they also offer options to fly from Silvermine over False Bay and from the mountains overlooking Hermanus.

SKYDIVING

Given the shaky rand, this is one of the cheapest places for you to learn to skydive or do a tandem dive. The view over Table Bay and the peninsula alone makes it worth it.

SKYDIVE CAPE TOWN

☎ 082 800 6290; www.skydivecapetown.za.net

Based about 20km north of the city centre in Melkbosstrand, this experienced outfit offers skydives for R1200 per person.

SURFING & SAND BOARDING

The Cape Peninsula has fantastic surfing possibilities, from gentle shore breaks ideal for beginners to 3m-plus monsters for experts only. There are breaks that work on virtually any combination of wind, tide and swell direction: for tips on choosing one, see the boxed text opposite and check the daily surf report (☎ 082 234 6353; www.wavescape .co.za) for more details.

If you don't want to get wet there's always sand boarding, which is just like snowboarding except on sand dunes.

DOWNHILL ADVENTURES Map p206

☎ 422 0388; www.downhilladventures.com; cnr Orange & Kloof Sts, Gardens

As well as mountain-biking trips, these totally adrenaline-focused guys run a surf school with introductory courses for R350. They got the craze for sand boarding going in the Cape and their trip to Betty's Bay is R500.

GARY'S SURF SCHOOL Map p209

☎ 788 9839; www.garysurf.co.za; Surfer's Corner, Muizenberg

Genial surfing coach Gary Kleinhan claims he can get anyone who can swim to stand on a board within a day; if you don't get up, you don't pay for the two-hour lesson (R380). His shop, the focus of Muizenberg's surf scene, rents out boards and wet suits for R100 each per day. It also runs sand-boarding trips to the dunes at Kommetjie (R250).

WINDSURFING & KITE BOARDING

With all that summer wind it's hardly surprising that the Cape coast is a favourite spot for windsurfers and kite boarders. Bloubergstrand (Map pp196–7) is a popular location, as is the lagoon in Langebaan (Map p146), further north.

WINDSWEPT

☎ 082 961 3070; www.windswept.co.za

Mike Tomlin runs windsurfing and kite-boarding camps out of his base in Bloubergstrand. A three-hour beginner's course costs R450, or if you know the ropes you can hire a board from R250. Packages including accommodation are available.

(Continued on page 123)

1 *Rhodes Memorial (p71), granite memorial to Cecil John Rhodes, Rondebosch* 2 *Voting Mural (p61), Parliament Street*
3 *Chiappini Street, Bo-Kaap, Muslim–Cape Malay area (p60)*
4 *Mosaic of Nelson Mandela at African Image shop (p126)*

1 *Guga S'Thebe Arts & Cultural Centre (p78), girls' dance group* 2 *Jazz musician at Green Dolphin live music venue (p104)* 3 *Old Mutual Building (p26)* 4 *Brett Murray sculpture 'Africa' (p29)*

1 *The Nose Wine Bar (p100),*
Cape Quarter cafés, Waterkant
2 *Vin de Constance, Klein*
Constantia (p36) 3 *Manor House,*
Groot Constantia vineyard (p36)
4 *Groot Constantia vineyard (p36)*

1 *Just Nuisance statue (p76), Simon's Town* **2** *Big houses on the slopes of Lion's Head (p63), Table Mountain* **3** *Dutch café (p92), Waterkant* **4** *Castle of Good Hope (p60), pentagonal fort built 1666–79*

1 *Afternoon tea at Mount Nelson Hotel (p136)* **2** *Africa Café interior (p87)* **3** *Cape Quarter cafés, Waterkant (p91)* **4** *Cara Lazuli restaurant (p87)*

1 Metropole Hotel, lounge (p98)
2 Planet bar (p99) at Mount Nelson Hotel 3 Drumming at Drum Café (p105) 4 'Mince' drag show at On Broadway (p106)

1 Mosaic-tiled pool at the Backpack (p137) *2* Kensington Place (p136) *3* Vicky's B&B (p144), Khayelitsha *4* Head South Lodge (p141), staircase and reception

1 Monkeybiz dolls (p128), Bo-Kaap
2 Wola Nani (p128) papier-mâché bowls 3 Greenmarket Square with old town house, Art Deco buildings and market (p129)
4 Streetwires workshop (p128), Bo-Kaap

(Continued from page 114)

CAPE SPORT CENTRE

☎ 022-772 1114; www.capesport.co.za

Based in Langebaan, Cape Sport Centre has more than 10 years' experience and can arrange windsurfing, kite boarding and kayaking.

WATCHING SPORT

Tickets & Reservations

COMPUTICKET

☎ 083 915 8000; www.computicket.co.za

Cape Town's computerised booking agency handles ticketing for all major sporting events. There are outlets in the Golden Acre Centre (Map pp200–2), at the Waterfront (Map pp203–5), in the Gardens Centre (Map p206) and in Sea Point's Adelphi Centre (Map p207) among other places.

CRICKET

NEWLANDS CRICKET GROUND

Map pp198–9

☎ 657 3300, 657 2099 (ticket hotline); Camp Ground Rd, Newlands

Venue for all international matches, Newlands vies with Australia's Adelaide Oval for the title of world's prettiest cricket ground. The season runs from September to March with the day–night matches drawing the biggest crowds. Grab a spot on the grass bank to soak up the festive atmosphere. Tickets cost about R50 for local matches and up to R200 for internationals.

FOOTBALL

With tickets costing just R20 attending the footy (soccer) in Cape Town is not only cheap, but also a hugely fun and loud night out with Capetonian supporters taking every opportunity to blow their plastic trumpets. The season runs from August to May. Ajax Cape Town, affiliated with the Dutch club Ajax Amsterdam, plays matches at Newlands Rugby Stadium (Map pp198–9; see Rugby, below). Matches are sometimes also played at Green Point Stadium (Map pp203–5) off Beach Rd in Green Point, and Athlone Stadium (Map pp196–7), off Klipfontein Rd in Athlone. This last stadium is home to the 2002 national champions, Santos as well as Hellenic. Tickets can be purchased through Computicket (see this page).

HORSE-RACING

If you like to watch or bet on the horses, races are held every Wednesday and Sunday. For more information contact the Western Province Racing Club (☎ 551 2110).

KENILWORTH RACE COURSE

Map pp196–7

☎ 700 1600; Rosemead Ave, Kenilworth

On the first Saturday in February, grab your fanciest hat and outfit and come here for the highlight of the year's racing calendar – the J&B Met (p9).

Weather Tips for Beach Babes & Surfers

The following are some local tips if the wind is up and you're deciding which beach to sun on or surf off:

- If the wind is a northerly or northeasterly (mainly from April to September), head to the Bloubergstrand area. You'll avoid the cloud and rain, usually closer to Table Mountain, and the beaches are more pleasant because the wind is offshore and cooling, rather than chilly.
- During the westerlies (from November to April), the coastal area between Muizenberg and Simon's Town is shielded from the worst of the wind by the mountains.
- If the wind is a southerly or southwesterly (throughout the summer), head for Llandudno and Sandy Bay. Sandy Bay in particular is shielded by the Sentinel (the tall mountain to the south), and can be gloriously warm when everywhere else is miserable.
- The most famous wind, the Cape doctor, is lifted by Table Mountain, so beaches on the western seaboard such as Camps Bay and Llandudno are protected.
- Kalk Bay is protected from the Cape doctor. A 'bubble' seems to form against the mountain and creates an area of calm, while just down the road in Fish Hoek, the wind howls onshore.

RUGBY

NEWLANDS RUGBY STADIUM

Map pp198–9

☎ 659 4600; Boundary Rd, Newlands

This hallowed ground of South African rugby is home to the Stormers. Tickets for Super 12 games cost R55 to R65 in seats, R35 to R45 in the stands. Tickets for international matches cost about R250 to R300.

YACHTING

ROYAL CAPE YACHT CLUB

Map pp198–9

☎ 421 1354; www.rcyc.co.za; Duncan Rd, Foreshore

Races known as 'the Wags' are held every Wednesday afternoon at the club. Get there at 4.30pm if you want to take part, otherwise it's a 6pm start. Anyone with sailing knowledge can participate – you'll be assigned to a boat.

Shopping

Shopping

From splendid local wines to a cornucopia of colourful crafts, both traditional and contemporary, the temptation to spend up a storm in Cape Town is irresistible. There are many locally designed products (see boxed text opposite) as well as pieces from across the country and the whole continent. Prices might be a bit higher than in other parts of South Africa, but the range and quality of products is practically unsurpassed. And with some items, such as Wola Nani's papier-mâché bowls and picture frames and Monkeybiz's bead dolls and tapestries, you'll be helping people who are struggling with poverty and AIDS.

If you're looking for simple gifts but don't want tacky tourist stuff (of which there's plenty), certainly consider some of the ingenious township-produced crafts made from recycled drink or oil cans and old food labels. Places to check out include Greenmarket Square and St Georges Mall, which is thronged with stalls Monday to Friday. For more upmarket shopping, Cape Town has troves of antiques and collectibles for sale, often at reasonable prices; prime hunting grounds include Church St, Long St and Main Rd in Kalk Bay. The local art, particularly ceramics, is also excellent.

Cape wines are of an extremely high quality and very cheap by international standards; consider having a few cases shipped home. The fashion scene is beginning to take off, with Cape Town having hosted a successful fashion week for local designers such as Maya Prass and the guys and girls behind Icuba and Hip Hop.

Not everywhere in the city is a shoppers' paradise (Sea Point and Camps Bay for example have few unique stores). The City Bowl is best explored during the week; it's dead from Saturday afternoon to Monday morning, when you can expect the already heavy crowds at mega shopping complexes, such as the Waterfront and Canal Walk, to swell. Capetonians in the know favour the new smaller shopping centres, such as the Cape Quarter in the Waterkant, and the Lifestyles on Kloof and the Gardens Centre, both in Gardens.

Opening Hours
Most shops, particularly those in the City Bowl area, are open from 9am to 5pm Monday to Friday and 9am to 1pm Saturday. If opening hours are not given in the listings in this chapter you can assume these hours apply. Shopping centres keep longer hours: check out the Waterfront, Cavendish Square and Canal Walk centres, which are open daily.

Consumer Taxes
South Africa has a value-added tax (VAT) of 14% but foreign visitors can reclaim some of their VAT expenses on departure. For details see p176.

Bargaining
When buying handicrafts from street hawkers and at some market stalls, bargaining is expected but isn't the sophisticated game that is often played in Asia. Don't press too hard.

CITY CENTRE

CITY BOWL & BO-KAAP

AFRICAN IMAGE Map pp200–2 *Arts & Crafts*
☎ 423 8385; cnr Church & Burg Sts, City Bowl
Fab range of new and old craft and artefacts at reasonable prices. You'll find a lot of township crafts here as well as wildly patterned shirts. The

branch at Victoria Wharf in the Waterfront (Map pp203–5) stocks a more upmarket range.

AFRICAN MUSIC STORE
Map pp200–2 *Music*
☎ 426 0857; 134 Long St, City Bowl
The knowledgeable staff here can advise you on the big selection of local music including all top jazz, kwaito and dance and trance recordings.

Top Five Best Buys

- **Boogie Lights** – the distinctive metal and coloured perspex wall lights of artist Brett Murray (see p29) are as redolent of Cape Town as Table Mountain. Look for them at African Image (opposite) and Bread & Butter (p131).
- **Clementina Ceramics** – Clementina van der Walt's colourfully patterned ceramics and homewares are on sale at her gallery in Kalk Bay (p132) as well as at the restaurant Africa Café (p87).
- **Monkeybiz bead-work** – get in on this brilliant township womens' empowerment project breathing new life into the art of bead-work. Hand over your credit card at the headquarters in the Bo-Kaap (p128), at outlets in Cape Town Tourism (p177) or at Carrol Boyes at the Waterfront (p130).
- **Wine** – South African wines offer incredible taste and value. For recommendations chat to the folks at Vaughn Johnson's Wine & Cigar Shop (p131).
- **Wola Nani** (p128) – it's easy to support this AIDS and HIV education project by buying groovy safety-pin and bead bracelets and kaleidoscopic papier-mâché bowls and picture frames. Heartworks (p129) and Montebello (p132) also stock its goods.

ATLAS TRADING COMPANY

Map pp200–2   *Food*

☎ 423 4361; 94 Wale St, Bo-Kaap

Atlas provides the Cape Muslim community with more than 100 different herbs and spices. It's a wonderfully atmospheric place and the proprietors will happily share some local recipes with you.

AVA GALLERY Map pp200–2   *Art*

☎ 424 7436; 35 Church St, City Bowl

Exhibition space for the nonprofit Association for Visual Arts (AVA), which shows some very interesting work by local artists.

BEAD CENTRE OF AFRICA

Map pp200–2   *Jewellery*

☎ 423 4687; 207 Long St, City Bowl

For an enormous range of beads, many in African designs, check out this long-running store which also stocks ethnic jewellery.

BELL-ROBERTS ART GALLERY

Map pp200–2   *Art & Books*

☎ 422 1100; www.bell-roberts.com; 199 Loop St, City Bowl

Discover many up-and-coming local artists, many working in new media, at this stylish gallery and art-book publisher.

CAROLINE'S FINE WINE CELLAR

Map pp200–2   *Wine*

☎ 419 8984; 15 Long St, City Bowl

Caroline Rillema's quarter century of experience in the wine industry shows at this cellar stocking more than 12,000 different wines. You can also enjoy lunch in Long St (see p87).

CLARKE'S Map pp200–2   *Books*

☎ 423 5739; www.clarkesbooks.co.za; 211 Long St, City Bowl

Clarke's stocks the best range of books on South Africa and the continent, and a great second-hand section. If you can't find it here, it's unlikely to be at the many other bookstores along Long St (there's no harm in browsing).

Clothing Sizes
Measurements approximate only, try before you buy

Women's Clothing

Aus/UK	8	10	12	14	16	18
Europe	36	38	40	42	44	46
Japan	5	7	9	11	13	15
USA	6	8	10	12	14	16

Women's Shoes

Aus/USA	5	6	7	8	9	10
Europe	35	36	37	38	39	40
France only	35	36	38	39	40	42
Japan	22	23	24	25	26	27
UK	3½	4½	5½	6½	7½	8½

Men's Clothing

Aus	92	96	100	104	108	112
Europe	46	48	50	52	54	56
Japan	S		M	M		L
UK/USA	35	36	37	38	39	40

Men's Shirts (Collar Sizes)

Aus/Japan	38	39	40	41	42	43
Europe	38	39	40	41	42	43
UK/USA	15	15½	16	16½	17	17½

Men's Shoes

Aus/UK	7	8	9	10	11	12
Europe	41	42	43	44½	46	47
Japan	26	27	27½	28	29	30
USA	7½	8½	9½	10½	11½	12½

HILTON WEINER

Map pp200–2   *Clothing & Accessories*

☎ 424 102; 55-57 Burg St

Achieve that cool 'Out of Africa' look with the classy linen suits and shirts at this local up-market chain unisex fashion store.

MEMEME

Map pp200–2   *Clothing & Accessories*

☎ 424 0001; 279 Long St, City Bowl; 🕙 10.30am-5pm Mon-Sat

Typical of the funky boutiques blooming along Long St, Mememe is a showcase for young Capetonian designers such as Richard de Jager, Carine Terreblanche and Kirsty Bannerman (one of the owners).

MONKEYBIZ Map pp200–2   *Crafts*

☎ 426 0145; www.monkeybiz.co.za; 43 Rose St, Bo-Kaap

Ceramicists Barbara Jackson and Shirley Fintz joined with Mataphelo Ngaka in 2000 to kick-start a revival of the ancient tradition of bead-work. The colourful products, including long legged dolls, animals and bags, all made by women in the townships, are brilliant. Turn up on Friday morning to meet the women artists at this main showroom, which is shared with the head office of Carrol Boyes (p130). There's a plan to launch a project to custom-bead clothing.

PAN AFRICAN MARKET

Map pp200–2   *Crafts*

☎ 426 4478; www.panafrican.co.za; 76 Long St, City Bowl

A microcosm of the continent with a bewildering range of art and craft. There's also a cheap café and music store packed into its three floors.

PEANUT GALLERY Map pp200–2   *Art*

☎ 426 5404; www.thepeanutgallery.co.za; 66 Church St, City Bowl

Hoping to discover the next big name in South African art? This vibrant gallery showcases young artists starting out and has some very affordable pieces.

PETER VISSER GALLERY

Map pp200–2   *Art & Crafts*

☎ 423 7870; 117 Long St, City Bowl

A long-established dealer with an excellent range of contemporary and traditional South African ceramics, jewellery, paintings, prints and sculpture.

Wirework sculpture from Streetwires (see below), Bo-Kaap

STREETWIRES Map pp200–2   *Crafts*

☎ 426 2475; www.streetwires.co.za; 77 Shortmarket St, Bo-Kaap; 🕙 9am-5pm Mon-Fri

Watch wire sculpture artists at work at this social upliftment project for young blacks and coloureds. It stocks an amazing range including working radios and chandeliers.

STURK'S TOBACCONISTS

Map pp200–2   *Tobacco*

☎ 423 3928; 54 Shortmarket St, City Bowl

Established in 1793, this is the place to pick up a cigar to enjoy at one of Cape Town's several cigar bars.

SURF ZONE

Map pp200–2   *Surf & Swimwear*

☎ 426 4226; 45 Castle St, City Bowl

All the usual international labels, including Rip Curl and Billabong, in what is claimed to be the biggest range of surfwear, wetsuits and boards in Africa.

WELLINGTON FRUIT GROWERS

Map pp200–2   *Food*

☎ 461 7160; 96 Darling St, City Bowl

A Cape Town institution, this long, narrow shop sells a huge range of nuts, dried and glace fruit, deli items, tinned foods and *lots* of sweets (candy).

WOLA NANI Map pp200–2   *Crafts*

☎ 423 7385; www.wolanani.co.za; 76 Long St, City Bowl

Wola Nani (Xhosa for 'we embrace and develop each other') is an NGO that addresses the needs of those infected with HIV and AIDS. Buy a decorated light bulb, papier-mâché bowl, safety-pin bracelet with bead or wire detail and you'll be helping a worthy cause

Top Five Markets

At Cape Town's many craft markets it's possible to find authentic items of quality associated with traditional cultures, but there's also an awful lot of cheap stuff generated solely for the tourist trade. As well as the markets listed below, check out the informal cluster of traders beside Cape Town train station in the City Bowl (Map pp200–2), on the seaside road to Hout Bay (Map p210) and on the M65 at Scarborough on the way to the Cape of Good Hope (Map pp196–7). The market at Grand Parade (Map pp200–2) on Wednesday and Saturday doesn't sell much of interest to visitors, but it's much livelier than the others, with people scrambling for bargains, mainly clothing.

- **Green Point Market** (Map pp203–5; ☎ 083 321 2072; Green Point Stadium, Western Blvd, Green Point; ⊙ 8.30am-6pm Sun) – this craft and flea market held in the main parking lot in front of the stadium is one of the best places to hunt for inexpensive African art, fabrics and clothes.
- **Greenmarket Square** (Map pp200–2; ☎ 083 692 2864; cnr Shortmarket & Berg Sts, City Bowl; ⊙ 9am-4pm Mon-Sat) – cobbled Greenmarket Square, the old market and gathering place of Cape Town, is one of the most vibrant spots in the city centre. Check out the street performers and the satirical, anti-corporate T-shirts of the Laugh It Off label.
- **Kirstenbosch Craft Market** (Map pp196–7; ☎ 671 5468; cnr Kirstenbosch & Rhodes Drs, Newlands; ⊙ 9am-5pm last Sun of month) – proceeds from this crafts market go to the development fund for Kirstenbosch Gardens.
- **Milnerton Flea Market** (Map pp196–7; Paarden Eiland, Milnerton; ⊙ 7am-3pm Sat & Sun) – you may be wondering what on earth you're doing out in this windswept and industrial corner of Cape Town, but insider knowledge pins this as the city's best market for genuine antiques at bargain prices. Hunt around between the old car parts and cool drink stands for collectable china, glass and furnishings.
- **Khayelitsha Craft Market** (Map pp196–7; ☎ 361 2904; St Michael's Church, Ncumo Rd, Harare, Khayelitsha; ⊙ 9am-4pm Mon & Thu) – this is a great place to look for interesting souvenirs, and you can be sure that your money goes directly to the people who need it most. A Marimba band sometimes plays and you can buy its CDs.

GARDENS & TAMBOERSKLOOF

AFROGEM Map p206   *Jewellery*
☎ 424 8048, 64 New Church St, Gardens; ⊙ 8.30am-6pm Mon-Sat
Produces jewellery and other items from semi-precious stones, gold and silver. You can call in and see how it's done on a free guided tour.

GARDENS CENTRE
Map p206   *Shopping Centre*
☎ 465 1842; Mill St, Gardens
Handy to the backpacker hostels, the Gardens Centre covers all the bases with good cafés, bookshops, an Internet café, Pick 'n' Pay and Woolworths supermarkets, a Flight Centre and a Cape Union Mart camping supplies shop.

HEARTWORKS Map p206   *Crafts*
☎ 424 8419; 98 Kloof St, Gardens
One of Cape Town's best-value and varied range of crafts, including Wola Nani goods, mealie bags made in Hout Bay, telephone wire baskets from Natal and Mustardseed and Moonshine ceramics. It also has a branch in the Gardens Centre (see above).

HOTCHI-WITCHI Map p206   *Antiques/Kitsch*
☎ 082 955 0054; 90 Kloof St, Tamboerskloof
A good place to browse for antiques and bric-a-brac such as animal skulls, *Biggles in Africa* books, and old cameras.

ICUBA Map p206   *Clothing & Accessories*
☎ 419 5763; www.icuba.co.za; Gardens Centre, Mill St, Gardens
Darlings of Cape Town's streetwear fashion scene, the Icuba guys have caught everyone's eyes with their irreverent slinky designs, perfect for a night of clubbing. There's also a branch next to the **East of Eden** store (see p130) in the Cape Quarter.

LIFESTYLES ON KLOOF
Map p206   *Shopping Centre*
50 Kloof St, Gardens
One of the city's trendiest shopping centres with an intriguing range of fashion and footwear boutiques, Exclusive Books, Woolworths, the good **Wine Concepts** and the second **Labia cinema** (see p107).

PHOTOGRAPHERS GALLERY
Map p206   *Art*
☎ 422 2762; 87 Kloof St, Gardens
A fabulous gallery upstairs from a classy interior décor shop. Inside you'll find classic prints by the likes of George Hallett, including his famous 'First Encounter' portrait of Nelson Mandela and photographs he took in District Six during the 1960s. Other artists to look out for include Lien Botha and Conrad Botes of Bitterkomix fame (see p29).

ATLANTIC COAST
GREEN POINT, WATERFRONT & WATERKANT

AFRICAN ART FACTORY
Map pp203–5 *Crafts*

☎ 421 9910; www.africanartfactory.co.za; Block E, Old City Hospital Complex, 2 Portswood Rd, Waterfront

This partnership project of designers and craftspeople produces colourful ceramics, wireworks and so forth within the old City Hospital grounds.

AFRICA NOVA Map pp203–5 *Art & Crafts*
☎ 425 5123; Cape Quarter, 72 Waterkant St, Waterkant; 9am-5pm Mon-Fri, 10am-2pm Sat & Sun

One of the most stylish, contemporary and desirable collections of African textiles, art and craft. It's known for the original potato-print fabrics made by women in Hout Bay, where you'll find another branch of the shop on Main Rd.

CAPE UNION MART
Map pp203–5 *Outdoor Gear*

☎ 419 0019; www.capeunionmart.co.za; Victoria Wharf, Waterfront; 8.30am-11pm

Set yourself up for everything from a hike up Table Mountain to a Cape-to-Cairo safari at this impressive outdoors shop. There are many other branches around the city (☎ 0800 034 000 for details).

CARROL BOYES Map pp203–5 *Homewares*
☎ 424 8263; www.carrolboyes.co.za; Shop 6180, Victoria Wharf, Waterfront

Sensuous designs in pewter and steel give a fun feel to cutlery, kitchen and homewares. Here, as at Carrol Boyes' head office on 43 Rose St, you can buy Monkeybiz's rainbow-hued bead-works (see p128).

EAST OF EDEN Map pp203–5 *Kitsch*
☎ 425 9147; Shop A17 Cape Quarter, 72 Waterkant St, Waterkant; 10am-8pm Mon-Fri; 10am-6pm Sat

The lifestyle side of Icuba brings a quirky interiors vision to Cape Town from kitsch drinking mats and clocks incorporating Tretchikoff prints (p29) to Asian ephemera.

EVERARD READ Map pp203–5 *Art*
☎ 418 4527; 3 Portswood Rd, Waterfront; 9am-6pm Mon-Sat

A top gallery for contemporary South African art, Everard Read is well worth a browse.

EXCLUSIVE BOOKS Map pp203–5 *Books*
☎ 419 0905; Victoria Wharf, Waterfront; 9am-10.30pm Mon-Thu, 9am-11pm Fri & Sat, 10am-9pm Sun

Exclusive Books stocks an excellent range including some books in French. There are also branches at **Cavendish Square** (Map pp198–9) and **Lifestyles on Kloof** (Map p206).

INDIA JANE
Map pp203–5 *Clothing & Accessories*

☎ 421 3517; 125 Waterkant St; 9.30am-5.30pm Mon-Sat

The sexy, silky clothes at India Jane's boutiques reflect the stylish, laid-back atmosphere of the city and include the India-meets-Africa designs of local hot young designer Maya Prass. Other branches are on **Main Rd, Kalk Bay** (Map p209) and on **Cavendish St, Claremont** (Map pp198–9).

MICHAEL STEVENSON
CONTEMPORARY Map pp203–5 *Art*
☎ 421 2575; www.michaelstevenson.com; Hill House, De Smidt St, Green Point

One of the city's best exhibitions spaces is put to good use displaying the works of up-and-coming and established South African artists such as Hilton Neil, Bernie Searle and Brett Murray.

NAARTJIE Map pp203–5 *Children's Clothing*
☎ 421 5819; Victoria Wharf, Waterfront; 9am-9pm

This global brand started out as a stall on Greenmarket Square. The nicely designed cotton children's clothing is instantly appealing and an adult range of garments here is also offered. There's another branch in **Cavendish Square** (Map pp198–9) and a **factory shop** (Map p210; ☎ 790 3093; Victoria Ave, Hout Bay).

RED SHED CRAFT WORKSHOP
Map pp203–5 *Crafts*

☎ 408 7847; Victoria Wharf, Waterfront; 9am-9pm

This permanent market focuses on local crafts including ceramics, textiles and the brightly painted metal cut-outs of Tintown (Shop 36). You can sometimes see artists at work.

A SUITABLE BOY
Map pp203–5 *Clothing & Accessories*

☎ 421 3517; 125 Waterkant St; 9.30am-5.30pm Mon-Sat

Upstairs from India Jane is the men's collection of designer clothes including desirables by Icuba, Wylde Oscar and Craig Fraser.

TRAVELLERS BOOKSHOP

Map pp203–5 *Books*

☎ 425 6880; Victoria Wharf, Waterfront; ◷ 9am-9pm

Travellers Bookshop stocks all the practical reading material you might need for your travels in Africa and further afield. It also has a good general range of books on Cape Town and South Africa.

VAUGHN JOHNSON'S WINE & CIGAR SHOP Map pp203–5 *Wine*

☎ 419 2121; Dock Rd, Waterfront; ◷ 9am-6pm Mon-Fri, 10am-5pm Sat & Sun

Practically every wine you could wish to buy (plus a few more) is sold here. It's open, unlike most wine sellers, on Sunday.

WATERFRONT CRAFT MARKET

Map pp203–5 *Crafts*

☎ 408 7842; Dock Rd, Waterfront; ◷ 9.30am-6pm

Also known as the Blue Shed, this eclectic arts and crafts market between the Aquarium and CD Wherehouse harbours some great buys. Search out **Afri-can Guitars** (☎ 552 4044; www .africanguitars.com) which makes and sells the all-electric township 'blik' guitars made from oil cans, wood and fishing wire. Also **Get Wired** jewellery, made by women in Crossroads, is some the most imaginative and beautiful you'll find in Cape Town.

WATERFRONT WORLD OF WINE

Map pp203–5 *Wine*

☎ 418 0001; www.waterfrontworldofwine.com; Clock Tower Centre, Waterfront; ◷ 9am-9pm

Taste before you buy at this well-stocked wine merchant with an enticing prospect across the bustling Waterfront, and knowledgeable staff. Tastings start from R4 per wine.

SOUTHERN SUBURBS

BREAD & BUTTER

Map pp198–9 *Gifts & Interior Design*

☎ 671 4204; Shop F56A Cavendish Square, Cavendish St, Claremont

This eclectic shop carries work by cutting-edge local artists, including wall lights by Brett Murray (p29). Check out the cute ballet-style pumps and mirrors by Doreen Southwood, Chiquita bags, each one unique, and the computerised art of Peter Eastman.

Top Five Shopping Strips & Malls

- **Long Street, City Bowl** (Map pp200–2) – already packed with second-hand book, craft and antique shops, this ornate Victorian street is also developing a reputation for its fashion boutiques.
- **Victoria Wharf** (Map pp203–5; ☎ 408 7600; www.waterfront.co.za; Waterfront; ◷ 9am-9pm) – all the big names in South African retail are here, plus some groovy craft outlets, and they're all open long hours.
- **Main Rd, Kalk Bay** (Map p209) – the place to browse for antiques, curios and colourful crafts, interspersed with several pleasant cafés.
- **Canal Walk** (Map pp196–7; ☎ 555 3100; www .canalwalk.co.za; Ratanga Junction, Century City, Milnerton; ◷ 9am-9pm) – brags of being the largest mall in Africa with some 450 shops, 50-odd restaurants and 18 cinema screens. The food court is so big that acrobatics shows are often held over the diners. Drive here along the N1.
- **Cavendish Square** (Map pp198–9; ☎ 671 8042; www.cavendish.co.za; Cavendish St, Claremont; ◷ 9am-6pm Mon-Thu, 9am-9pm Fri, 9am-6pm Sat, 10am-4pm Sun) – in and around this luxurious shopping mall you'll find clothes by many of Cape Town's top fashion designers, as well as supermarkets, department stores and two multiplex cinemas. It's close to Clarmenont Station on the Simon's Town train line.

HABITS Map pp198–9 *Clothing & Accessories*

☎ 671 7330; www.habits.co.za; 1 Cavendish Close, Cavendish St, Claremont

The clothes for women designed by Jenny le Roux are classical and practical, and are made from linen, cotton and silk. Her Bad Habits label is for younger women.

HIP HOP Map pp198–9 *Shopping Centre*

☎ 674 4605; 12 Cavendish St, Claremont;
◷ 9am-5.30pm Mon-Fri, 9am-4pm Sat, 10am-2pm Sun

Hip Hop is another Cape Town fashion success story for designers Kathy Page-Wood and Cheryl Arthur. The clothes appeal to all shapes and sizes and are suitable for all occasions. Drop by the **factory outlet** (Map pp200–2; ☎ 465 7511; Roeland St, City Bowl) for bargains.

LOOK & LISTEN Map pp198–9 *Music*

☎ 683 1810; Cavendish Square, Cavendish St, Claremont

This CD and video megastore has an impressive range and some discount prices. There's also a branch at **Canal Walk** (Map pp196–7).

Top Five Craft Shops

- **African Image** (p126)
- **Africa Nova** (p130)
- **Artvark** (p132)
- **Heartworks** (p129)
- **Montebello** (p132)

MNANDI TEXTILES & DESIGN

Map p208   *Clothing & Textiles*
☎ 447 6814; 90 Station St, Observatory
Mnandi sells cloth from all over Africa and clothing printed with everything from ANC election posters to animals and traditional African patterns. You can have clothes tailor-made. The Xhosa women and Desmond Tutu cloth dolls are also darling.

MONTEBELLO Map pp198–9   *Crafts*
☎ 685 6445; 31 Newlands Ave, Newlands; ☺ 9am-5pm
A worthy development project promoting good local design and creating jobs in the craft industry. An example is Thando Papers, started by Joseph Diliza who had the idea of turning invasive reeds from urban rivers into exclusive paper products. On weekdays you can visit the artists' studios; a good café, the **Gardener's Cottage** (see p94), is also here.

YOUNG DESIGNERS EMPORIUM

Map pp198–9   *Clothing & Accessories*
☎ 683 6177; Shop F50, Cavendish Square, Cavendish St, Claremont
It's a bit of a jumble but you'll most likely find something groovy to suit among the street clothes and accessories for both him and her by new South African designers.

FALSE BAY
MUIZENBERG & KALK BAY
ARTVARK Map p209   *Crafts*
☎ 788 5584; 48 Main Rd, Kalk Bay; ☺ 10am-6pm
One of the better shops in Kalk Bay specialising in local artists' paintings, pottery and crafts. It also has goods from India and Central America.

BELLE OMBRE ANTIQUES

Map p209   *Antiques & Crafts*
☎ 788 9802; 19 Main Rd, Kalk Bay; ☺ 10am-5pm
Appealing Cape country antiques and African pieces including wood carvings from Ethiopia and Namibia are sold here. In a shady garden behind, you'll find the **Blue Brinjal** restaurant.

CAPE TO CAIRO

Map p209   *Gifts & Interior Design*
☎ 788 4571; 100 Main Rd, Kalk Bay; ☺ 9.30am-5.30pm
It's like stepping into Aladdin's cave. There's a colourful collection of interior design items and gifts from around Africa and overseas.

CLEMENTINA CERAMICS & ALBIE BAILEY A.R.T. GALLERY

Map p209   *Art & Crafts*
☎ 788 8718; www.clementina.co.za; 20 Main Rd, Kalk Bay; ☺ 10am-5pm Tue-Sun
There's a continuously changing display of one-off works by Clementina van der Walt and other artists here, as well as a full selection of Clementina's distinctive tableware, hand-painted in bright overglaze colours. Attached is the relaxed **Café des Arts** where you can take tea in a courtyard overlooking the bay.

COOK'S ROOM & ART ETC T-SHIRTS

Map p209   *Shopping Centre*
☎ 788 6348; Petticoat Lane, Kalk Bay; ☺ 9am-5pm
There's a well-edited collection of kitchenware and gadgets from yesteryear. Also check out Jack de Klerk's witty and colourful **ART etc T-shirts** hanging outside. He's only here on the weekends (otherwise call him on ☎ 083 672 0429) and has 80 different hand-painted designs; an exploding volcano's tag lines are 'Hots for you' and 'Be my lava'.

GINA'S STUDIO Map p209   *Crafts*
☎ 788 8159; 38 Palmer Rd, Muizenberg; ☺ 10am-noon Tue, 10am-4pm Wed-Fri, 10am-1pm Sat.
Austrian Gina Niedeheumer's talents lie in creating unique quilts, patchworks and toys as well as hand-dyed wool and designing knitwear. His daughter's gingerbread houses and decorated biscuits are also a delight.

QUAGGA ART & BOOKS Map p209   *Books*
☎ 788 2752; 84 Main Rd, Kalk Bay; ☺ 9.30am-5pm Mon-Sat, 10am-5pm Sun
Visit if you're looking for old editions and antiquarian books as well as art, tribal art and artefacts.

WHATNOT & CHINA TOWN

Map p209   *Homewares*
☎ 788 1823; 70 Main Rd, Kalk Bay; ☺ 9.30am-5pm Mon-Sat, 10am-5pm Sun
Sift through this huge collection of old china and porcelain to find rare designs by Clarice Cliff and Royal Doulton.

Sleeping

Sleeping

Accommodation may not be the bargain it once was, but Cape Town's range of places to stay remains impressive at all levels, with backpackers and those in search of a characterful guesthouse especially well catered for. What follows is a selection of the better places we've come across.

If there's somewhere you particularly want to stay, plan ahead, especially if you're visiting during school holidays from mid-December to the end of January and at Easter when many places quickly become fully booked. Also consider the location and your planned activities. For example, if you plan to hit the beaches, then suburbs along the Atlantic or False Bay coast will make better sense than, say, Gardens or City Bowl. If you have transport, then anywhere is OK, but remember to inquire about the parking options when making a booking and check whether there's any charge for parking (anything from R20 to R40 per day for city-centre hotels).

> ## Top Five Sleeps
> - B&B – **Villa Papillon** (p137)
> - Backpackers – **the Backpack** (p137)
> - Luxury Hotel with spa – **Arabella Sheraton** (p139)
> - Boutique Hotel – **Kensington Place** (p136)
> - Sea views – **Ellerman House** (p141)

Price Ranges

We quote the rack rates here for rooms with en suite bathrooms, during high season and including VAT of 14%. There is also a 1% tourism promotion levy on your bill, but some places, particularly the budget ones, include this in the room rates. It's always worth your while asking about special deals, and rates for longer stays are definitely negotiable.

Mid-range accommodation choices start at R350 per double with bathroom. Anything that costs less appears under the heading 'Cheap Sleeps' at the end of each section.

For long-term rental options and accommodation agencies, see p170, check the ads in the local newspapers (see p175) or enquire at **Cape Town Tourism** (p177) about what deals may be available on serviced apartments.

CITY CENTRE

CITY BOWL

The City Bowl has a lot going for it. It's an interesting area to walk around during the day with the Company's Gardens, buzzing St Georges Mall, Greenmarket Square and the Long St shops on hand, as well as top museums, cafés and restaurants. At weekends, though, it's very quiet as practically all the shops are shut.

CAPE HERITAGE HOTEL

Map pp200–2 *Boutique Hotel*
☎ 424 4646; www.capeheritage.co.za; 90 Bree St; s/d from R725/1000; Ⓟ
Enjoy the gracious Cape Dutch–meets–contemporary style of this delightful boutique hotel that's part of the Heritage Square redevelopment of 18th-century buildings. Each of

the 15 air-conditioned rooms is individually decorated, and some have four-poster beds.

CAPE TOWN LODGE Map pp200–2 *Hotel*
☎ 422 0030; www.capetownlodge.co.za; 101 Buitengracht St; s/d from R795/895; Ⓟ
There are some nice African craft touches to the décor of this well-located business hotel that has a small plunge pool in its courtyard. Request a room with a mountain view.

METROPOLE HOTEL

Map pp200–2 *Boutique Hotel*
☎ 423 7247; www.metropolehotel.co.za; 38 Long St; s/d from R400/1100; Ⓟ
The ancient cast-iron elevator is still in place, but otherwise the Metropole has been given a complete makeover to become a super-smooth boutique hotel, all minimalist lines and soothing colours, aimed at the gay and

*Wallpaper**-reader market. Go for the larger superior rooms with their ostrich trimmed bedsteads. The on-site restaurant **Veranda** (see p89) and bar **M Bar** (see p98) also get top marks.

TOWNHOUSE Map pp200–2   *Hotel*
☎ 465 7050; www.townhouse.co.za; 60 Corporation St; s/d R471/866; **P**

Newly renovated rooms just add to the appeal of this often recommended hotel with good service and high standards. The rates rise only slightly in summer; ask for a room with a view of the mountain. It also has a small pool and gym.

TUDOR HOTEL Map pp200–2   *Hotel*
☎ 424 1335; www.tudorhotel.co.za; Greenmarket Sq, 153 Longmarket St; s/d with breakfast R420/640

Since the jazzy upgrade of its common areas the Tudor Hotel has become a whole lot more appealing. The rooms are not as impressive and vary greatly in size and ambience; ask to see a few before deciding. Family rooms at R640 are good value.

Cheap Sleeps
LONG ST BACKPACKERS
Map pp200–2   *Hostel*
☎ 423 0615; www.longstreetbackpackers.co.za; 209 Long St; dm/s/d R70/110/180

This, the first of the Long St hostels, still stands out from the pack. In a block of 14 small flats, with four beds and a bathroom in each, accommodation is arranged around a leafy, quiet courtyard and decorated with funky mosaics.

OVERSEAS VISITORS CLUB
Map pp200–2   *Hostel*
☎ 424 6800; www.ovc.co.za; 230 Long St; dm R65

Only dorms are available in this nice old building, with high-quality facilities and a pub-like bar. A good backpackers to stay at if you're looking to avoid a rowdy atmosphere but still be in a handy location. There's a 10% discount for HI members.

PARLIAMENT HOTEL Map pp200–2   *Hotel*
☎ 461 6710; www.parliamenthotel.co.za; 9 Barrack St; s/d with breakfast R250/350; **P**

This is one of the best inexpensive central hotels. It's not very flash but it's friendly, and has spotless, good-sized, air-conditioned rooms and a café.

ST PAUL'S B&B GUEST HOUSE
Map pp200–2   *B&B*
☎ / fax 423 4420; 182 Bree St; s/d with breakfast R120/200

If a backpackers is not your scene then opt for this great, budget place with neat, airy rooms and a quiet courtyard. All rooms share bathrooms and there are no other facilities, but Long St is a trice away.

GARDENS, HIGGOVALE, ORANJEZICHT & TAMBOERSKLOOF

As you rise up the slopes of Table Mountain, the suburbs become increasingly ritzier, culminating in wind-sheltered Higgovale. This is the domain of the boutique guesthouse, a brand of accommodation in which Cape Town has cornered the market. If you don't have wheels or don't fancy the slog up and down the hill each day, it's better to stay in Gardens with its easier access to the city.

AMSTERDAM GUEST HOUSE
Map p206   *B&B*
☎ 461 8236; www.amsterdam.co.za; 19 Forest Rd, Oranjezicht; s/d with breakfast R596/695; **P**

Head up the mountain to Oranjezicht to find this friendly, exclusively gay male guesthouse. There's a range of rooms, all pretty comfortable with good facilities, including pool, sundeck, sauna and an extensive video library. Rates are a third less out of season.

Sleeping – City Centre

BELMONT HOUSE Map p206 *B&B*

☎ 461 5417; www.capeguest.com/belmont/; 10 Belmont Ave, Oranjezicht; s/d with breakfast R220/440
At the cheaper end of the scale, the rooms in this smart guesthouse are small, but nicely decorated. There is a kitchen for guests' use and a garden.

CAPE MILNER Map p206 *Hotel*

☎ 426 1101; www.threecities.co.za; 2A Milner Rd, Tamboerskloof; s/d with breakfast R1230/2460; (P)
Another old hotel goes all contemporary and minimalist. The cold monochrome décor is softened by the friendliness of the staff and good views of the mountains from its terrace where you'll also find a pool.

CAPE TOWN HOLLOW Map p206 *Hotel*

☎ 423 1260; www.capetownhollow.co.za; 88 Queen Victoria St, Gardens; s/d with breakfast R480/780; (P)
Overlooking the Company's Gardens, this recently upgraded and renamed mid-range hotel has pleasant rooms and good facilities for the price, including a pool, small gym, business centre and restaurant.

DUNKLEY HOUSE Map p206 *B&B*

☎ 462 7649; www.dunkleyhouse.com; 3B Gordon St, Gardens; d/ste with breakfast R750/990
Ultra-stylish guesthouse close to the media enclave of Dunkley Square and the Company's Gardens. The rooms are in neutral tones, all with CD players and satellite TV, and there's a plunge pool in the courtyard.

FRITZ HOTEL Map p206 *B&B*

☎ 480 9000; www.fritzhotel.co.za; 1 Faure St, Gardens; s/d with breakfast from R500/550; (P)
There's a tasteful mix of Art Deco, 1950s and modern furnishings in the rooms at this small guesthouse, which is popular with media types doing business in the area.

HEMINGWAY HOUSE Map p206 *B&B*

☎ 461 1857; www.hemingwayhouse.co.za; 1 Lodge Rd, Oranjezicht; d with breakfast R1300 or R1600.
This is an utterly gorgeous guesthouse set in an old masonic lodge. The four double rooms are located one in each corner of the house around a vine-shaded courtyard with a sunken pool. A nice touch is that laundry is included in the rates.

IKHAYA GUEST LODGE

Map p206 *B&B/Serviced Apartments*

☎ 461 8880; www.ikhayalodge.co.za; Dunkley Square, Gardens; s/d with breakfast R560/840, apt R810/1140; (P)
Bags of African style at this excellent option in the trendy media district. The luxurious self-catering lofts are worth checking out, especially for the panoramic views across to Lion's Head.

KENSINGTON PLACE Map p206 *Hotel*

☎ 424 4744; www.kensingtonplace.co.za; 38 Kensington Cres, Higgovale; d with breakfast R2400; (P)
Nestled discreetly in leafy Higgovale, Kensington Place has eight spacious and tastefully decorated rooms all with balconies, satellite TV and DVD players, free Internet access, fresh fruit and flowers. Add a small pool and faultless service and you have Cape Town's ultimate boutique hotel.

MONTAGUE HOUSE Map p206 *B&B*

☎ 424 7337; www.montaguehouse.net; 18 Leeuwenhof Rd, Higgovale; s/d with breakfast R995/1300
The plays of Shakespeare inspired the delightful design of the five rooms at this luxurious guesthouse. It offers great views, a plunge pool and king-size four-poster beds.

MOUNT NELSON HOTEL Map p206 *Hotel*

☎ 483 1000; www.mountnelsonhotel.orient-express.com; 76 Orange St, Gardens; d/ste from R4660/6990
Pith-helmeted doormen greet you at Cape Town's most famous hotel, the sugar pink–coated 'Nellie'. Surrounded by seven acres of grounds and dating from 1899, the feel is very much end of Empire. The rooms are on the chintzy side but full of character. Even if you don't stay, drop by for afternoon tea or a meal at **Cape Colony** (see p90).

PARKER COTTAGE Map p206 *B&B*

☎ / fax 424 6445; www.parkercottage.co.za; 3 Carstens St, Tamboerskloof; d with breakfast from R550
Elegant Victorian mansion with eight individually decorated double rooms, two with air conditioning. The owners plan a plunge pool for the lovely garden.

TABLE MOUNTAIN LODGE Map p206 *Hotel*

☎ 423 0042; www.tablemountainlodge.co.za; 10A Tamboerskloof Rd, Tamboerskloof; d with breakfast R483
An older crowd frequents this classy, comfortable small hotel with just eight rooms. There's

a tiny Scottish themed bar and equally diminutive plunge pool in the sheltered grounds.

VILLA BELMONTE Map p206   *Hotel*
☎ 462 1576; www.villabelmontehotel.co.za; 33 Belmont Ave, Oranjezicht; s/d from R970/1290

Top-class luxury accommodation is offered at this ornately Italianate villa with huge pool and excellent facilities including a good restaurant. You can choose city or mountain views from the rooms.

VILLA PAPILLON Map p206   *B&B*
☎ 462 6850; www.villa-papillon.com; 7 Labouners St, Oranjezicht; s/d with breakfast R912/1140

We know its regular guests would prefer us to keep this place a secret, but the time has come to sing the considerable praises of Villa Papillon. Individually styled rooms have great themes including Japanese, funky 1950s and the silky, flowery papillon suite with a king-sized bed and an oversized shower. The 1862 villa is surrounded by lush gardens and has a dip pool.

Cheap Sleeps

ASHANTI LODGE Map p206   *Hostel*
☎ 423 8721; www.ashanti.co.za; 11 Hof St, Gardens; dm/d with shared bathroom R85/250; guesthouse d R320

Super-popular party hostel in a big, brightly painted old house with a fantastic view of Table Mountain from its deck. For something quieter, opt for the excellent en-suite rooms

in two separate National Monument houses around the corner. There is a 5% discount for HI members and camping is on offer at R55 per person.

THE BACKPACK Map p206   *B&B*
☎ 423 4530; www.backpackers.co.za; 74 New Church St, Tamboerskloof; dm/s/d with shared bathroom R85/220/285, d 360; Ⓟ

Not too laid-back, not too loud, guests love the Backpack and it's easy to see why. For years it has stayed ahead of the crowd by constantly adapting, yet always offering top-notch accommodation for the price and wonderfully clued-up service from its travel desk.

OAK LODGE Map p206   *Hostel*
☎ 465 6182; oaklodge@intekom.co.za; 21 Breda St, Gardens; dm/d from R70/210

A hippy air still pervades this one-time commune, now the most chilled hostel in Cape Town. It's taken over nearly all the flats in the attached block, which are a great long-term accommodation option with kitchens and bathrooms.

ZEBRA CROSSING Map p206   *Hostel*
☎ / fax 422 1265; www.zebra-crossing.co.za; 82 New Church St, Tamboerskloof; dm/s/d with shared bathroom R70/140/190

Peaceful hostel that's known for its quiet, no-frills atmosphere. There's a piano to tinkle in the lounge and good views of Lion's Head from some rooms.

Fancy a drink? A deck with a view at Ashanti Lodge (p137)

ZINDIGO LODGE Map p206   *Hostel*

☎ 461 4978; www.zindigo.co.za; 2 Vredehoek Ave, Gardens; dm/s/d with shared bathroom R70/180/280

Not too many hostels in Cape Town can claim to be both deaf and gay friendly. Zindigo is a pleasant place in a convenient location with a relaxed vibe; expect holistic therapies and massages rather than rave parties.

ATLANTIC COAST

CAMPS BAY, HOUT BAY & NOORDHOEK

As this is one of Cape Town's trendiest beachside suburbs you'll pay handsomely for the privilege of bedding down in Camps Bay. Hout Bay has a less fashionable, more village-like feel and is a good compromise if you don't want to be in the city centre but don't want to be too far from beaches and vineyards either. Noordho k offers leafy surrounds, a splendid quiet beach and serenity.

BAY HOTEL Map p208   *Hotel*

☎ 438 4444; www.thebay.co.za; 69 Victoria Rd, Camps Bay; d from R2690; Ⓟ

A hang-out for the well heeled that's just a stone's toss from the beach but also has a good-sized pool. The air-conditioned rooms in white and earth tones are soothing and spacious, the ones with sea views are pricier (R3860).

CHAPMAN'S PEAK HOTEL
Map p210   *Hotel*

☎ 790 1036; info@chapmanspeakhotel.co.za; Main Rd, Hout Bay; s/d with breakfast R500/700; Ⓟ

There are just 10 rooms at this convivial inn at the start of Chapman's Peak Drive, with a good pub and restaurant. The rooms aren't huge but are nicely furnished and most have sea views.

FLORA BAY RESORT
Map p210   *Serviced Aparments*

☎ / fax 790 1650; www.florabayresort.co.za; Chapman's Peak Dr, Hout Bay; apt from R385; Ⓟ

There are 27 self-catering units, all sea-facing, at this old-fashioned complex, with the benefit of a private beach. The newly furnished units start at R505.

HOUT BAY MANOR Map p210   *Hotel*

☎ 790 0116; www.houtbaymanor.co.za; Baviaanskloof Rd, Hout Bay; s/d with breakfast R925/1550; Ⓟ

The original building at this small luxury hotel dates from 1871. The rooms are big and attractively furnished with a floral motif, some with four-poster beds. There's also a pool.

Spa Wars

In the competitive environment of Cape Town's accommodation market, the latest star addition to the facilities at top-end hotels is the spa. All are open to nonguests for a fee.

Leading the way is the sleek, contemporary **Altira Spa** (☎ 418 3555; www.altiraspa.com) at the top of the **Arabella Sheraton** (opposite). Floor to ceiling windows afford great views; you can swim laps looking out at the Waterfront or relax in the Jacuzzi while gazing up at Table Mountain. There's a full gym, a sauna, a steam room and foot baths. Dermalogica and Barbor products are used in the treatment rooms and the staff are very professional.

Not to be outdone, the **Cape Grace** (p140) has also recently added the **Spa** (☎ 410 7140; www.capegrace.com/spa). Decorated in vibrant, warm and earthy colours there's both an African and spice route theme going on here with some massages apparently incorporating traditional San methods and treatments using Melissa products. And its treatment rooms also overlook Table Mountain.

The **Twelve Apostles** (opposite) goes for a radically different approach at its **Sanctuary Spa** (☎ 437 9000; www.12apostleshotel.com/spa.htm), which is built underground in a mock cave that looks like it could be the set from a James Bond movie, a feeling that is compounded when you get a look at the state-of-the-art contraptions in the treatment rooms. This is a Clarins domain and has Cape Town's only Rasul chamber (a Middle Eastern sauna) as well as a flotation pool.

An hour's drive northwest of the city near Paarl is the largest spa of all, the **Santé Wellness Centre** (☎ 875 8200; www.santewellness.co.za) part of the luxurious new **Winelands Hotel** (see p156). The centre makes much of its vinotherapy regime (R1645 with lunch) which includes a shiraz body rub, chardonnay cocoon wrap and cabernet sauvignon bath! There are lots of other treatments available as well as a gym and both indoor and outdoor pools.

LICHTENSTEIN CASTLE Map p210 *B&B*

☎ 790 2213; www.lichtensteincastle.co.za; Harbour Rd, Hout Bay; s/d with breakfast R375/550; **P**

Overlooking Hout Bay, on an easily-missed dirt lane just past Mariner's Wharf lies this architectural oddity. This replica of Bravaria's Schloss Lichtenstein is kitsch but not without merit. The main hall, with its vaulted beamed ceiling and baronial fireplace, makes a fine place to cosy up in winter.

MONKEY VALLEY BEACH NATURE RESORT

Map pp196–7 *B&B/Serviced Apartments*

☎ 789 1391; www.monkeyvalleyresort.com; Mountain Rd, Noordhoek; s/d with breakfast from R1100/1200, apt R2600; **P**

An imaginatively designed small resort with rustic cabins shaded by a milkwood forest, this place is good for kids and offers plenty of activities; however, with the wide beach moments away you might not need any distraction.

PLACE ON THE BAY

Map p208 *Serviced Apartments/Hotel*

☎ 438 7060; www.theplaceonthebay.co.za; cnr Fairways & Victoria Rds, Camps Bay; studio apt from R2000; hotel s/d with breakfast R1300/2600; **P**

A good range of smart modern studios and bigger apartments with a pool and views of the beach. Rates are slashed out of season. The same management runs the nearby Fairways, a classy hotel in the Victorian mould.

PRIMI ROYAL Map p208 *Boutique Hotel*

☎ 438 2741; www.primi-royal.com; 23 Camps Bay Dr, Camps Bay; d from R1500; **P**

All of the 10 rooms are individually decorated at this comfortable, sleek boutique hotel which overlooks Camps Bay but is set away from the main drag. Rose petals scattered across the bed linen on welcome is a nice touch.

TWELVE APOSTLES HOTEL

Map p208 *Hotel*

☎ 437 9000; www.12apostleshotel.com; Victoria Rd, Camps Bay; s/d from R3670/3760; **P**

Much controversy attended the building of this lumpen white complex in the middle of a nature reserve. The sea views are naturally wonderful. The interior design, OTT to the max (think leopard skin patterned carpet in the bar, mirrored ceilings in some rooms), grows on you and what's not to like about a hotel with its own mini cinema **Cine 12** (p107) and a luxury spa **Sanctury Spa** (see boxed text opposite)?

Cheap Sleeps
STANS HALT YOUTH HOSTEL

Map p208 *Hostel*

☎ / fax 438 9037; www.hisa.org.za/stanshalt.htm; The Glen, Camps Bay; dm R45; **P**

How much longer Stans Halt Youth Hostel will remain at its idyllic location, in the one-time stables of the Round House hunting lodge, is anyone's guess. The HI hostel is slated to move to Deer Park in Vredehoek, but if it's still open the dorms here are among the cheapest and most peaceful in Cape Town. It's a steep 15-minute walk to the nearest shops and restaurants in Camps Bay. If you're coming by public transport, the easiest way is to take a shared taxi to the top of Kloof Nek, then walk down Kloof Rd towards Camps Bay.

GREEN POINT, WATERKANT & WATERFRONT

Midway between the city centre and the prime beaches, this trio of suburbs has a lot going for it. The attractions of the Waterfront need little further elaboration but if you want to escape the crowds you probably won't fare much better in the Waterkant which is currently Cape Town's hottest locale and the apex of gay Cape Town. A good compromise is Green Point's fine range of guesthouses and backpackers.

ARABELLA SHERATON GRAND HOTEL Map pp203–5 *Hotel*

☎ 412 9999; www.arabellasheraton.com/capetown; Convention Sq, Lower Long St, Foreshore; d/ste with breakfast from R2960/4900; **P**

This is a sleek, contemporary, business-focused hotel attached to the new Cape Town International Convention Centre. Check-in is like entering an airport, but the corporate feel is softened by warmer colours in the rooms and sweeping views of the city, mountains and sea. Excellent facilities include the roof-top Altira Spa (see boxed text opposite).

BREAKWATER LODGE Map pp203–5 *Hotel*

☎ 406 1911; www.breakwaterlodge.co.za; Portswood Rd, Waterfront; s/d from R310/430; **P**

This former jail has been transformed into a decent if unexciting mid-range hotel, one of the few of the more affordable options at the Waterfront. The cheapest rooms are small and have a shower rather than a bath.

CAPE GRACE Map pp203–5 *Hotel*

☎ 410 7100; www.capegrace.com; West Quay, Waterfront; s/d with breakfast from R4085/4200; P

More like an exclusive yet welcoming club than a hotel. There's understated luxury in most rooms (go for the ones facing Table Mountain), an excellent restaurant **One.Waterfront** (see p90), the Bascule Bar and a colourfully decorated spa (see boxed text p138).

CAPE STANDARD

Map pp203–5 *Boutique Hotel*

☎ 430 3060; www.capestandard.co.za; 3 Romney Rd, Green Point; s/d R550/700; P

At this appealing, secluded hotel, choose between a whitewashed beach house–chic room downstairs or a more edgy, contemporary style room upstairs. All have big, mosaic-tiled bathrooms, and there's a small pool and a sun deck.

DE WATERKANT LODGE & COTTAGES
Map pp203–5

Boutique Hotel/Serviced Apartments

☎ /fax 419 1097; www.dewaterkant.co.za; 20 Loader St, Waterkant; s/d with breakfast R550/900; apt R1200

Choose either the beautifully restored lodge, discreetly located in the heart of the Waterkant, with its magnificent roof-top views, or one of the self-catering cottages, each individually decorated with top-quality art and antiques.

DE WATERKANT VILLAGE Map pp203–5

Boutique Hotel/Serviced Apartments

☎ 422 2721; www.villageandlife.com; Loader St, Waterkant; s/d R600/900; apt from R900

Village and Life manages many top-quality self-catering properties around Cape Town, the bulk of which are in the Waterkant nearby the sales office and reception on Loader St. This hotel on the corner of Napier and Waterkant Sts has a plunge pool and rooms with glossy magazine–style furnishings.

DUNGARVIN HOUSE Map pp203–5 *B&B*

☎ /fax 434 0677; kom@mweb.co.za; 163 Main Rd, Green Point; s/d with breakfast R320/540; P

The German-speaking owner of this nicely restored Victorian mansion has young children and keeps plenty of cuddly toys on hand, making this a very child-friendly option.

TABLE BAY Map pp203–5 *Hotel*

☎ 406 5000; www.suninternational.com/resorts/tablebay/; Quay 6, Waterfront; d/ste from R4350/7375

Luxurious behemoth, with 329 smartly decorated rooms, including ones for the disabled. The facilities include a business centre, a gym, a decent-sized pool, and a glitzy lobby where you can take afternoon tea (R75 or R85 with champagne) with a view of Table Mountain.

VICTORIA JUNCTION

Map pp203–5 *Hotel/Serviced Apartments*

☎ 418 1234; www.proteahotels.co.za; cnr Somerset St & Ebenezer Rd, Green Point; s/d with breakfast R965/1376, apt s/d R1526/1876; P

Popular, arty hotel and serviced self-catering apartments which is part of the Protea chain. The rooms are loft-style with exposed brick walls. It also has a pool.

VILLAGE LODGE Map pp203–5 *B&B*

☎ /fax 421 1106; reservations@thevillagelodge.com; 49 Napier St, Waterkant; s/d R350/550

Smart small guesthouse with two locations – one close by the Waterkant clubs for party animals, the other higher on the hill for those looking to avoid the action. There's a cute café attached where you can take breakfast, and a shop selling local ceramics and glass.

Cheap Sleeps

BIG BLUE Map pp203–5 *B&B*

☎ 439 0807; www.bigbluebackpackers.hostel.com; 7 Vesperdene Rd, Green Point; dm/d with shared bathroom R80/220, d 270; P

The most happening hostel in Green Point is a colourful, quirky affair with a grand hallway, a zen garden and a pool.

ST JOHN'S WATERFRONT LODGE

Map pp203–5 *B&B*

☎ 439 1404; www.stjohns.co.za; 6 Braemar Rd, Green Point; dm/d with shared bathroom R80/180, d 220

This often-recommended hostel is a large, relaxed and friendly place with very good facilities, including a large garden and two pools.

SEA POINT TO BANTRY BAY

Sea Point and the adjacent suburbs of Fresnaye and Bantry Bay are all good choices for a seaside base, with usually more realistic prices than Camps Bay further down the coast.

Sleeping – Atlantic Coast

ELLERMAN HOUSE Map p207 *Hotel*

☎ 430 3200; www.ellerman.co.za; 180 Kloof Rd, Bantry Bay; s/d with breakfast & sea view from R3500/ R4200; ste R8100; [P]

Unsurpassed luxury is available at this ultra-exclusive landmark overlooking the Atlantic with just nine rooms and two suites. The Regency-style furnishings are complemented by a tasteful range of local art. Rates include airport transfers, laundry, all drinks (save vintage wine and champagne) and secretarial services.

HEAD SOUTH LODGE
Map p207 *Boutique Hotel*

☎ 434 8778; www.headsouth.co.za; 215 Main Rd, Green Point; s/d with breakfast R595/695; [P]

A homage to the 1950s with its retro furnishings and fabulous collection of Tretchikoff prints (p29) hung throughout the well-maintained building. The 15 rooms are spacious, the location good and there's a tiny plunge pool in the front garden.

HUIJS HAERLEM Map p207 *B&B*

☎ 434 6434; www.huijshaerlem.co.za; 25 Main Dr, Sea Point; s/d with breakfast R680/980; [P]

Up one of the steeper slopes of Sea Point, this excellent gay-owned guesthouse comprises of two houses decorated in top quality antiques joined by delightful gardens in which you'll find a decent-sized pool. Some of the nine rooms even have Internet connections.

OLAF'S GUEST HOUSE Map p207 *B&B*

☎ 439 8943; www.olafs.co.za; 24 Wisbeach Rd, Sea Point; s/d with breakfast R590/810

Gorgeous place with eight individually decorated rooms and a plunge pool in the front garden. German is spoken here.

RITZ Map p207 *Hotel*

☎ 439 6010; gkhotels@iafrica.com, cnr Main & Camberwell Rds, Sea Point; s/d with breakfast R690/790; [P]

Nothing like its London namesake, but not bad as mid-range hotels go. Great views all round from the spacious rooms in this easily spotted tower block with a revolving restaurant on top.

VILLA ROSA Map p207 *B&B*

☎ 434 2768; www.villa-rosa.com; 277 High Level Rd, Sea Point; s/d with breakfast R410/615; [P]

Quaint guesthouse offering tastefully decorated rooms with high ceilings and huge bathrooms.

WINCHESTER MANSIONS HOTEL
Map p207 *Hotel*

☎ 434 2351; www.winchester.co.za; 221 Beach Rd, Sea Point; s/d with breakfast from R1150/1500; [P]

This Cape Dutch–style beauty has recently added a top floor with more modern rooms, and a heated pool. You'll pay more for sea views, but the courtyard fountain is lovely too. Sunday brunch with live jazz is held from 11am to 2pm for R125.

Cheap Sleeps
PLANET AFRICA
Map p207 *Hostel/Hotel/Serviced Apartments*

☎ 434 2151; www.planetafrica.co.za; 17 Kei Apple Rd, Fresnaye; dm/d/apt with breakfast R115/494/R787; [P]

Some R16 million has been spent on this stylish African-themed complex which provides practically every variation of room from luxury dorms to well-equipped self-catering apartments. It's lacking atmosphere, but is clearly a place for backpackers who want to be pampered. There's a pool you can actually swim in and a huge bar and a restaurant.

LION'S HEAD LODGE Map p207 *Hotel*

☎ 434 4163; www.lions-head-lodge.co.za; 319 Main Rd, Sea Point; d R330;

The rates at this decent, but old-fashioned budget hotel fall if you stay longer than one night. It has a reasonable-sized pool and a bar, and does three-course Sunday lunches for R55. Sharing the hotel's facilities is **Aardvark Backpackers** (☎ 434 4172; dm/d R80/280) which has its dorms in converted flats. There's a useful travel centre and a 10% discount for HI members.

SOUTHERN SUBURBS

Observatory and Pinelands, populated with bohemian types and students from the nearby university, are only a few minutes from the city by car or train, and have good nightlife and places to eat. For something more salubrious and leafy you won't go far wrong with hotels in Newlands and in and around the vineyards at Constantia.

ALPHEN Map pp196–7 *Hotel*

☎ 794 5011; www.alphen.co.za, Peter Cloete Ave, Hohenhot; s/d with breakfast R945/1230; [P]

Close by the vineyards, Alphen is in a National Monument Cape Dutch manor, shaded by old oak trees. As you'd expect the rooms are very chintzy, but the facilities including a pool and a restaurant are good.

CONSTANTIA UITSIG Map pp196–7 *Hotel*
☎ 794 6500; www.constantiauitsig.co.za; Spaanschemat River Rd, Constantia; s/d from R2300 ; **P**
Suitably exclusive and salubrious hotel set within the vineyard of the same name; there are beautiful gardens, a pool and three top-notch restaurants to choose from.

VINEYARD HOTEL Map pp198–9 *Hotel*
☎ 683 3044; www.vineyard.co.za; Colinton Rd, Newlands; s/d from R795/1095; **P**
Handy for both Kirstenbosch Botanical Gardens and the cricket, you want to choose a room at this very appealing hotel overlooking the lovely gardens and the mountains. It's also worth visiting for tea in the lounge (June to September only; R58).

Cheap Sleeps
GREEN ELEPHANT Map p208 *Hostel*
☎ 448 6359; greenelephant@iafrica.com; 57 Milton Rd, Observatory; dm/s/d/tr with shared bathroom R75/160/250/295, d R280
Split between two houses, the Green Elephant is a deservedly popular alternative to the city-centre hostels. It's spacious, colourful and generally quiet, with a tree-climbing dog for entertainment.

LIGHTHOUSE FARM LODGE
Map p208 *Hostel*
☎ / fax 447 9177; msm@mweb.co.za; Violet Bldg, Oude Molen Village, Alexandria Rd, Mowbray; dm/d with shared bathroom R50/150; **P**
This is the nicer of two hostels on the grounds of an old hospital that's been turned into a farm and alternative community of artists (see p70). It's a very simple but relaxed place and you can pay your way by working on the organic farm. It's best if you have your own transport, but it's within walking distance of Pinelands train station and there's good security around the complex.

FALSE BAY
MUIZENBERG & KALK BAY
If you want to be close by the beach but away from the crowds in the city centre,

then these suburbs are good options. Facing onto False Bay, rough-edged Muizenberg is a top surf spot, while the more genteel Kalk Bay is a hot spot for antique and craft shoppers.

CHARTFIELD GUEST HOUSE
Map p209 *B&B*
☎ 788 3793; www.chartfield.co.za; 30 Gatesville Rd, Kalk Bay; s/d with breakfast & shared bathroom from R200/220; s/d with breakfast from R300/R340; self-catering flat R200
There's a variety of good-value, large rooms here, several with sweeping views of False Bay. It also has a coffee shop.

INN AT CASTLE HILL Map p209 *B&B*
☎ 788 2554; www.castlehill.co.za; 37 Gatesville Rd, Kalk Bay; s/d with breakfast R300/600; **P**
Some of the convivial rooms in this renovated Edwardian home overlook the bay and all are decorated with works by local artists.

JOAN ST LEGER LINDBERGH ARTS
CENTRE Map p209 *B&B*
☎ 788 2795; artcentre@linbergh-arts.co.za; 18 Beach Rd, Muizenberg; s/d with breakfast R300/350; **P**
One of the four Herbert Baker–designed houses that make up the arts centre has been converted into a lovely B&B, decorated in 1920s style. There are just two rooms either side of a spacious lounge.

Cheap Sleeps
BLUE OCEANS Map p209 *Hostel*
☎ 788 9780; www.blueoceans.50g.com; 3 Church Rd, Muizenberg; dm R65, s or d 200; **P**
New backpackers making all the right moves. Owner Jason has fashioned a relaxed, brightly painted place out of this spacious old house with a big garden. While waiting for your laundry, you can work out on its mini multigym.

SIMON'S TOWN, BOULDERS & CAPE POINT
Further down the False Bay coast, and a good half-hour's drive from the city centre is Simon's Town and nearby Boulders where you can bunk down beside the penguins. It's an attractive, quiet place, but if

you really want to get away from it all, one self-catering option at Cape Point is also worth considering.

BOULDERS BEACH LODGE

Map p210   *B&B/Serviced Apartments*

☎ 786 1758; www.bouldersbeach.co.za; 4 Boulders Pl, Boulders Beach; s/d with breakfast R450/750, apt with breakfast R1000; ℗

Close by the penguin colony, this smart guesthouse, with rooms decorated in wicker and wood, also has a range of self-catering units and a pleasant café called the Penguin Point Restaurant with an outdoor deck.

BRITISH HOTEL

Map p210   *Serviced Apartments*

☎ /fax 786 2214; www.british-hotel.co.za; 90 St George's St, Simon's Town; apt from R1000

These stylish and quirkily decorated apartments with amazingly spacious bathrooms are set around a lovely courtyard. They're ideal for groups of friends or a family.

LORD NELSON INN Map p210   *B&B*

☎ 786 1386; 58 St George's St, Simon's Town; s/d with breakfast R350/500

Above a small, old-fashioned pub, this is a pleasant, refurbished place, with plain but smart rooms. Some overlook the sea (which is largely obscured by a shed in the naval dockyards).

OLIFANTSBOS

Map pp196–7   *Self-Catering Cottage*

☎ 701 8692; www.cpnp.co.za; Cape Point; Cottage R1500, dm in annexe R150; ℗

Imagine having Cape Point to yourself once the crowds have gone, and waking up just steps away from the Atlantic pounding on the beach. Make it happen at this white-washed cottage and dorm annexe that both sleep up to six.

Cheap Sleeps
SIMON'S TOWN BACKPACKERS

Map p210   *Hostel*

☎ 786 1964; www.capepax.co.za; 66 St George's St, Simon's Town; dm/d R70/200

Brightly painted rooms, a laid-back atmosphere and lots going on including bike hire, kayaking to Boulders beach and trips to Cape Point make this one very cool backpackers.

CAPE FLATS
LANGA & KHAYELITSHA

It's not for everyone, but bedding down in Langa or Khayelitsha is highly recommended if you want to experience life in the townships and go beyond token meetings with locals. Of the B&Bs listed here, only Vicky's is in an original shack; the other three are in brick buildings in the more developed parts of the township.

Cheap Sleeps
KOPANONG Map pp196–7   *B&B*

☎ / fax 361 2084; kopanong @xsinet.co.za; Site C-329 Velani Cres, Khayelitsha; s/d with breakfast R210/360; ℗

All the home comforts are in place at the most upmarket of Khayelitsha's B&Bs, run by the dynamic Thope Lekau, who's also a registered guide and experienced development worker. There are two stylishly decorated rooms, one with en suite bathroom, the other with its own separate shower. A three-course dinner is R60 for vegetarian, R80 for meat.

MAJORO'S B&B Map pp196–7   *B&B*

☎ 361 3412 or ☎ 082 537 6882; 69 Helena Cres, Graceland, Khayelitsha; s/d with breakfast and shared bathroom R180/360; ℗

Maria Maile is the very friendly and warm proprietress of this B&B in a quiet part of Khayelitsha. She can put up four people in her very homely rooms. Dinner is available on request for R80. There's safe parking should you choose to drive here.

MALEBO'S Map pp196–7   *B&B*

☎ 361 2391 or ☎ 083 475 1125; 18 Mississippi Way, Graceland, Khayelitsha; s/d with breakfast & shared bathroom R185/300

In the spacious, modern home of Lydia Masoleng there are three rooms for guests. The welcome is warm and dinner is available for R50.

NOMZI'S Map pp196–7   *B&B*

☎ 694 5926; harlemtours@absamail.co.za; 56 Harlem Ave, Langa; s/d R150/300

Nomzi Delima and her grandson Eric run this simple two-room B&B in Langa, the closest township to the city centre. The rooms have en suite bathrooms and there's Internet access available. Across the road is the restaurant Lelapa (see p96).

VICKY'S Map pp196–7   *B&B*

☎ 387 7104 or ☎ 082 225 2986; www.journey
.digitalspace.net/vicky.html; Site C-685A, Khayelitsha;
s/d with breakfast & shared bathroom R170/340

If you really want to know what it's like to live in a Cape Flats shack then a visit to Vicky Ntozini is essential. The home Vicky shares with her family was built of scrap but is charming nonetheless. There are two comfy rooms for guests and, since we last visited, an inside bathroom with toilet and shower courtesy of an international hotel chain. Apart from Vicky's bountiful hospitality, there's the bonus of Cape Town's other **Waterfront**, a long-running and lively *shebeen*, right across the road.

Excursions

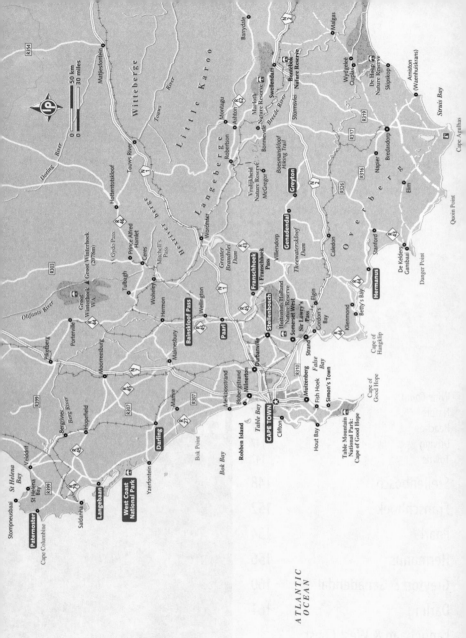

Excursions

For some a day trip to Cape Point or out into the townships of the Cape Flats will be diversion enough from the delights of central Cape Town. But with the city's excellent roads it hardly takes any more time or effort to venture further afield and discover some of the surrounding area too. Western Cape province has some truly beautiful scenery and interesting old towns, some tucked away in wine country first planted with vines over three centuries ago. There are also pristine beaches devoid of the crowds, and opportunities for hiking into mountains every bit as spectacular as Table Mountain.

WINE COUNTRY

The wine-producing country around Stellenbosch (p148), Franschhoek (p152) and Paarl (p154) is known as the Boland (meaning 'Upland'). Dramatic mountain ranges shoot up to over 1500m, with the vineyards forming a patchwork on their slopes and in the fertile valleys. Stellenbosch is the area's most interesting and lively town, Franschhoek has the best location and dining scene, and Paarl is a busy commercial centre with plenty to see. All three are historically important and attractive, and promote routes around the surrounding wineries; see p36–42. It's possible to see all three towns on day trips from Cape Town but you'll have a much more pleasant time of it if you spend the night and take your time.

NATURE

Although whales are common during the winter and spring season in False Bay (p75), the focus of whale-watching action is at Hermanus (p156). This pleasant coastal town is also a good base for other nature-focused adventures including shark-cage diving at nearby Gansbaai and exploring the Fernkloof Nature Reserve. Bird watchers will want to beat a path to the West Coast National Park (p162), which hosts huge numbers of migratory wading birds as well as spectacular stretches of *fynbos* (literally 'fine bush', primarily proteas, heaths and ericas) bursting with wildflowers between August and October.

BEACHES

If you're looking to swim in the sea rather than make a mad dash in and out of the water to avoid hypothermia, then head south of Cape Town to beaches at and around Hermanus (p156), which are lapped by the warmer waters of the Indian Ocean. For those made of sterner stuff Langebaan (p162) and the pretty fishing village of Paternoster (p163) along the west coast provide a bracing introduction to the chilly Atlantic.

DRIVING

The Four Passes Route heading through Franschhoek, and the Bainskloof Pass (p156), northwest of Paarl are among the most spectacular mountain passes in the country and worth travelling along back and forth to the Winelands in their own right. If it's ocean views and thrilling coastal driving that you hanker for, then take the cliff-hugging R44 around False Bay to Hermanus; it's a route in the same class as Cape Town's famous Chapman's Peak Drive.

TOWNS

Darling (p161), a charming small town in the Swartland north of Cape Town, is best known as the home of Pieter-Dirk Uys's alter-ego Evita Bezuidenhout (p107). Even more picturesque is **Greyton** (p160), in the shadow of the Riviersonderendberg, and nearby **Genadendal**, the oldest mission station in South Africa. If you have time, this is a wonderful area to go hiking in, the **Boesmanskloof Trail** across to McGregor being the highlight.

STELLENBOSCH

After Cape Town, leafy Stellenbosch is the oldest European town in South Africa. It was established on the banks of the Eerste River by Governor van der Stel in 1679 and remains one of the best-preserved in the country. The town is full of architectural gems (Cape Dutch, Georgian and Victorian) and is shaded by enormous oak trees. Apart from relishing its role as the hub of the Winelands, at the heart of a network of well over 100 different wineries, it also enjoys the gravitas of being a university town. You can organise a winery tour here (p150) or attend one of its frequent arts and culture festivals (p151).

Transport

Distance from Cape Town to Stellenbosch 46km
Direction East
Travel time 1hr
Car Take N2 and then the R310; alternatively continue to the junction with the R44.
Train Metro trains run roughly every 1½ hours from Cape Town to Stellenbosch (economy/1st-class R7.50/12).

The Afrikaans-language University of Stellenbosch, established in 1918, continues to play an important role in Afrikaner politics and culture. It has more than 17,000 students, which means the town's nightlife can get wild during term time – visit in February at the start of the academic year for the Venster Versiering festival and you'll see what we mean!

The train station is a short walk west of the centre. The train line effectively forms the western boundary of the town, and the Eerste River, the southern. Dorp St, which runs roughly parallel to the river, is the old town's main street and is lined with numerous fine old buildings. The commercial centre lies between Dorp St and the university to the east of the Braak, the old town square. A lovely way to get acquainted with the town is to take a walking tour (below).

If you only have a short amount of time, the priority should be the **Village Museum**, a group of carefully restored and period-furnished houses dating from 1709 to 1850. The main entrance leads into the oldest of the buildings, the Schreuderhuis. The whole block, bounded

Stellenbosch Walking Tour

Start at the publicity association on Market St and head northwest to the **Braak**, the old town square, where you'll find several old buildings, including the **VOC Kruithuis**, an 18th-century powder magazine.

Cross the Braak and turn left (north) up Bird St, right on to Beyers St, left on to Andringa St and right on to Victoria St. Follow Victoria St and you'll come to the **University of Stellenbosch**. This pretty campus is crammed full of Cape Dutch buildings, as befits the country's (and thus the world's) leading Afrikaans university.

Find your way back to Victoria St and head west until you come to Neethling St. Turn right, walk past the **Botanical Gardens** to the junction with Van Riebeeck St, turn right again (some of the fine old homes around here offer accommodation) and continue to Ryneveld St, on the edge of the town centre. Turn left down Ryneveld St to visit the **Village Museum**.

Follow Ryneveld St south on to Dorp St, one of Stellenbosch's oldest and most impressive streets, then turn right. Continue down Dorp St to Aan de Wagenweg where you'll turn left to reach the Eerste River; the willow-shaded restaurant **De Oewer** (p150) is a good spot to revive.

Retrace your steps across the bridge back to Dorp St, cross over and turn up Market St to return to where you started. On the way back you'll pass the elegant 18th-century **Van der Bijlhuis**, now occupied by an architect's office.

STELLENBOSCH

0 |————| 300 m
0 |————| 0.2 miles

SIGHTS & ACTIVITIES	(pp148–50)
Bergkelder	1 A4
Botanical Gardens	2 D5
Fick House (Burgerhuis)	3 B5
Grosvenor House	4 D5
St Mary's on the Braak Church	5 C5
Simonsberg Cheese Factory	6 A3
Toy & Miniature Museum	7 B5
Van Der Bijlhuis	8 B5
Village Museum (Dorp Museum)	9 D5
VOC Kruithuis	10 B5

EATING	🍴	(pp150–1)
De Oewer		11 A6
De Soete Inval		12 B5
De Volkskombuis		13 A6
Decameron Italian Restaurant		14 D5
Fishmonger		15 D5
Mugg & Bean		16 C5

The Naked Truth	17 C4
Wijnhuis	18 C5

DRINKING	🍷	(p151)
Bohemia		19 C4
De Akker		20 B6
Dros		21 C5
Hidden Cellar		(see 20)
Java Café		22 C5
Nu Bar		23 C5
Terrace		24 B5
Tollies		25 B4

SHOPPING	🛍	
Ex Libris		26 C5
Exclusive Books		27 C5
Oom Samie se Winkel		28 B6
Shopping Mall		29 C5

SLEEPING	🏠	(pp151-2)
D'Ouwe Werf		30 C5
De Goue Druif		31 B5
Stellenbosch Hotel		32 C5
Stumble Inn		33 B5

TRANSPORT	
Minibus Taxis	34 C4
Minibus Taxis	35 C5

INFORMATION	
Easy Rider Wine Tours	(see 33)
Fandangos Internet Café	36 C5
Fandangos	(see 25)
Hospital	37 D3
Post Office	38 C5
Rennies Travel	39 C5
Stellenbosch Publicity Association	40 B5

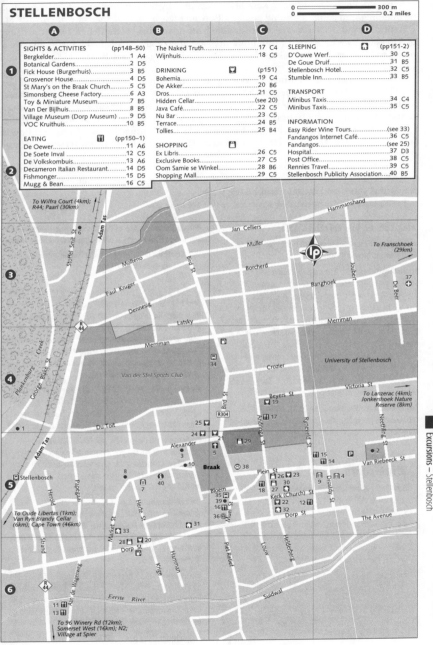

by Ryneveld, Plein, Drostdy and Kerk Sts, is occupied by the museum and includes most of the buildings and some charming gardens. **Grosvenor House** is on the other side of Drostdy St.

Behind the publicity association, in another historic building, is the delightfully surprising **Toy & Miniature Museum**. Many of the miniatures are amazingly detailed; the highlights are a model railway set and houses made entirely of icing sugar – get the guide to point out some of the best pieces.

At the north end of the Braak (Town Square), an open stretch of grass, you'll find the neo-Gothic **St Mary's on the Braak Church**, completed in 1852. To the west is the **VOC Kruithuis**, built in 1777 to store the town's weapons and gunpowder and now housing a small military museum. On the northwest corner is **Fick House**, also known as the Burgerhuis, a fine example of Cape Dutch–style from the late 18th century. Most of this building is now occupied by Historical Homes of South Africa, established to preserve important architecture.

If you're looking for a hike or mountain-bike scramble, drive or cycle out to the small **Jonkershoek nature reserve** around 8km southeast of town along the WR4. Set within a timber plantation you'll find walking and biking trails.

For details of recommended wineries in the area see p37.

Sights & Information

Jonkershoek nature reserve (Map p149; ☎ 866 1560; admission car/bicycle R110/5)

Stellenbosch Publicity Association (Map p149; ☎ 883 3584; www.stellenboschtourism.co.za; 36 Market St; 8am-6pm Mon-Fri, 9am-5pm Sat, 10am-4pm Sun) Pick up the excellent brochure *Discover Stellenbosch on Foot* (R2), with a walking-tour map and information on many of the historic buildings (also available in French and German). Also useful is the free brochure *Stellenbosch Wine Routes*, which gives information about opening times and tastings at many nearby wineries. Guided walks leave from the publicity association at 10am and 3pm. They cost R50 per person (minimum three people).

Toy & Miniature Museum (Map p149; ☎ 887 7888; cnr Market & Herte Sts; adult/child R5/1; 9.30am-5pm Mon-Sat, 2-5pm Sun, closed Sun May-Aug).

Wine Tours

Easy Rider Wine Tours (Map p149; ☎ 886 4651; www.jump.to/stumble; 12 Market St) This long-established company offers good value for a full day trip (R250 including lunch and all tastings). The wineries visited sometimes change but on the schedule at the time of research was Boschendal, Delaire, Fairview and Simonsig.

Anne Lee Steyn (Map p149; ☎ 083 631 5944; famsteyn@mweb.co.za)Ms Steyn is a knowledgeable Stellenbosch-based guide who can arrange walking tours of the local wineries in the Simonsberg area. The walk (R295 including a picnic lunch and tastings) is around 8km.

Village Museum (Map p149; ☎ 887 2902; 18 Ryneveld St; adult/child R15/10; 9.30am-5pm Mon-Sat, 2-5pm Sun)

VOC Kruithuis (Map p149; Powder House; admission free; 9.30am-1pm Mon-Fri)

Eating

96 Winery Rd (Map p149; ☎ 842 2945; Zandberg Farm, Winery Rd; mains R70; noon-3pm daily, 7-9.30pm Mon-Sat) Off the R44 between Stellenbosch and Somerset West is one of the most respected restaurants in the area, known for its dry aged beef. It has a relaxed style and a belief in simply cooked real food.

De Oewer (Map p149; ☎ 886 5431; Aan de Wagenweg; mains R70) Next to De Volkskombuis, De Oewer has an open-air section shaded by willow trees beside the river. It offers lighter meals with a more Mediterranean emphasis.

De Soete Inval (Map p149; ☎ 886 4842; 5 Ryneveld St; mains R50) Known primarily for offering a choice of 40 different pancakes, this cheerful place also does a fine Indonesian *rystafel* (rice with many dishes) with six dishes for R75 or a half portion for R50.

De Volkskombuis (Map p149; ☎ 887 2121; Aan de Wagenweg; mains R75) An atmospheric place specialising in traditional Cape Malay cuisine, the terrace looks across fields to Stellenbosch Mountain. You can try sample plates of famous Cape Malay savoury and sweet dishes. Booking is advisable.

Decameron Italian Restaurant (Map p149; ☎ 883 3331; 50 Plein St; mains R40-50; lunch & dinner Mon-Sat) Considered the town's best Italian restaurant it's good for either a quick pizza or a full meal. It has outdoor seating for those balmy evenings.

Fishmonger (Map p149; ☎ 887 7835; cnr Ryneveld & Plein Sts; mains R50; lunch & dinner) The choice for seafood. It's a snazzily designed place with a relaxed vibe. A platter goes for a reasonable R70.

Java Cafe (Map p149; ☎ 887 6261; cnr Church & Andringa Sts; snacks from R15) A good range of drinks and snacks are available at this stylish café, with pavement tables. It also offers Stellenbosch's cheapest Internet access.

Moyo (Map p149; ☎ 809 1100; Spier Estate, Vlottenburg; buffet R150 or R98 per kilo) This place brings a fantasy vision of Africa to the midst of the Spier wine estate. It's a lot of fun, with face painting, roving musicians and dancers, and alfresco dining in tents and up in the trees. The buffet is extensive and tasty, but if you're not that hungry, you can also pay per kilo of food.

Mugg & Bean (Map p149; ☎ 883 2972; Muel St; mains from R30) A reputable chain café, it's a good choice for breakfast with bagels, huge muffins, and self-service bottomless cups of coffee.

Naked Truth (Map p149; ☎ 882 9672; 62 Andringa St; mains from R20) A funky café decorated with some intriguing pieces of local art and photography and a quiet courtyard. The menu includes wraps, Thai curry and tempting home-made desserts.

Wijnhuis (Map p149; ☎ 887 7196; Andringa St; mains R50-100) A stylish option with indoor and outdoor dining areas, an extensive menu and a wine list stretching to 350 different labels. Around 20 wines are available by the glass and tastings of six wines cost R20.

Entertainment

Clustered together in the complex just off Bird St and north of the Braak, are some of the liveliest bars: **Dros** (Map p149; ☎ 886 4856), the **Terrace** (Map p149; ☎ 887 1942) and Tollies. You can eat at them all, but that's not what most patrons have in mind. If you're looking for a slightly more sophisticated option try Fandangos, which is a cocktail bar and Internet cafe in the same complex. (The other branch of Fandangos on Muel St is just an Internet café.)

Bohemia (Map p149; ☎ 882 8375; cnr Andringa & Victoria Sts) There is live music every Tuesday, Thursday and Sunday. Try the novelty hubble-bubble pipes (R25) with a range of different tobaccos.

De Akker (Map p149; ☎ 883 3512; 90 Dorp St) This is another classic student drinking hole with pub meals from under R30. Upstairs is the Hidden Cellar, where bands occasionally play.

Nu Bar (Map p149; ☎ 886 8998; 51 Plein St) With more of a club feel, Nu Bar has a small dance floor beyond the long bar. The DJ pumps out hip-hop and house.

Sleeping

De Goue Druif (Map p149; ☎ 883 3555; goedruif .hypermart.net; 110 Dorp St; s/d with breakfast R600/650) The name of this charming guesthouse in an old Cape Dutch building, run by a couple from Belgium, means 'the golden grape'. They also have a small gym, pool and sauna.

De Oude Meul (Map p149; ☎ 887 7085; www.deoude meul.snowball.co.za; 10A Mill St; s/d with breakfast R175/350) Above an antiques shop in the centre of town, the accommodation here is very reasonable for the price (which is lower in winter). Some rooms have balconies and air con, and there's off-street parking.

D'Ouwe Werf (Map p149; ☎ 887 4608; www.ouwewerf .com; 30 Church St; s/d with breakfast R700/990) This is an appealing, old-style hotel (dating back to 1802) with a good restaurant. It's worth dropping by the shady courtyard for lunch. The more expensive luxury rooms are furnished with antiques and brass beds.

Lanzerac (Map p149; ☎ 887 1132; www.lanzerac .co.za; Jonkershoek Valley; s/d/ste with breakfast R1990/2700/3315) Based around a 300-year-old manor house and winery is this ultra-luxurious place. You don't even need plug adaptors since the spacious rooms are equipped with a range of sockets! Some suites have their own private pools.

Stellenbosch Hotel (Map p149; ☎ 887 3644; www .stellenbosch.co.za/hotel; cnr Dorp & Andringa Sts; s/d with breakfast from R489/365) A comfortable country-style hotel, some rooms have four-poster beds while others have self-catering facilities. A section dating from 1743 houses the Jan Cats Brasserie, a good spot for a drink.

Stumble Inn (Map p149; ☎ 887 4049; www.jump.to /stumble; 12 Market St; camp sites per person R40, dm R60, d with shared bathroom R160) With a lively and welcoming atmosphere this place is split over two old houses, one with a small pool and the other with a pleasant garden.

Special Events

The **Oude Libertas Amphitheatre** (Map p149; ☎ 809 7380; www.oudelibertas.co.za) and the **Spier wine estate** (Map p37; ☎ 809 1100; www .spier.co.za) both hold performing arts festivals between January and March.

The **Van der Stel Festival** at the end of September and early October combines the festival of music and arts with the festival of food and wine.

The owners are travellers themselves and are a good source of information. Stumble Inn also runs Easy Rider Wine Tours (see p150) which rents bicycles for R50 per day.

Village at Spier (Map p37; ☎ 809 1100; www.spier .co.za; Vlottenburg; d/ste with breakfast R1290/1950) Forgo the usual Cape Dutch style in favour of a design copying the brightly painted houses found in Cape Town's

Bo-Kaap. Rooms are large and well appointed and there's a pool.

Wilfra Court (Map p149; ☎ /fax 889 6091; 16 Hine St, Cloetsville; s/d with breakfast R210/360) In this homely place run by a friendly former mayor and his wife, there are only two rooms so book ahead. It's a fair way from the town centre so get directions.

FRANSCHHOEK

The booming village of Franschhoek, nestled in one of the loveliest settings in the Cape, is crammed with many fine restaurants and wineries. You could find yourself lingering here longer than you expected to – not a bad thing since Franschhoek is a good base from which to visit both Stellenbosch and Paarl as long as you have transport.

The town is clustered around Huguenot St. At the southern end it reaches a T-junction at Huguenot Memorial Park. Here you'll find the mildly diverting **Huguenot Memorial Museum** which celebrates the 200 French Huguenots who settled in the region in the 17th century. It houses the genealogical records of their descendants, as well as some hefty Cape Dutch furniture. Some of the names of the original settlers, such as Malan, De Villiers, Malherbe and Roux, are among the most famous Afrikaner dynasties in the country. Behind the main complex is a pleasant café, in front is the **Huguenot Monument**, three interlocking arches symbolising the holy trinity, and across the road is the museum's annexe, with displays on the Anglo-Boer War and natural history.

Continue northeast along the R45 to cross the spectacular Franschhoek Pass. Together with the Helshootge Pass on the R310, and Viljoens Pass and Sir Lowry's Pass (the most stunning of the lot) on the R321, this

Transport

Distance from Cape Town to Franschhoek 71km
Direction East
Travel time From Cape Town 2hrs; from Stellenbosch 40mins; from Paarl 30mins.
Car Follow the N1 and then stick on the R310 through Stellenbosch and over the Helshootge Pass to the junction with the R45, where you take a right turn.
Taxi Take a shared taxi from Stellenbosch to Pniel where you should be able to change to another shared taxi heading to Franschhoek from Paarl.

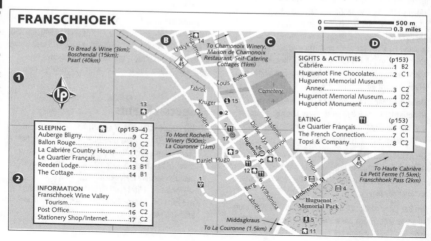

FRANSCHHOEK

0 — 500 m
0 — 0.3 miles

SIGHTS & ACTIVITIES (p153)
Cabrière.................................1 B2
Huguenot Fine Chocolates.........2 C1
Huguenot Memorial Museum
  Annex..................................3 C2
Huguenot Memorial Museum.....4 D2
Huguenot Monument................5 C2

EATING (p153)
Le Quartier Français................6 C2
The French Connection.............7 C1
Topsi & Company....................8 C2

SLEEPING (pp153–4)
Auberge Bligny......................9 C2
Ballon Rouge.........................10 C2
La Cabrière Country House.......11 C2
Le Quartier Français...............12 C2
Reeden Lodge........................13 B1
The Cottage..........................14 B1

INFORMATION
Franschhoek Wine Valley
  Tourism..............................15 C1
Post Office............................16 C2
Stationery Shop/Internet...........17 C2

To Bread & Wine (3km);
Boschendal (15km);
Paarl (40km)

To Chamonoix Winery,
Maison de Chamonoix
Restaurant, Self-Catering
Cottages (1km)

Louis Botha
Fabriek
Kruger
Cemetery

To Mont Rochelle
Winery (500m);
La Couronne (1km)

Daniel Hugo

Middagkraus
To La Couronne (1.5km)

To Haute Cabrière
La Petit Ferme (1.5km);
Franschhoek Pass (2km)

Huguenot
Memorial Park

152

forms part of the **Four Pass Route** that makes for a cracking day's driving to and from Cape Town or Stellenbosch.

For details of Franschhoek's **wineries**, some of which can be visited on foot from the town, see p39. There's also the option of taking a horse-riding tour of the area with the **Mount Rochelle Equestrian Centre**.

Wining and dining apart, there's some decent walks in the surrounding mountains – the staff at **Franschhoek Wine Valley Tourism** can provide a map of suggested routes and issue permits (R10) for walks in nearby forestry areas. There are also plenty of galleries and designer shops to mop up any spare cash. In particular, visit **Huguenot Fine Chocolates**. An empowerment programme helped give the two local coloured guys who run this Belgium-style chocolate shop a leg up and now people are raving about their confections. Call a day in advance to arrange a tour and chocolate-making demonstration including tasting of samples (R12).

Sights & Information

Franschhoek Wine Valley Tourism (Map p152; ☎ 876 3603; www.franschhoek.org.za; Huguenot St; ☼ 9am-6pm Mon-Fri, 9am-5pm Sat, 10am-5pm Sun Sep-Apr) Call ahead for opening hours in other months.

Huguenot Fine Chocolates (Map p152; ☎ 876 4096; 62 Huguenot St)

Huguenot Memorial Museum (Map p152; ☎ 876 2532; Lambrecht St; adult/child R5/2; ☼ 9am-5pm Mon-Sat, 2-5pm Sun)

Huguenot Monument (adult/child R3/1; ☼ 9am-5pm)

Mont Rochelle Equestrian Centre (☎ 083 300 4368; fax 876 2363; horse riding per hr R80).

Eating

Bread & Wine (Map p152; ☎ 876 3692; Môreson Wine Farm, Happy Valley Rd, La Motte; mains R60; ☼ noon-6pm Tue-Sun) Hidden away down a dirt road as you approach town along the R45, Bread & Wine is worth searching out for its breads, pizzas, cured meats and tasty Mediterranean-style cuisine.

French Connection (Map p152; ☎ 876 4056; 48 Huguenot St; mains R50; ☼ lunch & dinner) A deservedly popular place with chequered red tablecloths that give it that ooh-la-la factor. The menu features bistro-style food done to perfection.

Haute Cabrière Cellar (Map p152; ☎ 876 3688; Franschhoek Pass Rd; mains R80-90; ☼ noon-3pm daily & 7-9pm Wed-Mon) In a dramatic dining space in a cellar cut into the mountain side, each dish can be had either as a starter or main and all are paired with a Cabriére wine.

La Petite Ferme (Map p152; ☎ 876 3016; Franschhoek Pass Rd; mains R80; ☼ noon-4pm) A must-visit for foodies who hanker for romantic views, boutique wines and smoked, de-boned salmon trout, the delicately flavoured signature dish. There's a helipad should you feel like choppering in from Cape Town and some luxurious rooms if you can't bear to leave.

Le Quartier Français (Map p152; ☎ 876 2151; 16 Huguenot St; mains R75; ☼ lunch & dinner) This place dazzles with the quality and creativity of its cooking; try dishes such as double-baked beetroot and rocket soufflé, lemon verbena roasted chicken, or the divine plum tartlet with currant syrup and verjuice. The hotel's bar does lighter meals for around R50.

Topsi & Company (Map p152; ☎ 876 2952; 7 Reservoir St; mains R50-75; ☼ 12.30-3pm & 7.30-10pm Wed-Mon) Run by Topsi Venter, who should be accorded national treasure status, this place is quirky and very relaxed. Topsi pops out from her open kitchen to serve the totally delicious food and chat with guests; you can BYO wine.

Sleeping

Auberge Bligny (Map p152; ☎ 876 3767; www.blingny .co.za; 28 Van Wyk St; s/d with breakfast R590/680) This guesthouse in a Victorian homestead has nine pleasant rooms, a shady garden and pool.

Ballon Rouge (Map p152; ☎ 876 2651; www.ballon -rouge.co.za; 7 Reservoir St East; s/d with breakfast R500/600) A small hotel with good quality rooms opening on to the stoop. There's a restaurant and pool.

Cottage (Map p152; ☎ 876 2392; thecottage55@iafrica .com; 55 Huguenot St; s/d R250/320) There is just one cottage sleeping two, or four at a pinch, but it's a beauty. It's private, quiet, and is a few minutes' walk from the village centre.

Chamonix cottages (Map p152; ☎ 876 2494; www .chamonix.co.za; Uitkyk St; cottages from R480) Pleasant cottages sleeping up to four are set in the middle of the vineyards. It's a 10-minute walk uphill north of Huguenot St.

La Cabrière Country House (Map p152; ☎ 876 4780; www.lacabriere.co.za; Middagkrans Rd; d with breakfast R950) A modern boutique guesthouse that's a refreshing break from all that Cape Dutch architecture. There are only four sumptuously decorated rooms, very personal service, a pool and sweeping views to the mountains.

La Couronne (Map p152; ☎ 876 2770; www.lacouronne hotel.co.za; Robertsvlei Rd; d with breakfast from R1800) A boutique hotel and restaurant partly built into the hills, this place offers gilt-edged luxury and magnificent views across the valley.

Le Quartier Français (Map p152; ☎ 876 2151; www .lequartier.co.za; 16 Huguenot Rd; d from R2350) This is one of the best places to stay in the Winelands. Set around a leafy courtyard and pool, guest rooms are very large with fireplaces, huge beds and stylish décor. There's also a fine restaurant here (see p153).

Reeden Lodge (Map p152; ☎ 876 3174; www.reedenlodge.co.za; end of Fabriek St; cottages from R380) The lodge offers well-equipped self-catering cottages sleeping up to six people. They're based on a farm about 10 minutes' walk from town. It's good if you've got kids – there are sheep, a tree house, a pool and lots of space.

PAARL

Less touristy and more spread out than Stellenbosch, Paarl is a large commercial centre surrounded by mountains and vineyards on the banks of the Berg River. There are several vineyards and wineries within the sprawling town limits, including the huge Kooperatieve Wijnbouwers Vereeniging, better known as the KWV (p41).

Transport

Distance from Cape Town to Paarl 56km
Direction Northeast
Travel time 1hr by car
Car Take the N1 from Cape Town.
Bus All the major long-distance bus companies (p166) offer services which pass through Paarl. The bus segment between Paarl and Cape Town costs R90.
Train Metro trains run roughly every hour between Cape Town and Paarl (economy/first class R8.50/14.5, 1¼ hours) from Monday to Friday. The services are less common on weekends. Take care to travel on trains during the busy part of the day, as robberies have been reported. You can travel by train from Paarl to Stellenbosch: take a Cape Town–bound train and change at Muldersvlei.

The surrounding valley was settled by Europeans in the 1680s, and Paarl was established in 1720. It became a centre for wagon-building, but the town is most famous for its important role in the development and recognition of Afrikaans as a language in its own right (opposite).

Paarl is not really a town to tour on foot, but there is still quite a lot to see and do. Paarl's main street, imaginatively called Main St, runs 11km along the entire length of the town, parallel to the Berg River and the train line. It's shaded by oaks and jacarandas and is lined with many historic buildings. The busy commercial centre is around Lady Grey St near where you'll find the fascinating **Paarl Museum** housed in the Old Parsonage (Oude Pastorie), built in 1714. It has an excellent collection of Cape Dutch antiques and relics of Huguenot and early Afrikaner culture. There's a bookcase modelled on King Solomon's temple and display sections on the 'road to reconciliation', the old mosques of the local Muslim community and the Khoisan.

A short walk south of the Paarl Museum is the marginally interesting **Afrkaans Language Museum**. The birth of Afrikaans is chronicled in the former home of Gideon Malherbe, the meeting place for the Association of True Afrikaners and the birthplace of the first Afrikaans newspaper. The house has been painstakingly restored.

Afrikaans is further celebrated at the giant needle-like **Taal Monument** up on highlands overlooking the town to the west. This is the Paarl Mountain Nature Reserve dominated by three giant granite domes; they apparently glisten like pearls if they are caught by the sun after a fall of rain – hence 'Paarl'. The reserve has mountain *fynbos* with a particularly large number of proteas. There's a cultivated wildflower garden in the middle that's a nice spot for a picnic, and numerous walks with excellent views over the valley. Access is from the 11km-long Jan Phillips Dr, which skirts the eastern edge of the reserve. The picnic ground is about 4km from Main St. A map showing walking trails is available from Paarl Tourism.

For details of wineries in and around Paarl see p41. At the Winelands Hotel you'll also find a luxurious spa, the **Santé Wellness Centre** (p138). Also see the Activities chapter for details of hot-air balloon trips (p113) you can organise out of Paarl.

The Official Birth of Afrikaans

In 1875 Arnoldus Pannevis, a teacher at Paarl Gymnasium High School, inspired a number of Paarl citizens to form the Genootskap van Regte Afrikaners (the Association of True Afrikaners). They developed and formalised the grammar and vocabulary of a language that was developed over 200 years from the interaction of the Dutch with their slaves and the indigenous inhabitants of the Cape. Many of the founding members of the association were actually descendants of the French Huguenots.

A small press was set up in the house of Gideon Malherbe and the first issue of an Afrikaans newspaper, *Die Afrikaanse Patriot*, was published followed by many books. Afrikaans was proclaimed an official language in 1925 and is protected under South Africa's new constitution.

Sights & Information

Afrikaans Language Museum (Map p155; ☎ 8721 3441; Pastorie Ave; adult/child R5/2; ◷ 9am-1pm & 2-5pm Mon-Fri)

Paarl Museum (Map p155; ☎ 872 2651; www.museums.org.za/paarlmuseum; 303 Main St; adult/child R5/donation; ◷ 10am-5pm Mon-Fri)

Paarl Tourism (Map p155; ☎ 872 3829; www.paarlonline.com; 216 Main St; ◷ 9am-5pm Mon-Fri, 9am-1pm Sat, 10am-1pm Sun) Has an excellent supply of information on the whole region and helpful staff.

Taal Monument (Map p155; Paarl Mountain Nature Reserve, Jan Phillips Dr; adult/child R5/2; ◷ 8am-5pm)

Eating

Bosman's (Map p155; ☎ 863 2727; Grande Roche, Plantasie St; mains R140; ◷ lunch & dinner) If money is no object, try this ritzy restaurant. It's undoubtedly classy, with chandeliers inside, flickering candles outside and a wine list that runs to more than 50 pages! There are various set menus from R175 for three courses.

Kostinrichting (Map p155; ☎ 871 1353; 19 Pastorie Ave; mains R30; ◷ lunch Mon-Sat) Ideal if you're looking for a pleasant central café. It's in a Victorian building that was once a school and has an attached craft shop.

Marc's Mediterranean Cuisine and Garden (Map p155; ☎ 863 3980; 129 Main Rd; mains R60-75; ◷ noon-3pm Tue-Sun & 6pm-late Mon-Sat) Marc's is the current favourite of restaurant reviewers, and with good reason. Patron Marc Friedrich has created a light and bright place

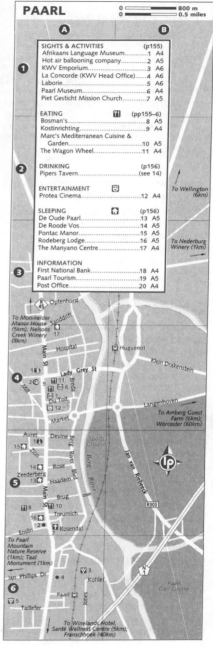

Detour: Bainskloof Pass

The Bainskloof Pass is one of the country's great mountain passes, with a superb caravan park halfway along. It's a magical drive, which would be even better to experience on bicycle. Colonial engineer Andrew Bain developed the road through the pass between 1848 and 1852. Other than having its surface tarred, the road has not been altered since, and is now a national monument.

The R301 runs from Wellington, 13km north of Paarl, across Bainskloof to meet another road running south to Worcester and north to Ceres. There are several nearby walks including the five-hour **Bobbejaans River Walk** to a waterfall. This walk actually starts back at Eerste Tol and you need to buy a permit (R30), which is available from the Cape Nature Conservation desk at **Cape Town Tourism** (p177).

The **Patatskloof Trail** is a long day walk that begins and ends at the **Oasis Tea Room** (☎ 873 4231; ☾ 8.30am-6pm Thu-Sun), on the road leading up to the pass from Wellington. You can make it an overnight walk by arranging to stay in a cave on the trail.

with food to match and a Provençal-style garden to dine in. Try the meze plate (R45) for lunch.

Wagon Wheel (Map p155; ☎ 872 5265; 57 Lady Grey St; mains R70; ☾ noon-2pm Tue-Fri & 6pm-late Tue-Sat) More than your average steak joint, this cosy wood-panelled restaurant has won many awards and packs them in nightly. Next door is Gabi's, a continental-style café-bar and a nonsmoking section for the restaurant.

Sleeping

Amberg Guest Farm (Map p155; ☎ /fax 862 0982; amberg@mweb.co.za; R101 along Du Toits Kloof Pass; s/d with breakfast R250/380) Accommodation is in cottages (one of which is self-catering for R300) with spectacular views. There's also a pool and the Swiss-style Amberg Country Kitchen, which serves Swiss specialities.

De Oude Paarl (Map p155; ☎ 872 1002; www.deoude paarl.com; 132 Main St; s/d with breakfast R650/930) This new boutique-style hotel has rooms with antique touches and a secluded courtyard with pool at the back. Attached are shops selling a good selection of wine and delectable but pricey Belgian chocolates.

De Roode Vos (Map p155; ☎ /fax 872 5912; 152 Main St; s/d R150/240) Next to the reliable bistro Pipers Tavern is one of Paarl's cheaper guesthouses. It offers unspectacular but clean lodgings and is about as cheap as you'll get in central Paarl.

Manyano Centre (Map p155; ☎ 872 2537; manyanocentre@cci.org.za; Sanddrift St; dm with full

board R110) This enormous accommodation complex has sparse three-bed dorms; you'll need to bring a sleeping bag. Call in advance, especially on weekends when it fills up with groups. Huguenot train station is closer than the main Paarl station.

Mooikelder Manor House (Map p155; ☎ 869 8787; www.capestay.co.za/mooikelder; Main Rd, Noorder Paarl; s/d with breakfast R275/500) Around 5km north of the town centre in an elegant homestead once occupied by Cecil Rhodes, this is a lovely quiet spot amid citrus orchards. There's plenty of antique atmosphere in the rooms and a pool outside.

Pontac Manor (Map p155; ☎ 872 0445; www.pontac .com; 16 Zion St; s/d with breakfast R770/1050) This small, stylish, Victorian-era hotel commands a good view of the valley. The rooms are comfortable, there's one self-catering cottage, and there's a pool and a recommended restaurant.

Rodeberg Lodge (Map p155; ☎ 863 3202; www .rodeberg.co.za; 74 Main Rd; s/d with breakfast R280/420) Good rooms (some with air con and TV) are sensibly located away from the busy main road. The hosts are friendly and breakfast is taken in the conservatory, opening on to a leafy garden.

Winelands Hotel (Map p155; ☎ 875 8100; www .southernsun.com; Klapmuts; ste with breakfast R2300) Paarl's luxury option. The newly planted vines are yet to fill out, so the surrounding countryside is looking a bit barren and dusty. Inside the hotel rooms it's king-sized beds, the latest in audio-visual equipment and decadent bathrooms all the way. Attached to the hotel is the luxurious spa complex Sante Wellness Centre (see p138)

HERMANUS

Particularly popular with Capetonian families on holiday between December and January, the tourist mecca of Hermanus was originally a fishing village and still retains vestiges of its heritage. It's now best known as a place to view whales (p159) and to dive with great white sharks. It's a pleasant place with some appealing beaches, most of which

HERMANUS

| | 0 ——— 400 m |
| | 0 ——— 0.2 miles |

SIGHTS & ACTIVITIES (p158)
Hermanus Harbour Museum.............1 C3
Museum Annexe.........................2 C3
Shark Lady Adventures.................3 C3
Whale-Watching Car Park...............4 C4

EATING (pp158–9)
Bientang's Cave.........................5 D3
Burgundy Restaurant....................6 C3
Marimba Cafe...........................7 C3
Rossi's Pizzeria & Italian Restaurant...8 C3
Savannah Café......................(see 12)
Fisherman's Cottage....................9 C3

DRINKING (p159)
Zebra Crossing.........................10 C3

SHOPPING
Long St Arcade Centre.................11 C3
Village Square Shopping Centre......12 C3

SLEEPING (pp159–60)
Auberge Burgundy.....................13 C3
Hermanus Backpackers.................14 B2
Hermanus Esplanade...................15 B2
Kenjockity Guesthouse................16 C3
Marine Hermanus......................17 D3
Moby's Traveller's Lodge.............18 C3
Windsor Hotel........................19 C3
Zoete Inval Travellers Lodge.........20 A2

INFORMATION
First National Bank...................21 C3
Hemmingway's Bookshop...........(see 26)
Hermanus Internet &
  Information Café.....................22 C3
Hermanus Tourism.....................23 D2
Hospital.............................24 A3
Post Office..........................25 C3
The Book Cottage.....................26 C3

Excursions – Hermanus

are west of the town centre. Rocky hills, vaguely reminiscent of Scotland, surround the town, and there are good walks and a nature reserve, protecting some of the prolific *fynbos*. The town centre, easily negotiated on foot and east of the new harbour, is well endowed with restaurants and shops. There's a small **market** daily at Lemms Corner in the Market Square off Main Rd; on Saturday a craft market is held there, too.

The old harbour clings to the cliffs in front of the town centre; here you'll find a small and generally uninteresting **harbour museum** and a display of old fishing boats. The museum's annexe, in the old schoolhouse on the market square, displays some evocative old photographs of the town and its fishermen.

Transport

Distance from Cape Town to Hermanus 122km
Direction Southeast
Travel time 2hrs
Car The fastest route is to take the N2 from Cape Town. It's not that much longer, and makes for a far more attractive drive, if you follow the R44 through Strand, Gordon's Bay and around Cape Hangklip.
Bus There are no regular bus services to Hermanus, but plenty of organised bus tours from Cape Town; inquire with Cape Town Tourism (p177).

From the old harbour take the **Cliff Path Walking Trail** that meanders east along the sea to Grotto Beach, a long narrow surf beach with excellent facilities. The walk takes about 1½ hours and along the way you'll pass Kraiiwater, a good whale watching lookout, and Laangbai and Voelklip beaches.

The 1400-hectare **Fernkloof Nature Reserve**, 5km east of town, is worth a visit if you are interested in *fynbos*. They have identified 1100 species so far. There is a 60km network of hiking trails for all fitness levels.

See p113 for details of sea kayaking in the harbour and p110 for details of shark-cage diving at Gansbaai.

Travel Tip

There's been an explosion of places to stay in Hermanus over the last few years, but in the holiday season the town can still be bursting at the seams, so take care to book ahead. Hermanus Tourism will help you and there are agencies such as **Whale Route Accommodation** (☎ 028-314 1566; www.hermanus.co.za/accom/whaleroute) and the **Hermanus Accommodation Centre** (☎ 028-313 0004; www.fire.adept.co.za/hermanus/accom.html), which lets houses and books other accommodation.

Sights & Information

Fernkloof Nature Reserve (Map p157; ☎ 028-313 8100; Fir Ave; admission free; ☺ 9am-5pm)

Hermanus Harbour Museum (Map p157; ☎ 044-312 1475; adult/child R2/1; ☺ 9am-1pm & 2-5pm Mon-Sat, noon-4pm Sun)

Hermanus Internet & Information Café (Map p157; ☎ 028-313 0277; Waterkant Bldg, Main Rd; per hr R40;

☺ 8am-8pm Mon-Fri, 9am-8pm Sat) Offers reliable and speedy Internet connections.

Hermanus Tourism (Map p157; ☎ 028-312 2629; www.hermanus.co.za; Old Station Bldg, Mitchell St; ☺ 9am-5pm Mon-Sat, noon-5pm Sun) Has a large supply of information about the area, including walks and drives in the surrounding hills, and can book accommodation.

Eating & Drinking

Bientang's Cave (Map p157; ☎ 028-312 3454; Marine Dr; mains R55) Nestled in the cliffs beside the water this really *is* a seaside cave, containing a good seafood restaurant with a children's menu.

Burgundy Restaurant (Map p157; ☎ 028-312 2800; Marine Dr; mains R60-95) Booking is essential at the Burgundy, one of the most acclaimed and popular restaurants in the province. It's in a pair of cottages, which are the oldest buildings in town (1875), with a garden and sea views. The menu is mostly seafood with a different vegetarian dish each day.

Fisherman's Cottage (Map p157; ☎ 028-312 3642; Lemms Corner; mains R22-75) Good cheap seafood is on

---

Coastal Route to Hermanus

Hugging False Bay, the R44 from Cape Town runs through Strand and towards Hermanus around Cape Hangklip. It's a thrilling coastal drive, the best of which is between Gordon's Bay and Kleinmond, and the views are stunning. At times it feels as if the road is going to disappear into the sea. On one side is blue-green water, on the other are rock-strewn cliffs.

At **Stony Point**, just before you reach the small, scattered holiday village of Betty's Bay, take a short stroll to the look out point for a colony of **African penguins**. It's very picturesque with crashing waves and a sea of black and white birds. In Betty's Bay itself you'll find the **Harold Porter National Botanical Gardens** (☎ 028-272 9311; adult/child R7/3; ☺ 8am-4.30pm Mon-Fri, 8am-5pm Sat & Sun), definitely worth visiting. There are paths exploring the area and, at the entrance, tearooms and a formal garden where you can picnic. Try the **Leopard Kloof Trail** (3km return), which leads through fern forests and up to a waterfall. Coming from Cape Town look for the turn-off to the gardens after driving through Betty's Bay.

Close to a wild and beautiful beach, **Kleinmond** is in a state of revival. The Harbour Rd area is quickly becoming quite chic and makes for a great place to spend an afternoon, eat some fresh seafood and browse through the art gallery and little shops. Stop by the **Abalone Hatchery** (☎ 028-271 5681; Harbour Rd; admission R8; ☺ 9am-4pm Mon-Fri) where South Africa's six abalone species are grown for export. It's a tiny place but worth a stroll. The area also has some reliable swells for surfers and some good walking.

Watching the Whales

Between June and November, there can be up to 70 whales in the bay at once as southern right whales *(Eubalaena australis)* come to Walker Bay to calve. South Africa was a whaling nation until 1976 – this species was hunted to the verge of extinction but its numbers are now recovering. Humpback whales *(Megaptera novaeangliae)* are also sometimes seen.

Whales often come very close to shore and there are some excellent vantage points from the cliff paths that run from one end of Hermanus to the other. The best places are Castle Rock, Kraal Rock and Sievers Point. There's a telescope on the cliff top above the old harbour.

The people of Hermanus took the seasonal arrival of the whales for granted and only recently bothered to tell the outside world the whales were regular visitors. Now, however, the tourism potential has been recognised and just about every business in town has adopted a whale logo. There's a whale-spotters hotline (☎ 0800 228 222) and a whale crier, who walks around town blowing on a kelp horn and carrying a blackboard that shows where whales have been recently sighted. A **Whale Festival** is held in late September or early October.

Despite all this hoopla, boat viewing of whales is banned in the bay (as are jet skis) and boats are strictly regulated outside the bay. There are only two boat-viewing operators licensed to operate in the seas outside the bay: **Southern Right Charters** (☎ 082 353 0550) and **Hawston Fishers** (☎ 082 396 8931). They charge around R250 for a one- to two-hour trip.

Although Hermanus is the best known whale-watching site, whales can be seen all the way from False Bay (Cape Town) to Plettenberg Bay and beyond. The west coast also gets its share. Check out www.cape-whaleroute.co.za for more information.

---

offer at this cute restaurant in a whitewashed cottage draped with fishing nets.

Marimba Cafe (Map p157; ☎ 028-312 2148; 108D Main Rd; mains R40-75) The lively atmosphere matches the eclectic menu at this recommended restaurant where you can eat traditional African dishes from around the continent. The bar is perfect for a drink.

Rossi's Pizzeria & Italian Restaurant (Map p157; ☎ 028-312 2848; 10 High St; mains R22-40) Delicious smells enchant your senses upon entering this low-key family restaurant that focuses on pizza and pasta.

Savannah Café (Map p157; ☎ 028-312 4259; Village Theatre, Marine Dr; mains from R20; ☽ breakfast & lunch) Watch the whales frolic in the sea while eating the 'Whale of a Breakfast' – eggs, juice, coffee, bacon, chips, mushrooms and *boerewores* (sausages) among other items.

Zebra Crossing (Map p157; ☎ 028-312 3906; 121 Main Rd; mains R20-30) This stylish DJ bar with a funky zebra theme is *the* late-night spot to party on the weekends, and popular with backpackers. At other times there's an open fire and pool tables. Food is burgers and sandwiches.

Sleeping

Auberge Burgundy (Map p157; ☎ 028-313 1202; www.hermanus.co.za/accom/auberger; 16 Harbour Rd; s/d with breakfast R450/900) This is a wonderful place, built in the style of a Provençal villa, with fine facilities (including a pool), wrought iron balconies and unique art on the walls.

Hermanus Backpackers (Map p157; ☎ 028-312 4293; moobag@mweb.co.za; 26 Flower St; camp sites per person R40, dm R70, s/d with shared bathroom R100/200) This is a smashing place with clued-up staff, great décor and facilities including a reed-roofed bar and pool. Breakfast included.

Hermanus Esplanade (Map p157; ☎ 028-312 3610; clarkbro@hermanus.co.za; 63 Marine Dr; flats from R250)

Excursions – Hermanus

Detour: Around Hermanus

If you want to see whales in a much less commercialised environment, head south from Hermanus to the sleepy village of **De Kelders**. Next along is **Gansbaai**, an unprepossessing fishing town that is riding the wave of interest in shark-cage diving. If this is not your bag, then the nearby **Dyer Island**, where the sharks hang out, also hosts colonies of African penguins and seals; regular boat trips are available. On the unsealed inland route between Gansbaai and Cape Agulhas is **Elim**, a picturesque but poor Moravian mission village founded in 1824.

Some of these cheery self-catering apartments with colourful furniture overlook the sea; the lowest rates actually cover the whale-watching season from May to October.

Kenjockity Guesthouse (Map p157; ☎ 028-312 1772; kenjock@hermanus.co.za; 15 Church St; s/d R200/400) This guesthouse, the first in Hermanus, has a nice atmosphere and fair-sized rooms with wooden furniture and walls the same colour as the duvets.

Marine Hermanus (Map p157; ☎ 028-313 1000; www .marine-hermanus.co.za; Marine Dr; s/d with breakfast R1500/2500) Right on the sea with immaculate grounds and amenities, this place is as posh as a five-star hotel should be. The staff is very friendly and will work with what you're looking for – sea views or rooms with balconies. The hotel's two restaurants both face the sea and are open for dinner only. They serve nouveau South African cuisine. You can choose between two courses (R155) and three courses (R195).

Moby's Traveller's Lodge (Map p157; ☎ 028-313 2361; www.mobys.co.za; 9 Mitchell St; dm R70, s/d with shared bathroom R150/190) Travellers give this place rave reviews, and we agree. In a converted old hotel you can party the night away at the big bar, or chill out in the awesome rock pool with its own waterfall. Breakfast is included in the price and light snacks (R15) are available.

Windsor Hotel (Map p157; ☎ 028-312 3727; www .windsor-hotel.com; 49 Marine Dr; s/d with breakfast from 420/620) Situated on a cliff overlooking the ocean, naturally you'll want one of the more expensive sea-facing rooms that give you the opportunity to view whales without leaving your bed.

Zoete Inval Travellers Lodge (Map p157; ☎ 028-312 1242; www.zoeteinval.co.za; 23 Main Rd; dm R70, d with shared bathroom R300) More a guesthouse than a backpacker hostel, this is a quiet place with good amenities and nicely furnished rooms. Families are accommodated in 4-person doubles.

GREYTON & GENADENDAL

The neighbouring villages of Greyton and Genadendal are among the most pleasant in the Overberg region. Somewhat twee and polished, the whitewashed, thatched-roof cottages of Greyton may be a bit artificial but they are becoming very popular with Capetonians on the lookout for a relaxing country retreat. In contrast Genadendal, the oldest mission station in South Africa, founded in 1738, couldn't be more authentic. It has an uncontrived attractiveness and is still home to a predominantly coloured community.

Greyton, with plenty of accommodation, comes into its own as a base for **hiking** in the Riviersonderend Mountains which rise up in Gothic majesty immediately to the village's north. Apart from the **Boesmanskloof Trail** (below) there are several shorter walks, as well as the two-day **Genadendal Trail** for the serious hiker. This is a 25.3km circular route that begins and ends at Genadendal's Moravian Church; for more details pick up the Cape Nature Conservation leaflet at the **tourist information office**.

Some 3km west of Greyton, Genadendal was, for a brief time, the largest settlement in the colony after Cape Town. Entering the village from the R406, head down Main Rd until you arrive at the cluster of national monuments around Church Square. The Moravian

Boesmanskloof Trail

The Boesmanskloof Trail, administered by **Cape Nature Conservation** (www.capenature.org.za), runs for roughly 17km through the spectacular *fynbos*-clad Riviersonderend Mountains between Greyton and Die Galg, 15km south of McGregor. To hike the entire trail costs R40/50 per person one-way/round-trip plus another R25 per day permit fee. It takes between four and six hours one way, making an overnight stay in Greyton the preferred option. Alternatively you can stay at Whipstock Farm (☎ /fax 023-625 1733; whipstock@netactive.co.za; s/d R250/500) at the Die Galg end of the trail, 7km from McGregor. The friendly hosts will organise transfers to and from the trail head. At Die Galg you'll notice that the start of the trail marks the end of a long-abandoned project to construct a pass across the range. Only 50 people per day are allowed on the trail, so it's best to book in advance, especially for weekends and during the holidays; make inquiries with the Cape Nature Conservation desk at Cape Town Tourism (p177) or go to the **Greyton Municipal Offices** (☎ 028-254 9620).

Church is a handsome, simply decorated building; opposite you'll find the **tourist information centre**. There's a café here selling home-made bread and souvenirs including pottery.

The village's fascinating history is documented in the fine **Mission Museum** based in what was South Africa's first teacher training college. Elsewhere in this historic precinct is one of the oldest printing presses in the country, still in operation, and a water mill.

Sights & Information

Genadendal Mission Museum (☎ 028-251 8582; adult/child R7/2; ⏰ 9am-1pm & 2-5pm Mon-Thu, 9am-3.30pm Fri, 9am-1pm Sat)

Genadendal Tourist Information Centre (☎ 028-251 8291; ⏰ 8.30am-5pm Mon-Fri, 10am-1pm Sat)

Greyton Tourist Information Office (☎ 028-254 9414; ⏰ 10am-noon & 2.30-4.30pm Mon-Sat) On the village's main road.

Sleeping & Eating

High Hopes B&B (☎ /fax 028-254 9898; 89 Main Rd; d with breakfast from R450) One of the nicest places in town, High Hopes has tastefully furnished rooms, lovely gardens and a well-stocked library. Singles are negotiable and afternoon tea is thrown in for all guests. Convenient for hikers, it's the closest B&B to the start of the Boesmanskloof Trail.

Guinea Fowl (☎ 028-254 9550; longreyton.co.za; cnr DS Botha & Oak Sts; d with breakfast from R500) Comfortable and quiet, this guesthouse has a pool for summer, log fire for winter and good breakfasts year-round.

Posthaus Guesthouse (☎ 028-254 9995; fax 254 9920; Main Rd; d with breakfast from R400) Set around a pretty garden, the gimmick here is to name the rooms after Beatrix Potter characters (we told you Greyton was a twee

place). The attached English-style pub the **Ball & Bass** is a cosy place for a drink or meal.

Greyton Lodge (☎ 028-254 9876; greytonlodge@kingsley .co.za; 46 Main Rd; s/d with breakfast R450/600) A pair of stocks and rampant lion statues flank the entrance to this upmarket hotel in the old police station. There's a pool and a reasonably priced but unadventurous **bistro**, which is open from 7pm to 9pm daily.

Oak & Vigne Cafe (☎ 028-254 9037; DS Botha St; mains from R30) Evidence of the creeping 'yuppification' of Greyton is this trendy deli–art gallery–café, which is a fine place to grab a snack, chill out and watch the world go by.

Rosie's Restaurant (☎ 028-254 9640; 2 High St; mains from R40; ⏰ dinner only) The house specialities are wood-fired-oven pizzas (which are delicious and huge) and steaks.

Transport

Distance from Cape Town to Greyton 148km
Direction East
Travel time 2 hrs
Car From Cape Town follow the N2 to just before Caledon, then take the R406 which brings you to Genadendal, 3km before Greyton.

DARLING

Named after Lieutenant Governor Charles Henry Darling and founded in 1853, Darling was once a quiet little country town, principally famous for the displays of wildflowers in the surrounding Swartland (Black Land). Then actor and satirist Pieter-Dirk Uys opened a theatre in the town as a platform for his cast of flamboyant characters headed up by the irrepressible Tannie Evita Bezuidenhout (p107). Life in Darling has never been the same since.

Now Capetonians make the 70km trek north by the dozens on show nights to catch this uniquely South African brand of cabaret at **Evita se Perron** (p106). The theatre's splendidly kitsch **restaurant**, in a converted station building next to the railway, is worth a visit in its own right. Painted bright blues and reds, with pink lights

Transport

Distance from Cape Town to Darling 75km
Direction North
Travel time 1hr
Car Take the N1 then the N7 north until the turn off on to the R307. Alternatively take the R27 from Cape Town running through Milnerton and Bloubergstrand and look for the signs to Darling.
Train It's worth inquiring about the occasional Saturday excursions to Darling on the Spier Train (☎ 419 5222). The 2½-hour trip includes a picnic lunch and admission to the show at Evita se Perron.

strung from the ceiling and its walls are cluttered with old posters and paintings. Food is traditional Afrikaans – chicken pie and *bobotie* (curried mince with a topping of savoury egg custard, usually served on turmeric-flavoured rice). While you're here take a walk around the **sculpture garden** behind the theatre – pink tissue paper ostriches and green mermaids lounge in a sea of broken glass.

Darling is so close to Cape Town that there's no pressing need to stay overnight, but there are some nice guesthouses.

Sights & Information

Evita se Perron (☎ 022-492 2851; www.evita.co.za; Evita's Platform; tickets R75; performances 2pm & 8pm Sat, 2pm Sun; restaurant mains R20-40; ☉ lunch & dinner Tue-Sun)

Tourist Information (☎ 022-492 3361; Pastorie St)

Eating & Sleeping

Arum Inn (☎ 022-492 3195; 5 Long St; s/d R180/270) This guesthouse has lots of light and windows to make the big rooms feel especially spacious. Children are welcome.

Darling Guest House (☎ 022-492 3062; 22 Pastorie St; s/d with breakfast R195/330) An elegant and imaginatively decorated place.

Through the Looking Glass (☎ 022-492 2858; 19 Main Rd; breakfast R30) For afternoon tea or all day breakfast, don't miss this arty café, which also has an Internet connection.

LANGEBAAN & WEST COAST NATIONAL PARK

Its beautiful and unusual location overlooking the Langebaan Lagoon, has made Langebaan a favourite holiday destination with Capetonians. As such the town suffers from a number of poorly conceived property developments (such as the Club Mykonos Resort), so if you're looking for untouched scenery you might be happier elsewhere. This said Langebaan does support an excellent hotel, open-air seafood restaurants, phenomenal sunset views, superb sailing and windsurfing on the lagoon and a few good beaches, the best of which is **Langebaan beach**, in town, a favourite with swimmers.

The town is also the best base for exploring the **West Coast National Park**, 7km south of Langebaan. Encompassing the clear blue waters of the lagoon, home to an enormous number of migratory wading birds, the park covers around 18,000 hectares. It protects wetlands of international significance and important seabird breeding colonies. The wading birds flock here by the thousands in the summer. The most numerically dominant species is the delicate-looking curlew sandpiper, which migrates north from the sub-Antarctic in huge flocks. Flamingos, Cape gannets, crowned cormorants, numerous gull species and African black oystercatchers are also among the hordes. The offshore islands are home to colonies of jackass penguins.

The vegetation is predominantly made up of stunted bushes, sedges and many flowering annuals and succulents. There are some coastal *fynbos* in the east, and the park is famous for its wildflower display, which is usually between August and October. Several game species can be seen in the part of the park known as the Postberg section, which is open from August to September. Game species include a variety of small antelope, wildebeest, bontebok and eland.

Note that the roads in the park are dirt and can be quite heavily corrugated. The return trip from Langebaan to the northern end of the Postberg section is more than 80km; allow yourself plenty of time.

Transport

Distance from Cape Town to Langebaan 127km
Direction North
Travel time 1¼hr
Car Follow the R27 from Cape Town.
Bus West Coast Shuttle (☎ 083 556 1777) runs a minibus service (R60) from Cape Town to the Mykonos resort and casino.
Seaplane Contact Life Out There (☎ 082 413 6149; www.lifeoutthere.co.za) about chartering a seaplane from Cape Town to Langebaan.

Another place to visit while you're up here is the **West Coast Fossil Park** on the R45 about 16km northeast of Langebaan. The first bear discovered south of the Sahara, lion-sized sabre toothed cats, three-toed horses and short necked giraffes are all on display here. Tours to the excavation sites depart daily at 11.30am. Children can sieve for their own fossils in a special display area.

Dominated by an enormous iron-ore pier, navy yards and fish-processing factories is **Saldanha**, at the northern end of the same lagoon as Langebaan. Despite this, the town's bays are pleasant and, because they are sheltered, much warmer than the ocean. **Hoedjies Bay**, near the town centre, is the most popular for swimming.

See p113 for details of horse riding and p114 for windsurfing in the area.

West Coast Wildflower Shows

Between the end of August and mid October wildflowers bloom all over the Western Cape. Among the most spectacular displays are along the west coast. Contact Cape Town Tourism or the tourist offices in Darling and Langebaan to confirm dates. The West Coast National Park is a particularly attractive place to visit during this season.

Sights & Activities

Langebaan Tourist Information Centre (☎ 022-772 1515; www.langebaaninfo.com; end of Hoof St; ⊙ 9am-5pm Mon-Fri, 9am-12.30pm Sat, 9am-noon Sun)

West Coast Fossil Park (☎ 022-766 1606; www .museums.org.za/wcfp; admission R45; ⊙ 10am-4pm Mon-Fri, 10am-1pm Sat & Sun)

West Coast National Park (☎ 022-772 2144; admission non-flower/flower season R15/60; ⊙ 7am-7pm)

Sleeping & Eating

Club Mykonos (☎ 0800 226 770; theretha@clubmykonos .co.za; 4-person cabins R1550) There's a beautiful private beach here in a small cove with lots of shells. The resort is good for families as there is plenty here to entertain the kids. Greek themed and with pseudo Mediterranean architecture, you'll either love it or hate it. There are no less than six outdoor swimming pools, a casino, restaurants and an arcade.

Farmhouse (☎ 022-772 2062; www.thefarmhouse langebaan.co.za; 5 Egret St; s/d with breakfast R500/800; mains R50-80) This is by far Langebaan's best hotel, on a

hill overlooking the bay with lovely sunset views. Rooms are large with country décor and their own fireplaces. For such a classy place the restaurant is reasonably priced with a creative menu and a rustic, intimate dining room.

Oliphantskop Farm Inn (☎ /fax 022-772 2326; Main Rd; s/d R150/260; mains R50) An attractive place around 3km from town, across the road from the Mykonos resort complex, Oliphantskop's restaurant has a good reputation and nice ambience – cool and dark with rough white walls and a wooden ceiling. The menu is meat and seafood oriented and offers no veggie options.

Windstone Backpackers (☎ 022-766 1645; www.wind stone.co.za; Route 45; camping per person R50, dm R70, d R180) Facilities here are quite good, there's even an indoor swimming pool. The grounds are spacious with lots of trees and the accommodation rustic. Bring all the food and drinks you need for a stay as this place – it's kind of in the middle of nowhere.

Die Strandloper (☎ 022-772 2490; mains R95; ⊙ lunch Wed, Sat & Sun, dinner Wed-Sat) This rustic open-air seafood restaurant and bar on the beach is outside of the town on the way to the Mykonos resort, and has a seafood buffet. Call ahead to check it's open – sometimes it just closes.

PATERNOSTER

Paternoster, a clutch of simple whitewashed homes with green roofs up against the blue sea, sparkles in the sun and is a feast for the eyes. This sleepy fishing village apparently got its name (Latin for 'our father') after the locals rescued shipwrecked Portuguese sailors, who gave their thanks with many 'our father' prayers. It's a low-key kind of place with fishing as its lifeblood – although, as in Kalk Bay, the industry has recently been hit hard by the government decision to cut back on fishing licences. As the locals become impoverished, wealthy Capetonians looking for holiday houses have moved in. Property is now a hot commodity – there are sold signs left and right and new guesthouses are opening every day.

The surrounding countryside is attractive, the rolling hills scattered with strange granite outcrops. The **Cape Columbine Nature Reserve**, 3km past the town, protects 263 hectares of coastal *fynbos* around Cape Columbine. Further north along the coast is the similar village of

St Helena Bay, with a lovely sheltered stretch of water, but no real beach.

Paternoster is rather lacking in street signs, instead look out for the individual guesthouse signs. B&Bs are opening here on a daily basis, so it may be worth checking out a few places first. During the crayfish season (November 15 to late December) you will see the tasty crustaceans for sale on the side of the road for between R25 and R40.

Sights

Cape Columbine Nature Reserve (☎ 022-752 2718; adult/child R9/6; ☼ 7am-7pm)

Sleeping & Eating

Ahoy! Guesthouse & Restaurant (☎ /fax 022-752 2725; s/d R220/440; mains R20-70) Some of the nicest rooms in Paternoster are found here – all immaculate with a white theme. There's a very blue kitchen for self-catering and a *braai* (barbecue) area for cooking your own crayfish, and it's all just a two-minute walk to the beach. The

Transport

Distance from Cape Town to Paternoster 156km
Direction North
Travel time 2½hr
Car From Cape Town follow the R27 to its junction with the R45, turn right and continue through Vredenburg to the coast.

restaurant is seafood oriented. Try the big fish platter (R230), which includes crayfish and prawns and serves up to three people.

Paternoster Hotel (☎ /fax 022-752 2703; paternosterhotel @webnet.co.za; s/d R160/320) This rough-edged, quirky country hotel, virtually on the beachfront, is a popular venue for those interested in fishing. Its fish and crayfish *braais* are famous. Warning: the bar is a feminist's nightmare.

Voorstrandt Restaurant (☎ 022-752 2038; Strand loperweg; mains R40-95) You can hop from this designer red-and-green painted beach shack right on to the sand. Specialising in seafood, this is also an excellent spot to watch the sunset over a beer.

Directory

Directory

TRANSPORT

AIR

There are many direct international flights into Cape Town although sometimes you'll have to change planes at Johannesburg. Useful online ticket sellers include the following:

Cheapflights (www.cheap-flights.co.uk) – with links to online travel agents in the UK.

Flight Centre (www.flightcentre.com)

STA Travel (www.statravel.com)

Travel.com.au (www.travel.com.au) – bookings for travel out of and around Australia.

Zuji (www.zuji.com)

Airlines

Air Mauritius (Map pp200–2; ☎ 421 6294; 11th floor, Strand Towers, 66 Strand St, City Bowl)

Air Namibia (Map pp196–7; ☎ 936 2755; Cape Town International Airport)

British Airways (Map pp196–7; ☎ 934 0292; Cape Town International Airport)

KLM (Map pp198–9; ☎ 082 234 5747; Slade House, Boundary Terraces, 1 Mariendahl Lane, Newlands)

Lufthansa (Map pp200–2; ☎ 086 126 6554; 9th floor, Picbel Arcade, 58 Strand St, City Bowl)

Malaysia Airlines (Map pp200–2; ☎ 419 8010; fax 419 7017; 8th floor, Safmarine House, 22 Riebeeck St, City Bowl)

SAA (Map pp196–7; ☎ 936 1111; Cape Town International Airport)

Singapore Airlines (Map pp198–9; ☎ 674 0601; 3rd floor, Sanclaire, 21 Dreyer St, Claremont)

Virgin Atlantic (Map pp196–7; ☎ 683 2221; Cape Town International Airport)

Airport

Cape Town International Airport (Map pp196–7; ☎ 934 0407) is 20km east of the city centre, approximately 20 minutes' drive depending on traffic. Note that there is no petrol station at the airport, so if you're returning a rental car to the airport, refuel before you get there.

Several companies offer a shuttle service between the airport and the city and some hostels will pick you up for free if you have a booking. **Backpacker Bus** (☎ 082 809 9185; www.backpackerbus.co.za) picks up from hostels and hotels in the city and does airport transfers for R90 per person. Non-shared taxis are expensive; expect to pay R200.

BICYCLE

The Cape Peninsula is a great place to explore by bicycle, but there are many hills, and distances can be deceptively large – it's nearly 70km from the centre to Cape Point. Unfortunately, you are not supposed to take bicycles on suburban trains.

The following places have bicycle hire:

Atlantic Tourist Information Centre (Map p207; ☎ 434 2382; 243 Main Rd, Seapoint; 24-hour hire of bicycle/scooter R85/195)

Downhill Adventures (Map p206; ☎ 422 0388; www.downhilladventures.com; Orange St, Gardens; 24-hour bicycle hire R100)

BOAT

There are very few international cruise ships that stop in Cape Town at present, but there are plans to develop a new cruise passenger terminal at Duncan Dock on the foreshore so this might change (see also p57).

Water Taxis

There is a water taxi service between the Cape Town International Convention Centre (p60) and the Cape Grace (p140) at the Waterfront. The service runs every half hour from 9am to 7pm daily and costs R20 one way.

BUS

Interstate buses arrive at Cape Town Train station (Map pp200–2) where you'll find the booking offices for the three major bus companies:

Greyhound (☎ 505 6363; www.greyhound.co.za)

Intercape Mainliner (☎ 380 4400; www.intercape.co.za)

Translux (☎ 449 3333; www.translux.co.za)

Cape Town's local Golden Arrow public bus network is reliable, if a little run down. Most services stop running early in the evening. Buses are most useful for getting along the Atlantic coast from the city centre to Hout Bay (trains service the suburbs to the east of Table Mountain). When travelling short distances, most people wait at the bus stop and take either a bus or a shared taxi, whichever arrives first.

At the main bus station, the **Golden Acre Terminal** (Map pp200–2; Grand Parade, City Bowl), you'll find a helpful **bus information kiosk** (☎ 461 4365, 080 121 2111; 🕒 8am-7pm Mon-Fri, 7am-1.30pm Sat).

Bus Tickets

Destinations and off-peak fares (applicable from 8am to 4pm) from the city include the Waterfront (R2.50), Sea Point (R2.90), Kloof Nek (R2.90), Camps Bay (R4.20) and Hout Bay (R6.70). Peak fares are about 30% higher. If you're using a particular bus regularly, it's worth buying 'clipcards', with 10 discounted trips.

CAR
Buying a Car

Cape Town is the most pleasant place in South Africa to spend the week or two that it will inevitably take to buy a car. Prices tend to be a bit higher, so it's a good place to sell, but as the market is smaller you might wait longer. Cars from around Cape Town are more likely to be rusty than those kept inland, but as one dealer told us, 'What's wrong with rust? It just means that the car is cheaper'.

DEALERS

The main congregation of used-car dealers is on Voortrekker Rd (Map pp196–7) between Maitland and Bellville. Voortrekker Rd is the R102; the dealers start around Koeberg Rd and extend east for about 10km.

Some dealers might agree to a buy-back deal – try **Wayne Motors** (Map pp200–2; ☎ 465 2222; wancars@mweb.co.za; 61 Roeland St, City Bowl). They'll guarantee a buy-back price and don't deal in rock-bottom cars.

Dealers have to make a profit, so you'll pay less if you buy privately. The weekly classified-ads paper *Cape Ads* is the best place to look, or try its website (www.capeads.com). A useful website is www.autotrader.co.za.

MAKING THE DEAL

Whoever you're buying a car from, make sure its details correspond accurately with those on the ownership (registration) papers, that there is a *current* licence disk on the windscreen and that there's police clearance on the vehicle. The police clearance department can be contacted on ☎ 945 3891. Check the owner's name against their identity document, and check the engine and chassis numbers. Consider getting the car tested by an independent garage: try **Same Garage** (Map p207; ☎ 434 1058; 309 Main Rd, Sea Point). A full test can cost up to R500; less detailed tests are around R200.

Cheap cars are often sold without a roadworthy certificate. This certificate is required when you pay tax for a licence disk, and register the change-of-ownership form. 'Roadworthies' used to be difficult to get but some private garages are allowed to issue them; some will overlook minor faults. A roadworthy costs R220.

There seem to be very few quality used cars at low prices; a good car costs about R25,000. You will be lucky to find a decent vehicle for much less than R15,000 (anything cheaper than R8000 is definitely a gamble).

You might be thinking of getting a 4WD for a trans-Africa trip – Series 1, 2 and 3 Land Rovers cost anything in the region of R15,000 to R40,000 depending on their condition. A recommended contact in Cape Town is **Graham Duncan Smith** (☎ 797 3048), a Land Rover expert who has helped people buy these 4WDs in the past; he charges a consultation fee of R100, and R165 per hour for engineering work.

PAPERWORK

To register your newly purchased car, present yourself along with the roadworthy, a current licence disk, an accurate ownership certificate, a completed change-of-ownership form (signed by the seller), a clear photocopy of your ID (passport) along with the original, and your money to the City Treasurer's Department, **Motor Vehicle Registration Division** (Map pp200-2; ☎ 400 2385-9; Civic Centre, Foreshore; 🕒 8am-2pm Mon-Fri). Call ahead to check how much cash you'll need, but it will be under R300.

Insurance for third-party damages and damage to or loss of your vehicle is a very good idea as repairs are horrendously expensive. It's easy enough to take out a year's insurance but most travellers don't want that much. Unfortunately, if you want to buy insurance by the month it is surprisingly difficult to find an insurance company to take your money; it's even more difficult if you don't have a permanent address or a local bank account. You might be able to negotiate paying for a year's worth of insurance then getting a pro-rata refund when you sell the car, but get an agreement in writing, not just a vague promise. One recommended insurance agent is **African Independent Brokers** (☎ 086 000 1002).

Membership of the AA is highly recommended. It has an efficient vehicle breakdown service and a good supply of maps and information. (The important things to get are the window stickers you're given for breakdown service.) The joining fee is waived for members of many foreign motoring associations, so bring your membership details from home.

Driving & Parking

Driving in Cape Town is on the whole a pleasure. There's an excellent road and freeway system that, outside the morning and early-evening rush hours, carries surprisingly little traffic. The only downside is getting used to the sometimes erratic breaking of road rules by fellow drivers.

Road signs alternate between Afrikaans and English. You'll soon learn, for example, that Linkerbaan isn't the name of a town – it means 'left lane'.

Petrol stations are often open 24 hours; there's a useful one in the city on the corner of Annandale Rd and Hatfield St (Map p206) with a Woolworths convenience store attached. Petrol costs around R4.10 per litre, depending on the octane level you choose. Not all petrol stations accept credit cards and of those that do some will charge you a fee, typically 10%, to do so. An attendant will always fill up your tank for you, clean your windows and ask if the oil or water needs checking – you should tip them 10% for the service.

Parking on the street in the city centre has now been systemised. Council-employed parking attendants will provide you with a pre-paid ADO card with which to pay charges. These rechargeable cards cost R17 and each R3 unit covers 30 minutes of parking. The attendants will sell you a card and show you how to use it with the parking meter, which will be nearby. Often within the city centre there will be a one-hour limit on parking in a particular spot. This system is also in use in other parts of Cape Town. Otherwise you'll almost always find someone on the street to tip a small amount to (say R5) in exchange for looking after your car – and it's certainly a good idea to pay the street guys when parking anywhere at night.

Hire

Major local and international car hire companies in Cape Town include:

Avis (Map pp200–2; ☎ 086 102 1111; 123 Strand St, City Bowl)

Budget (Map pp200–2; ☎ 086 001 6622; 120 Strand St, City Bowl)

Imperial (Map pp200–2; ☎ 086 113 1000; cnr Loop & Strand Sts, City Bowl)

Smaller, cheaper companies come and go; you'll find plenty of brochures for them at Cape Town Tourism and all the hostels. The deals may look tempting, but read the small print (R99 a day is a rate that is seldom, if ever, available).

If you hire a 'category B' car (usually a smallish Japanese car such as a Toyota Corolla with a 1.6L motor, manual transmission and air con) for five days with at least 200 free kilometres per day, and collision and theft insurance, you'll pay in the region of R300 per day with the larger companies and from about R250 with the smaller companies. Many backpacker hostels can arrange better deals from around R200 per day or less.

If you're not looking for anything fancy try the **Happy Beetle Co** (☎ 426 4170; info@the happybeetleco.com) which rents out 1970s VW Beetles for R100 per day for up to 14 days and then R85 per day thereafter. It also has a few Vespa scooters for R125 per day.

South Africa is a big country but, unless you are a travel writer on a tight schedule, you probably don't need to pay higher rates for unlimited kilometres. For meandering around, 400km a day should be more than enough, and if you plan to stop for a day here and there, 200km a day might be sufficient.

However, if you're renting with an international company and you book through the branch in your home country, you'll probably get unlimited kilometres at no extra cost. At peak times in South Africa (mainly summer), even your local branch might tell you that unlimited-kilometre deals aren't available. Your travel agency might be able to get around this.

When you're getting quotes make sure that they include value-added tax (VAT), as that 14% slug makes a big difference.

One problem with nearly all car-rental deals is the excess: the amount you are liable for before the insurance takes over. Even with a small car you can be liable for up to R5000 (although there's usually the choice of lowering or cancelling the excess for a higher insurance premium). A few companies offer 100% damage and theft insurance at a more expensive rate. You may be charged extra if you nominate more than one driver. If a non-nominated driver has an accident, then you won't be covered by insurance. Always make sure you read the contract carefully before you sign.

Toll Roads

It costs R20 to drive along Chapman's Peak Drive (p69).

MOTORCYCLE RENTAL

The following places rent motorcycles:

Harley-Davidson Cape Town (Map pp200–2; ☎ 424 3990; www.harley-davidson-capetown.com; 45 Buitengracht St, City Bowl; ☺ 9am-5pm Mon-Sat). Rents a Harley 1340cc Big Twins or an MG-B convertible sports car for R1150 for 24 hours.

Le Cap Motorcycle Hire (Map p206; ☎ 423 0823; www.lecapmotorcyclehire.co.za; 45 New Church St, Tamboerskloof; motorcycle hire from R200; ☺ 9am-5pm Mon-Fri, 10am-1pm Sat)

RIKKI

Tiny open vans, called Rikkis, provide Asian-style transport in the City Bowl and nearby areas for low prices. They operate from 7am to 7pm Monday to Friday, and 7am to 2pm Saturday. They can be booked (☎ 423 4888) or hailed on the street and travel as far afield as Camps Bay and Observatory. A single-person trip from the main train station to Tamboerskloof costs R15; to Camps Bay is R25. A Rikki from the City Bowl to Kirstenbosch Botanical Gardens costs R70 for the first four people and R10 for each extra person. Rikkis also operate out of Simon's Town (☎ 786 2136); they meet all trains to Simon's Town and go to Boulders.

Although cheap and fun, Rikkis may not be the quickest way to get around, as there is usually a certain amount of meandering as passengers are dropped off, and they are notoriously slow to turn up to a booking.

TAXI

It's worth considering taking a non-shared taxi late at night or if you're in a group, but they're expensive (about R10 per kilometre). There is a taxi rank at the Adderley St end of the Grand Parade in the city, or call **Marine Taxi** (☎ 434 0434) or **Unicab Taxis** (☎ 447 4402).

Shared Taxi

Shared taxis cover most of the city with an informal network of routes. They're a cheap and efficient way of getting around. Useful routes are from Adderley St, opposite the Golden Acre Centre, to Sea Point along Main Rd (R2.50) and up Long St to Kloof Nek (R2).

The main rank is on the upper deck of the main train station (Map pp200–2) and is accessible from a walkway in the Golden Acre Centre or from stairways on Strand St. It's well organised, and finding the right rank is easy. Anywhere else, you just hail shared taxis from the side of the road. There's no way of telling which route a shared taxi will be taking except by asking the driver.

TRAIN

Metro commuter trains are a handy way to get around, although services have been cut back and there are few (or no) trains after 6pm on weekdays and after noon on Saturday. For information contact **Cape Metro Rail** (☎ 0800 656 463; www.capemetrorail.co.za).

Metro trains have first- and economy-class carriages only. The difference in price and comfort is negligible, although you'll find the first-class compartments to be safer on the whole.

The most important line for visitors is the Simon's Town line, which runs through Observatory and around the back of Table Mountain through upper-income white suburbs such as Rosebank, on to Muizenberg and the False Bay coast. These trains run at least every hour from around 5am to 7.30pm Monday to Friday (to 6pm on Saturday), and from 7.30pm to 6.30pm on Sunday. (Rikkis meet all trains and go to Boulders.) On some of these trains you'll find Biggsy's, a restaurant carriage and rolling wine bar. There's a small extra charge to use it.

Metro trains run some way out of Cape Town, to Strand on the eastern side of False Bay, and into the Winelands to Stellenbosch and Paarl. They are the cheapest and easiest means of transport to these areas; security is best at peak times.

Some economy/first-class fares include Observatory (R4.2/5.50), Muizenberg (R5.50/8.50), Simon's Town (R7.30/12), Paarl (R8.50/14.50) and Stellenbosch (R7.50/12).

The **Spier steam train** (☎ 419 5222) runs occasional trips to the Spier wine estate and Darling.

TRAVEL AGENCIES

Africa Travel Centre (Map p206; ☎ 423 5555; www.backpackers.co.za; the Backpack, 74 New Church St, Tamboerskloof) – books all sorts of tours and activities, including day trips, hire cars and extended truck tours of Africa.

Atlantic Tourist Information Centre (Map p207; ☎ 434 2382; www.capetowntravel.co.za; 242 Main Rd, Three Anchor Bay) – gay-run tour company and travel agent.

Flight Centre (Map p206; ☎ 461 8658; Gardens Centre, Mill St, Gardens)

Rennies Travel (Map pp200–2; ☎ 423 7154; 101 St George's Mall, City Bowl) – handles international and domestic bookings and is the agent for Thomas Cook travellers cheques. It can arrange visas for neighbouring countries for a moderate charge. There are also branches at Sea Point (Map p207; ☎ 439 7529; 182 Main Rd, Sea Point) and the Waterfront (Map pp203–5; ☎ 418 3744).

STA Travel (Map pp200–2; ☎ 418 6570; 31 Riebeeck St, City Bowl)

Wanderwomen (☎ 082 298 2085; www.wanderwomen .co.za) – travel agent and tour company run by women.

PRACTICALITIES

ACCOMMODATION

Accommodation listings in the Sleeping chapter (p133) are ordered by neighbourhood, then listed in alphabetical order with mid-range and top-end options, followed by 'cheap sleeps'. The average double room with bathroom generally costs around R600 including breakfast; prices are up to 50% lower from May to October, during Cape Town's winter season.

Cape Town Tourism (p177) runs an accommodation booking service and sometimes has special deals. Like any agency, it only recommends its members. You can also enquire with them about long-term rental deals, or you can check out what's available on the Web sites listed below.

Online Booking

There are many online booking services that cover Cape Town. Because most charge listings fees, the cheapest places usually aren't included.

www.bnb.co.za – a bed 'n' breakfast organisation with a number of members around the Cape Peninsula.

www.bookaholiday.co.za – for Cape Town and the Garden Route.

Lighting Up?

Most mid-range and top-end hotels in Cape Town have non-smoking rooms, and some even have non-smoking floors. Most B&Bs and backpackers are also non-smoking, at least in the bedrooms, although some provide a smoking area. Restaurants throughout the country have non-smoking sections.

www.hostelafrica.com – also takes Baz Bus bookings.

www.leisurestay.co.za – upmarket B&Bs and lodges.

www.portfoliocollection.com – for upmarket B&Bs, private game reserve lodges and boutique hotels.

www.wheretostay.co.za – covers most of the country, and also includes disabled-friendly listings.

www.accommodationshop.co.za – Sea Point-based agency specialising in long-term rentals.

BUSINESS

Cape Town is one of South Africa's major business centres. Top-end and many higher mid-range hotels provide business facilities, including conference rooms, private office space and secretarial services. To find out more about business opportunities contact the **Cape Town Regional Chamber of Commerce and Industry** (☎ 402 4300; www.caperegionalchamber.co.za; Cape Chamber House, 19 Louis Gradner St, Foreshore; 🕐 8.30am-4.45pm Mon-Fri) or the **city council** (www.capetown.gov.za).

Hours

Banking hours vary but are usually from 9am to 3.30pm Monday to Friday. Many branches also open from 8.30am to 11am Saturday. Post offices are usually open from 8.30am to 4.30pm Monday to Friday and 8am to noon Saturday.

Most shops are open from 8.30am to 5pm Monday to Friday and on Saturday morning. At major shopping centres such as the Waterfront, Canal Walk and Cavendish Square (p129) shops are open daily and for longer hours.

Cafés generally open from 7.30am to around 5pm daily. A few places (more usually in the City Bowl) are closed on Sunday or occasionally Monday. Restaurants open for lunch from 11.30am to 3pm, with dinner usually kicking off around 7pm and last orders at 10pm.

CHILDREN

Cape Town, with its fun family attractions such as the Two Oceans Aquarium and the Ratanga Junction amusement park, is a great place to bring the kids. South Africans tend to be family oriented, so most places cope with childrens' needs. 'Family' restaurants, such as the Spur chain, offer children's portions, as do some of the more upmarket places.

Many of the sights and attractions of interest to parents are also entertaining to kids. The Table Mountain cableway, the attractions at the Waterfront (especially the seals, which can usually be seen at Bertie's Landing), and Cape

Point, with its baboons and other animals, delight kids. The South African Museum has plenty to offer the younger visitor, including special shows at the Planetarium.

At the beach you'll have to watch out for rough surf, but there are some quiet rockpools as well as some sheltered coves. The Sea Point Pavilion has a great family swimming pool that is significantly warmer than the surrounding ocean. For our pick of the best children's entertainment see p78.

For tips on keeping children (and parents) happy on the road, check out Lonely Planet's *Travel with Children* by Cathy Lanigan.

Baby-Sitting

The following agencies can arrange child minders (from R30 per hour for a minimum of three hours, excluding transport expenses); you'll be charged more (R55 per hour) if you're staying in a five-star hotel:

Childminders (☎ 788 6788)

Super Sitters (☎ 439 4985)

CLIMATE

The weather is not really a critical factor in deciding when to visit Cape Town. Great extremes of temperature are unknown, although it can be relatively cold and wet for a few months in winter.

One of the Cape's most characteristic phenomena is the famous Cape doctor, a south-easterly wind that buffets the Cape and lays Table Mountain's famous 'tablecloth' (a layer of cloud that covers the City Bowl). It can be a welcome breeze in summer, but it can also be a wild gale, particularly in spring. When it really blows you know you're clinging to a peninsula at the southern end of Africa, and there's nothing between you and Antarctica.

In winter, between June and August, temperatures range from 7°C to 18°C with pleasant, sunny days scattered between the gloomy ones. From September to November the weather is unpredictable, with anything

from bright warm days to howling southeasterly storms and winds of up to 120km/h. (The wildflowers are at their best during August and September.) December to March can be very hot, although the average maximum temperature is only 26°C and the Cape doctor generally keeps things bearable. From March to April, and to a lesser extent in May, the weather remains good and the wind is at its most gentle.

For hourly updates on the weather, check www.weathersa.co.za.

CUSTOMS

South Africa, Botswana, Namibia, Swaziland and Lesotho are members of the South African Customs Union, which means that their internal borders are effectively open from a customs point of view. When you enter the union, however, there are the usual duty-free restrictions: you're only allowed to bring in 1L of spirits, 2L of wine and 400 cigarettes. Motor vehicles must be covered by a carnet. For more information, contact the **Department of Customs & Excise** (☎ 012-28 4308) in Pretoria.

DISABLED TRAVELLERS

People with limited mobility will not have an easy time in Cape Town. Special facilities are few and most wheelchair users will find travel easier with an able-bodied companion. The sight- or hearing-impaired traveller should have fewer problems.

There is some good news: an increasing number of places to stay have ramps and wheelchair-friendly bathrooms. There are a number of operators offering car hire, and assistance is usually available on regional flights.

Organisations

Some useful sources of information include the following:

National Council for Persons with Physical Disabilities in South Africa (☎ 011-726 8040; www.ncppdsa.co.za) – a helpful initial contact.

Access-Able Travel Source (www.access-able.com) – has lists of tour operators catering for travellers with disabilities.

Carpe Diem Tours (☎ /fax 027-217 1125) – specialises in tours for the physically challenged and the elderly in Western Cape and Northern Cape.

Central Reservations (www.centralres.co.za/disabled.html) – has a small listing of disabled-friendly accommodation.

Eco-Access (www.eco-access.org) – has an overview of disabled-related initiatives in South Africa.

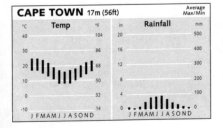

CAPE TOWN	17m (56ft)			Average Max/Min
°C	Temp	°F	in	Rainfall	mm

Linx Africa (www.linx.co.za/trails/lists/disalist.html) – for province-by-province listings of disabled-friendly trails.

South African Tourism (www.southafrica.net) – links on this Web site focus on disabled facilities in national parks.

DISCOUNT CARDS

You'll save a few rand at Hostelling International South Africa hostels and affiliated hostels with a Hostelling International (HI) card.

There's no real advantage in having a student card here since student discounts apply only to South African nationals.

ELECTRICITY

The electricity system is 220/230 volts AC at 50 cycles per second. Appliances rated at 240 volts AC will work. Plugs have three large round pins. Adaptors aren't that easy to find; we found one at the national camping supply and clothing store Cape Union Mart (p130). If your appliance doesn't have a removable lead, you can always buy a South African plug and have it wired on (assuming that the appliance takes AC and is rated at the correct voltage).

EMBASSIES & CONSULATES

Most foreign embassies are based in Johannesburg (Jo'burg), but a few countries also maintain a consulate in Cape Town. All of the following are consulates, except Italy, which is also an embassy.

Botswana (Map pp200–2; ☎ 421 1045; 5th floor, Southern Life Centre, 8 Riebeeck St, City Bowl)

Canada (Map pp200–2; ☎ 423 5240; 19th floor, Reserve Bank Bldg, 60 St George's Mall, City Bowl)

France (Map p206; ☎ 423 1575; 2 Dean St, Gardens)

Germany (Map p206; ☎ 424 2410; 74 Queen Victoria St, Gardens)

Italy (Map p206; ☎ 424 1256; 2 Grey's Pass, Queen Victoria St, Gardens)

Mozambique (Map pp200–2; ☎ 426 2944; Pinnacle Bldg, 8 Burg St, City Bowl)

UK (Map pp200–2; ☎ 405 2400; Southern Life Centre, 8 Riebeeck St, City Bowl)

USA (Map pp200–2; ☎ 421 4280; Broadway Centre, Heerengracht, City Bowl)

EMERGENCIES

In an emergency call ☎ 107; ☎ 112 if using a cell phone. Other useful phone numbers include the following:

Ambulance (☎ 10177)

Automobile Association (AA) emergency rescue (☎ 082 16111)

Fire brigade (☎ 535 1100)

Mountain Rescue Services (☎ 948 9900)

Police (☎ 10111)

Rape Crisis Centre (☎ 447 1467)

Sea Rescue (☎ 405 3500)

GAY & LESBIAN TRAVELLERS

Cape Town is Africa's premier gay destination. The Waterkant (Map pp203–5), the city's self-proclaimed gay village, is a grid of streets that will take you 10 minutes to wander around. There are also small gay scenes in Sea Point (Map p207) and around the northern end of Long St (Map pp200–2). The beaches to head for are Clifton No 3 (Map pp198–9), Camps Bay (Map p208) and Sandy Bay (Map pp198–9); the clothing-optional stretch of sand is discreetly located near Llandudno Bay. There are frequent parties and festivals including the Out in Africa gay and lesbian film festival (p10) and the Mother City Queer Project dance event every December (p103). There's even a gay dialect, see p15.

Further afield, consider visiting Darling (p153), which is home to Evita se Peron, the cabaret theatre of Pieter-Dirk Uys. Heading south down the coast there are a couple of gay guesthouses around Hermanus (p156). Further afield, Knysna, about 500km east of Cape Town, has made its mark as the gayest resort town on South Africa's Garden Route. It hosts the annual Pink Loerie Carnival (www.gaymay.co.za), four huge days of gay-and-lesbian partying, shows and a street parade. (For detailed information on Knysna and the Garden Route, see Lonely Planet's *South Africa, Lesotho & Swaziland*).

The useful *Pink Map* is updated annually and available from Cape Town Tourism. Like the similarly ubiquitous *Cape Gay Guide* booklet, it's free but contains only information on businesses that have paid for the advertising. The local listings magazine *Cape Etc* has details of gay events. The website www.gaynetcapetown.co.za has plenty of information specific to the city; for general information on the gay scene across South Africa check www.gaysouthafrica.org.za.

On the HIV/AIDS and counselling front, Cape Town's **Triangle Project** (☎ 448 3812; triangle@icon.co.za; 41 Salt River Rd, Salt River) is one of the leading support organisations, it offers legal advice and education programmes.

AIDS in Cape Town

South Africa is facing a health crisis in the form of HIV/AIDS. It's estimated that 1800 people catch HIV every day. Roughly 11% of the population is HIV positive and in Khayelitsha over a quarter of pregnant women attending antenatal classes test positive. It's predicted that there will be upwards of 2.5 million AIDS orphans in South Africa by 2010. After years of inaction the government is about to roll out one of the largest public health programmes in the world in relation to HIV – supplying 1.4 million people with medicine. A clinic in Langa was the first to supply HIV medicine as part of this programme in January 2004.

What can you do about this? First is to make sure you protect yourself while having sex; there's no excuse for not using a condom. Also you can buy goods from producers such as Wola Nani and Monkeybiz (p128) whose projects help support HIV positive women in the townships. If you want to help further, contact organisations such as **Nazareth House** (Map p206; ☎ 461 1635; www.nazhouse.org.za; 1 Derry St, Vredehoek) which provides a refuge for orphan babies and those that have HIV or have been abandoned or abused; and the **Treatment Action Campaign** (☎ 788 3507; www.tac.co.za) run by the antiapartheid activist Zachie Achmat, an HIV-positive man who has refused to take anti-retroviral medicine until it is free to all under the national health system. There is a **National AIDS Helpline** (☎ 0800 012 322; www.aidshelpline.org.za).

Cape Town's lesbian scene is pretty low-profile. One leading light is Michelle Petring who runs the shop **Rainbow Trade** (☎ 083 597 0868; www.rainbowtrade.co.za; 29A Somerset Rd, Waterkant), specialising in gay-pride goods and souvenirs. Also see the Entertainment chapter (p97) for details of regular lesbian parties at Cohibar and the Valve.

HEALTH

With the exception of AIDS (above), you need not worry about health issues when visiting Cape Town. The city's health services are generally excellent (for details of hospitals and clinics see p174). For more information on health in South Africa, read Lonely Planet's *Healthy Travel Africa* and *South Africa, Lesotho & Swaziland*.

HOLIDAYS

On public holidays government departments, banks, offices, post offices and some museums are closed. Public holidays in South Africa include the following:

New Year's Day 1 January

Easter (Good Friday/Easter Monday) March/April

Human Rights Day 21 March

Family Day 17 April

Constitution or Freedom Day 27 April

Workers' Day 1 May

Youth Day 16 June

Women's Day 9 August

Heritage Day 24 September

Day of Reconciliation 16 December

Christmas Day 25 December

Boxing Day (Day of Goodwill) 26 December

School Holidays

Cape Town experiences a big influx of domestic tourists in the school holidays and accommodation is at a premium. The dates differ slightly from year to year but are roughly mid-April (two weeks), late June to mid-July (three weeks), late September to early October (about one week) and early December to early February (about eight weeks).

INSURANCE

A travel-insurance policy to cover theft, loss and medical problems is a good idea. Although there are excellent private hospitals in South Africa, the public health system is underfunded and overcrowded, and is not free. Services such as ambulances are often run by private enterprise and are expensive. There is a wide variety of policies available, so check the small print. Some policies exclude 'dangerous activities', which can include scuba diving, motorcycling and even trekking. If such activities are on your agenda you don't want such a policy. A locally acquired motorcycle licence is not valid under some policies.

INTERNET ACCESS

Cape Town is one of the most wired cities in Africa. Most hotels and hostels have Internet facilities and in the city there are several handy Internet cafés, including one at Cape Town Tourism; it charges R15/48 for 15 minutes/one hour. Cheaper and quieter is the National Library in the Company's Gardens which charges R10 per 30 minutes. Internet cafés line Long St and Main Rd at Sea Point (Map p207) where you'll find some of Cape Town 's cheapest access rates, as low as R10 per hour. Try **Cafe Erté** (Map p207; ☎ 434 6624; 265A Main Rd, Sea Point), which is also a gay-friendly bar. At the Waterfront, Cape Town Tourism again has Internet access at its office, and there's also **Odyssey Internet** (Map pp203–5; ☎ 418 7289) above Cinema Nouveau in the Victoria Wharf shopping mall.

LEGAL MATTERS

The legal drinking age is 18 years, the same for driving. Breath testing for alcohol exists but given the lack of police resources and the high blood-alcohol level permitted (0.08%) drunk drivers remain a danger. It's highly unlikely that the police will bother you for petty breaches of the law, such as breaking the speed limit. This might sound like a pleasant state of affairs, but after you've encountered a few dangerous drivers strict cops seem more attractive. If your skin colour isn't white, you might receive less than courteous treatment if, say, you're pulled over for a traffic violation. A Western passport should fix things quickly, and make sure you have your driving licence to hand too.

The importation and use of illegal drugs is prohibited and punishable with imprisonment.

The age of consent for straight sex is 16 years, for homosexual sex 19 years.

MAPS

If you're staying for more than a week or so, and have a car, consider buying Map Studio's *Cape Town Streetfinder*. Lonely Planet's *Cape Town City Map* is useful if you plan to stick to the city centre only; it includes an index of street names. Otherwise Cape Town Tourism produces free maps that will serve most short-term visitors' needs.

MEDICAL SERVICES

Medical services are of a high standard in Cape Town. In an emergency contact the police (☎ 10111) to get directions to the nearest hospital. Many doctors make house calls; they're listed under 'Medical' in the phone book and hotels and most other places to stay can arrange a visit.

Groote Schuur Hospital (Map p208; ☎ 404 9111; Main Rd, Observatory) – in an emergency, you can go directly to its casualty department. As every local will proudly tell you while driving past on the N2, this is where in 1967 the late Dr Christiaan Barnard made the world's first successful heart transplant.

Christian Barnard Memorial Hospital (Map pp200–2; ☎ 480 6111; 181 Longmarket St, City Bowl) – the best private hospital; reception is on the 8th floor.

Clinics

SAA-Netcare Travel Clinic (Map pp200–2; ☎ 419 3172; Room 314, Fountain Medical Centre, Adderley St, City Bowl; ☺ 8am-5pm Mon-Fri, 9am-1pm Sat) – for vaccinations and travel health.

MONEY

The unit of currency is the rand (R), which is divided into 100 cents. The coins are one, two, five, 10, 20 and 50 cents, and R1, R2 and R5. The notes are R10, R20, R50, R100 and R200. The R200 note looks a lot like the R20 note, so check them carefully before handing them over. There have been forgeries of the R200 note; some businesses are reluctant to accept them. Rands are sometimes referred to as bucks.

ATMs

If your card belongs to the worldwide Cirrus network you should have no problem using ATMS in Cape Town. However, it pays to follow some basic procedures to ensure safety (opposite).

Changing Money

Rennies Travel (p169), a large chain of travel agencies, is the Thomas Cook agent. Rennies Travel also changes other brands of travellers cheques; its rates are good and it doesn't charge fees for changing travellers cheques (but does for cash).

There are American Express (AmEx) offices in Cape Town; these, like foreign-exchange bureaus, don't charge commission but will give you a lower rate of exchange than you'll generally get from a bank. AmEx has offices on Thibault Square at the end of St George's Mall (Map pp200–2; ☎ 408 9700) and outside the arcade at the Victoria & Alfred Hotel at the Waterfront (Map pp203–5; ☎ 419 3917; ☺ 10am-5pm daily). There's also an exchange office at Cape Town Tourism (Map pp200–2).

Most banks change travellers cheques in major currencies, with various commissions. First National Bank is an AmEx agent and its branches are supposed to change AmEx travellers cheques without charging commission, but some don't seem to know this and you might have to pay a transaction fee anyway. Keep at least some of your receipts when exchanging money because you'll need to reconvert leftover rand when you leave.

Directory – Practicalities

Beating the ATM Scams

If you are a victim of crime in Cape Town, it's most likely to occur at an automatic teller machine (ATM). There are dozens of scams that involve stealing your cash, your card or your personal identification number (PIN) – usually all three. Thieves are almost always well-dressed and well-mannered men.

The ATM scam you're most likely to encounter involves the thief tampering with the machine so your card becomes jammed. By the time you realise this you've entered your PIN. The thief will have seen this, and when you go inside to report that your card has been swallowed, he will take the card and leave you several thousand rand shorter. We make no guarantees, but if you follow the rules listed here you stand a better chance of avoiding this and other scams.

- Avoid ATMs at night and in secluded places. Rows of machines in shopping malls are usually the safest.
- Most ATMs have security guards. If there's no guard around when you're withdrawing cash, watch your back, or get someone else to watch it for you.
- Watch carefully the people using the ATM ahead of you. If they look suspicious, go to another machine.
- Use ATMs during banking hours and if possible take a friend. If your card is jammed in a machine then one person stays at the ATM and the other seeks assistance from the bank.
- When you put your card into the ATM press cancel immediately. If the card is returned then you know there is no blockage in the machine and it should be safe to proceed.
- Don't hesitate to be rude in refusing any offers of help to complete your transaction. If someone does offer, end your transaction immediately and find another machine.
- Carry your bank's emergency phone number, and if you do lose your card report it immediately.

Credit Cards

Credit cards, especially MasterCard and Visa, are widely accepted. Nedbank is an official Visa agent and Standard Bank is a MasterCard agent – both have branches across the country. For lost or stolen cards contact:

American Express (☎ 0860 003 768)

Diners Club (☎ 686 1990)

MasterCard (☎ 0800 990 418)

Visa International (☎ 0800 990 475)

NEWSPAPERS & MAGAZINES

Cape Town's two newspapers – the *Cape Times* (morning) and the *Cape Argus* (afternoon) – print practically the same news. The national daily *This Day* (www.thisdaysa.co.za) is a better read all round. Also worth a look is the tabloid *Sowetan*, the biggest-selling paper in the country, catering largely to a poorly educated audience but with a more balanced political and social outlook than most of the major white papers. The weekly *Mail & Guardian*, published Friday, includes excellent investigative and opinion pieces and a good arts review supplement. The *Independent on Sunday* is also good.

Cape Etc is a decent bi-monthly arts and listings magazine dedicated to what's going on around town. Pick up a copy of the *Big Issue*, the weekly magazine that helps provide an income for the homeless – it's a good read and a worthy cause. See also p17 for other national magazine recommendations.

PHARMACIES

Glengariff Pharmacy (Map p207; ☎ 434 1685; cnr Main Rd & Glengariff St, Sea Point; 8am-11pm Mon-Sat, 9am-11pm Sun)

Lite Kem Pharmacy (Map pp200–2; ☎ 461 8040; 24 Darling St, City Bowl; ☾ 8am-11pm daily)

POST

Most post offices are open from 8.30am to 4.30pm Monday to Friday and 8am to noon Saturday. Sending aerograms, letters up to 50g and standard-size postcards to Europe or the US costs R3.30. Internal delivery can be very slow and international delivery isn't exactly lightning-fast. If you ask someone in South Africa to mail you something, even a letter, emphasise that you need it sent by airmail, otherwise it will probably be sent by sea mail and could take months to reach you. If you're mailing anything of value consider using one of the private mail services; **Postnet** has offices across the city; you'll find them in all the major shopping malls.

The **General Post Office** (Map pp200–2; ☎ 464 1700; Parliament St, City Bowl) is upstairs, above the new shopping centre, and it has a poste restante counter.

RADIO

Most SABC radio stations (AM and FM) are broadcast nationally and play dreary music and stodgy chat, although the hour-long current affairs programmes are good. To check out the schedules go to www.sabc.co.za. Cape Town's talk radio station Cape Talk 567MW is a quick way to tune into local views and opinions on a variety of subjects. Other local radio stations include Fine Music Radio (101.3FM), KFM (94.5FM), P4 (104.9FM) and GHFM (which is to be found between 94 and 97FM).

SAFETY

Cape Town remains one of the most relaxed cities in Africa, which can instil a false sense of security. People who have travelled overland from Cairo without a single mishap or theft have been known to be cleaned out in Cape Town – generally when doing something stupid like leaving their gear on a beach while they go swimming.

Paranoia is not required, but common sense is. There is tremendous poverty on the peninsula and the 'informal redistribution of wealth' is reasonably common. The townships on the Cape Flats have an appalling crime rate and unless you have a trustworthy guide or are on a tour they are off-limits.

Care should be taken in Sea Point and quiet areas of the city centre, such as the Company's Gardens, at night. Walking to or from the Waterfront is not recommended at night either and you should take care during the day, sticking to the main route along the foreshore. The rest of Cape Town is reasonably safe. As always, listen to local advice. There is safety in numbers.

Swimming at any of the Cape beaches is potentially hazardous, especially for those inexperienced in surf. Check for warning signs about rips and rocks and only swim in patrolled areas.

The mountains in the middle of the city are no less dangerous just because they are in the city. Weather conditions can change rapidly, so warm clothing, water and a good map and compass are always necessary: see p64.

Another hazard of the mountains is ticks, which can get on to you when you brush past vegetation.

TAXES & REFUNDS

South Africa has a value-added tax (VAT) of 14% but foreign visitors can reclaim some of their VAT expenses on departure. This applies only to goods that you are taking out of the country; you can't claim back the VAT you've paid on food or car rental, for example. Also, the goods have to have been bought at a shop participating in the VAT foreign tourist sales scheme.

To make a claim, you need your tax invoice. This is usually the receipt, but make sure that it includes the following:

- the words 'tax invoice'
- the seller's VAT registration number
- the seller's name and address
- a description of the goods purchased
- the cost of the goods and the amount of VAT charged
- a tax invoice number
- the date of the transaction

For purchases over R2000, your name and address and the quantity of goods must also appear on the invoice. All invoices must be originals, not photocopies. The total value of the goods claimed for must exceed R250.

At the point of your departure, you will have to show the goods to a customs inspector. At airports, make sure you have the goods checked by the inspector before you check in your luggage. After you've gone through immigration, you make the claim and pick up your refund cheque – at Cape Town airport you can then cash it immediately at the currency exchange office (usually in rand or US dollars).

To save time, there's a VAT desk in the **Clock Tower Centre** (Map pp203–5; ☎ 405 4500; ⏰ 9am-8.30pm daily) at the Waterfront, which can take care of the paperwork, or Cape Town Tourism in the City Bowl (p177).

You can also make your claim at the international airports in Jo'burg, Cape Town and Durban, at the Beitbridge (Zimbabwe) and Komatipoort (Mozambique) border crossings and at major harbours.

TELEPHONE

Public telephones, which can be found across the city, take coins or phonecards. Local calls cost R1 for three minutes. Expect charges for calls from hotel rooms to be outrageous – never less than double what you would pay at a public phone and often a lot more. When using a coin phone you might find that you have credit left after you've finished a call. If you want to make another call don't hang up or you'll lose the credit. Press the black button under the receiver hook.

Cardphones are even easier to find than coin phones, so it's certainly worth buying a phonecard if you're going to make more than just the odd call. Cards are available in denominations of R10, R20, R50, R100 and R200 and you can buy them at Cape Town Tourism, newsagents and general stores.

South Africa's country code is ☎ 027 and Cape Town's area code is ☎ 021, as is Stellenbosch's, Paarl's and Franschhoek's. If a number given in this book doesn't have an area code, you can assume that it is in the ☎ 021 area. Sometimes you'll come across phone numbers beginning with ☎ 0800 or ☎ 0860; these prefixes indicate a toll-free number.

Mobile Phones

The cell phone (mobile phone) network covers most of the country, and cell phone ownership is widespread. The network operates on the GSM digital system. The three major mobile networks are **Vodacom** (www.vodacom .co.za), **MTN** (www.mtn.co.za) and **Cell C** (www .cellc.co.za). Hiring a cellphone is relatively inexpensive (all three companies have desks at Cape Town Airport), but call charges average about R2.50 per minute. Some car rental firms offer deals on cellphones. An alternative is to use your own phone (check ahead that it's compatible), and insert a local prepaid or pay-as-you-go SIM card from one of the three mobile networks. These cards are readily available at malls and shops in all larger cities and towns. The main mobile phone codes are 082 (Vodacom), 083 (MTN) and 084 (Cell C).

Cellurent (☎ 418 5656; www.cellurent.co.za) offers good rates for renting a phone; they'll deliver it to wherever you are in the city and pick up from you before you leave.

TELEVISION

South African Broadcasting Corporation (SABC; www .sabc.co.za) has three generally bland TV channels and one pay TV station. There's also **e-tv** (www.etv.co.za), a privately owned free-to-air station. Its news services are marginally more international than those of the other stations. Only the cheapest places to stay won't have M-Net, a pay station that shows standard fare and some good movies. CNN is much less widely available than it was. If you're lucky you'll get BBC World. Satellite digital TV is on the way.

Programming is similar to that in any US-dominated TV market: soaps, sitcoms, chat shows and infomercials dominate. Locally made programmes include tacky game shows, some reasonable children's programmes, a few music shows, and soaps such as *Isidingo* and *E Goli*. *Yizo Yizo*, set in a school and reflecting current realities, is one of the better dramas. For good current affairs documentaries tune into *Special Assignment* on SABC 2.

TIME

South African Standard Time is two hours ahead of Greenwich Mean Time (GMT; at noon in London it's 2pm in Cape Town), seven hours ahead of USA Eastern Standard Time (at noon in New York it's 7pm in Cape Town) and eight hours behind Australian Eastern Standard Time (at noon in Sydney it's 4am in Cape Town). There is no daylight saving.

TIPPING & BARGAINING

Tipping in bars and restaurants is usual; 10% to 15% is reasonable. Staff are often paid very low wages (or even no wages). This results in overfriendly service, which can be irritating. Tipping taxi drivers, petrol-pump attendants and so on is also common.

Bargaining is not a South African habit, but you'll often find that you can lower the price of accommodation when business is slow.

TOURIST INFORMATION

Cape Town Tourism (Map pp200–2; ☎ 426 4260; www .tourismcapetown.co.za; cnr Castle & Burg Sts, City Bowl; ☉ 8am-7pm Mon-Fri, 8.30am-2pm Sat, 9am-1pm Sun Dec-Mar, 8am-6pm Mon-Fri, 8.30am-1pm Sat, 9am-1pm Sun Apr-Nov) – very impressive and busy facility with advisers who can book accommodation, tours and rental cars. Western Cape Tourism has a desk here, and you can get advice on Cape Nature Conservation parks (☎ 426 0723) and the national parks and reserves (☎ 423 8005). There's also an adviser for safari and overland tours, an Internet café, a Monkeybiz outlet and a foreign-exchange booth. There are similar facilities at the Waterfront office of Cape Town Tourism (Map pp203–5; ☎ 405 4500; Clock Tower Centre, Waterfront; ☉ 9am-9pm).

Hout Bay Tourist Information Centre (Map p210; ☎ 790 1264; 4 Andrews Rd, Hout Bay; ☉ 9am-5.30pm Mon-Fri, 9am-1pm Sat & Sun Oct-Apr, 9am-5pm Mon-Fri May-Sept)

Muizenberg Tourist Information Centre (Map p209; ☎ 788 6193; the Pavilion, Beach Rd, Muizenberg; ☉ 9am-5.30pm Mon-Fri, 9am-1pm Sat)

Simon's Town Publicity Association (Map p210; ☎ 786 2436; 111 St George's St, Simon's Town; ☉ 9am-5.30pm Nov-Mar, 9am-5pm Mon-Fri, 9am-1pm Sat & Sun Apr-Oct)

VISAS

Visitors on holiday from most Commonwealth countries (including Australia and the UK), most Western European countries, Japan and the USA don't require visas. Instead, you'll be issued with a free entry permit on arrival. These are valid for a stay of up to 90 days. However, if

177

the date of your flight out is sooner than this, the immigration officer may use it as the date of your permit expiry unless you specifically request otherwise.

If you aren't entitled to an entry permit, you'll need to get a visa (also free) before you arrive. These aren't issued at the borders, and must be obtained at a South African embassy or consulate in your own country. Allow several weeks for processing. South Africa has consular representation in most countries. The web page of the South African High Commission in London (www.southafricahouse.com) has a helpful overview of visa requirements, and listings of which nationalities require visas.

For any entry – whether you require a visa or not – you need to have at least two completely blank pages in your passport, excluding the last two pages.

You can apply for a South African visa extension or a re-entry visa at the **Department of Home Affairs** (Map pp200–2; ☎ 462 4970; 56 Barrack St; ⊗ 8am-3.15pm Mon-Fri).

The **Visa Service** (Map pp200–2; ☎ 421 7826; 9th floor, Strand Towers, 66 Strand St) can arrange visas for countries outside South Africa.

WOMEN TRAVELLERS

Cape Town is generally safe for women travellers. In most cases, you'll be met with warmth and hospitality, and may find that you receive kindness and special treatment that you wouldn't likely be shown if you were a male traveller. That said, paternalism and sexism run strong, especially away from the city centre, and these attitudes – much more than physical assault – are likely to be the main problem.

South Africa's sexual assault statistics are appalling. Yet, while there have been incidents of female travellers being raped, these cases are relatively rare. It's difficult to quantify the risk of assault – and there is a risk – but it's worth remembering that plenty of women do travel alone safely in South Africa.

Following are some tips, and a few basic precautions:

- Outside Cape Town, it's worth dressing and behaving conservatively to help minimise unwanted attention.
- Use common sense and precaution, especially at night. Don't go out alone in the evenings on foot – always take a taxi; avoid isolated areas, roadways and beaches during both day and evening hours; avoid hiking alone; and don't hitch.
- Carry a mobile phone if you're driving alone.
- Make efforts to talk with local women – white and black – about what and where is OK, and what isn't.
- Be sensible, but don't let concerns on the issue ruin your trip.

WORK

Because of high unemployment and fears about illegal immigration from the rest of Africa, there are tough penalties for employers taking on foreigners without work permits. So far this doesn't seem to have stopped foreigners getting jobs in restaurants or bars in tourist areas, but this might change. Don't expect decent pay, something like R40–60 per hour plus tips (which can be good) is usual. The best time to look for work is from October to November, before the high season starts and before university students begin holidays. For information about volunteer work, see the boxed text on p173.

Language

Language

South Africa's official languages were once English and Afrikaans but nine others have been added: Ndebele, North Sotho, South Sotho, Swati, Tsonga, Tswana, Venda, Xhosa and Zulu.

Forms, brochures and timetables are usually bilingual (English and Afrikaans) but road signs alternate. Most Afrikaans speakers also speak good English, but this is not always the case in small rural towns and among older people. However, it's not uncommon for blacks in cities to speak at least six languages – whites can usually speak two.

In the Cape Town area only three languages are prominent: Afrikaans (spoken by many whites and coloureds), English (spoken by nearly everyone) and Xhosa (spoken mainly by blacks).

AFRIKAANS

Although Afrikaans is closely associated with Afrikaners, it is also the first language of many coloureds. Ironically, it was probably first used as a common language by the polyglot coloured community of the Cape, and passed back to whites by nannies and servants. Around six million people speak the language, roughly half of whom are Afrikaners and half of whom are coloured.

Afrikaans developed from the High Dutch of the 17th century. It has abandoned the complicated grammar and incorporated vocabulary from French, English, indigenous African languages and even Asian languages (as a result of the influence of East Asian slaves). It's inventive, powerful and expressive, but it wasn't recognised as one of the country's official languages until 1925; before which it was officially a dialect of Dutch.

Pronunciation

The following pronunciation guide is not exhaustive, but it includes the more difficult of the sounds that differ from English.

a	as the 'u' in 'pup'
e	when word stress falls on **e**, it's as in 'net'; when unstressed, it's as the 'a' in 'ago'
i	when word stress falls on **i**, it's as in 'hit'; when unstressed, it's as the 'a' in 'ago'
o	as the 'o' in 'fort', but very short
u	as the 'e' in 'angel' but with lips pouted
r	a rolled 'rr' sound
aai	as the 'y' in 'why'
ae	as 'ah'
ee	as in 'deer'
ei	as the 'ay' in 'play'
oe	as the 'u' in 'put'
oë	as the 'oe' in 'doer'
ooi/oei	as the 'ooey' in 'phooey'
tj	as the 'ch' in 'chunk'

Conversation & Essentials

Hello.	Hallo.
Good morning.	Goeiemôre.
Good afternoon.	Goeiemiddag.
Good evening.	Goeienaand.
Good night.	Goeienag.
Please.	Asseblief.
Thank you.	Dankie.
Thank you very much.	Baie dankie.
Yes.	Ja.
No.	Nee.
Do you speak English?	Praat U Engels?
Do you speak Afrikaans?	Praat U Afrikaans?
I only understand a little Afrikaans.	Ek verstaan net 'n bietjie Afrikaans.
Isn't that so?	Né?
What?	Wat?
How?	Hoe?
How many/much?	Hoeveel?
Where?	Waar?
When?	Wanneer?
How are you?	Hoe gaan dit?
Good, thank you.	Goed dankie.
Pardon.	Ekskuus.
Where do you live?	Waar woon U?
What is your occupation?	Wat is U beroep?
Where are you from?	Waarvandaan kom U?

from ...	van ...
overseas	oorsee
son/boy	seun
daughter/girl	dogter
wife	vrou
husband	eggenoot
mother	ma
father	pa
sister	suster
brother	broer
uncle	oom
aunt	tante
nice/good/pleasant	lekker
bad	sleg
cheap	goedkoop
expensive	duur
emergency	nood
party	jol

Transport

travel	reis
departure	vertrek
arrival	aankoms
to	na
from	van
ticket	kaartjie
single	enkel
return	retoer

Shopping & Services

art gallery	kunsgalery
at the corner	op die hoek
avenue	laan
building	gebou
butcher	slaghuis
church	kerk
city centre	middestad
city	stad
inquiries	navrae
exit	uitgang
information	inligting
left	links
office	kantoor
pharmacy/chemist	apteek
right	regs
road	pad
room	kamer
shop	winkel
shop that sells alcohol	drankwinkel
station	stasie
street	straat
tourist bureau	toeristeburo
town	dorp
traffic light	verkeerslig

Out & About

bay	baai
beach	strand
caravan park	woonwapark
field/plain	veld
game reserve	wildtuin
hiking trail	wandelpad
little hill (usually flat-topped)	kopje/koppie
main road	hoofweg
marsh	vlei
mountain	berg
point	punt
river	rivier
road	pad
shanty town	blikkiesdorp
utility/pick-up	bakkie

Time & Days

am	vm
pm	nm
daily	daagliks
public holiday	openbare vakansiedag
today	vandag
tomorrow	môre
yesterday	gister
soon	nou-nou

Monday	Maandag (Ma)
Tuesday	Dinsdag (Di)
Wednesday	Woensdag (Wo)
Thursday	Donderdag (Do)
Friday	Vrydag (Vr)
Saturday	Saterdag (Sa)
Sunday	Sondag (So)

Numbers

1	een
2	twee
3	drie
4	vier
5	vyf
6	ses
7	sewe
8	ag
9	nege
10	tien
11	elf
12	twaalf
13	dertien
14	veertien
15	vyftien
16	sestien
17	sewentien
18	agtien
19	negentien

Language

20	twintig
21	een en twintig
30	dertig
40	veertig
50	vyftig
60	sestig
70	sewentig
80	tagtig
90	negentig
100	honderd
1000	duisend

SOUTH AFRICAN ENGLISH

English has undergone some changes during its time in South Africa. Quite a few words have changed meaning, new words have been appropriated and, thanks to the influence of Afrikaans, a distinctive accent has developed. British rather than US practice is followed in grammar and spelling. In some cases British words are preferred to their US equivalents (eg 'lift' not 'elevator', 'petrol' not 'gas'). In South African English, repetition for emphasis is common: Something that burns you is 'hot hot'; fields after the rains are 'green green'; a crammed minibus is 'full full' and so on.

The Glossary at the end of this chapter includes many colloquial South African English expressions.

XHOSA

Xhosa is the language of the Xhosa people. It's the dominant indigenous South African language in Eastern Cape province, and is also spoken by many blacks in the Cape Town area.

It's worth noting that *bawo* is a term of respect that is used when addressing an older man.

Good morning.	Molo.
Good night.	Rhonani.
Do you speak English?	Uyakwazi ukuthetha isiNgesi?
Are you well?	Uphilile namhlanje?
Yes, I am well.	Ewe, ndiphilile.
Where do you come from?	Uvela phi na?
I come from ...	Ndivela e ...
When do we arrive?	Siya kufika nini na?
The road is good.	Indlela ilungile.
The road is bad.	Indlela imbi.
I'm lost.	Ndilahlekile.
Is this the road to ...?	Yindlela eya ...?
Would you show me the way to ...?	Ungandibonisa indlela eya ...?
Is it possible to cross the river?	Ungaweleka umlambo?
How much is it?	Yimalini?

day	usuku
week	iveki
month (moon)	inyanga
north	umntla
south	umzantsi
east	empumalanga
west	entshonalanga

Glossary

ANC – African National Congress

apartheid – literally 'the state of being apart'; the old South African political system in which people were segregated according to race

AWB – Afrikaner Weerstandsbeweging (Afrikaner Resistance Movement), an extremist right-wing group of Afrikaners; it seems to be fading from the scene

Bergie – homeless person

biltong – dried meat made from virtually anything

bobotie – a traditional Malay dish; delicate curried mince with a topping of savoury egg custard, usually served on turmeric-flavoured rice

boerewors – spicy sausages, often sold like hot dogs by street vendors; essential at any braai

Bokke – affectionate name for the South African national rugby team, the Springboks

bottle store – shop selling alcohol

braai – a barbecue featuring lots of grilled meat and beer ('and a small salad for the ladies'); a South African institution, particularly among whites

bredie – a traditional Cape Malay stew of vegetables and lamb, chicken, or fish

Broederbond – a secret society open only to Protestant Afrikaner men; highly influential under National Party rule

bru/boykie/bra/china – generally a male mate

buppie – black yuppie

cafe, kaffe – in some cases, a pleasant place for a coffee; in others, a small shop selling odds and ends, plus unappetising fried food

camp site – an individual pitch on a camping ground

camping ground – an area where tents can be pitched and caravans parked

Codesa – Convention for a Democratic South Africa

coloureds – South Africans of mixed race

comma – used instead of the decimal point, eg 10,5 ('ten comma five')

cool drink – canned soft drink

dinkie – the smallest size of wine bottle

dop – alcoholic drink

dorp – a rural settlement where a road crosses a river

DP – Democratic Party

drostdy – the residence of a landdrost

dumpie – the smallest size of beer bottle

eh – pronounced to rhyme with 'hay', an all-purpose ending to sentences, even very short ones such as 'Thanks, eh'.

eish! – expression of disbelief

farm stall – small roadside shop or shelter that sells farm produce

fynbos – the vegetation of the area around Cape Town, composed of proteas, heaths and reeds; literally 'fine bush'

hanepoot – a dessert wine made from the Mediterranean grape variety known as muscat of Alexandria

hectic – can mean either fantastic or chaotic

Homelands – reserves for the black peoples of South Africa, established under apartheid and reabsorbed into South Africa after 1994; also derisively called bantustans

Howzit? – all-purpose greeting

IFP – Inkatha Freedom Party

Izzit? – rhetorical question that most closely translates as 'Really?' It could mean 'Is it?', 'Is that so?', 'Did you?', 'Are you?', 'Is he?', 'Are they?', 'Is she?', 'Are we?', 'Amazing!' etc.

jol – party (used as a verb and as a noun); also any good time: 'How was Mozambique?' 'Yah, it was a jol, man.'

just now – indeterminate future, but reasonably imminent (see 'now' and 'now-now')

kaffe – see café

karamat – the tomb of a Muslim saint

kat – Afrikaans for shit

kiff – like lekker, something that's very cool

kingklip – an excellent firm-fleshed fish, usually served fried

kloof – ravine

kloofing – adventure activity involving climbing, jumping and swimming in kloofs

koesister (or koeksuster) – doughnut –like confection

KWV – Kooperatieve Wijnbouwers Vereeniging; the cooperative formed in 1918 to control minimum prices, production areas and quota limits in the wine industry

landdrost – an official representative of the colony's governor who acted as local administrator, tax collector and magistrate

lekker – cool, fantastic, something you love

line fish – catch of the day

location – another word for township, usually in a rural area

malva pudding – a delicious sponge dessert; sometimes called vinegar pudding, since it's traditionally made with apricot jam and vinegar

mealie – an ear of maize

mealie meal – finely ground maize

mealie pap – mealie porridge; the staple diet of rural blacks, often served with stew

melktert – custard tart

moerse – huge, massive, as in 'that was a moerse party!'

moffie – a gay man; formerly derogatory, but now appropriated by many in the gay community

Mother City – another name for Cape Town; probably so called because it was South Africa's first colony

NNP – New National Party

non-shared taxi – a taxi available for private hire, as distinct from a shared taxi

now – soon; eg 'I'll serve you now' means in a little while. 'Just now' means 'I understand that you're impatient, and I'll be with you soon', or 'When I can get around to it'.

now-now – immediately

NP – National Party

PAC – Pan-African Congress

Pagad – People against Gangsterism and Drugs

pap and sous – maize porridge with a sauce

plus-minus – approximately; eg 'How far is Dagsdorp?' 'Plus-minus 60km.'

poort – a mountain pass

renosterbos – literally 'rhinoceros bush'; a type of vegetation

Rikkis – tiny, open vans providing Asian-style transport in Cape Town's City Bowl and nearby areas at low prices

robot – traffic light

rondavel – a round hut with a conical roof, frequently seen in holiday resorts

russian – large red sausage, fried but often served cold

SABC – South African Broadcasting Corporation

samp – crushed maize used for porridge; known in Xhosa as umngqusho

SANDF – South African National Defence Force

sandveld – land consisting mainly of sand dunes

Shame! – What a pity!

shared taxi – a relatively cheap form of shared transport, usually a minibus; also known as a black taxi, a minibus taxi or a long-distance taxi

shebeen – a drinking establishment in a township; once illegal, now merely unlicensed

sif – horrible

sis – ugh

slots – poker machines

snoek – a firm-fleshed migratory fish that appears off the Cape in June and July, served smoked, salted or curried

Sorry! – often used to express sympathy for someone having a minor mishap. Also used to get attention, as in 'Excuse me'.

sourveld – barren land; land where little will grow

Spar – a supermarket chain; becoming a generic term for any large supermarket

spook and diesel – rum and Coke

spruit – shallow river

stad – Afrikaans for 'city centre'; used on road signs

strand – beach

sundowner – any drink, but typically alcohol, drunk at sunset

supper – main evening meal

Tavern of the Seas – Cape Town was once known this way, in the days when it had a reputation among sailors as a riotous port

Telkom – government telecommunications company

tickie box – public phone on private premises

township – black residential district, usually hidden on the outskirts of an otherwise white town

ubuntu – a Xhosa and Zulu word for humanity, often used to indicate traditional hospitality, but broader than that; it has spiritual overtones that suggest the connectedness of all living things

UDF – United Democratic Front

UDM – United Democratic Movement

umnqombothi – Xhosa for rough-and-ready home-brewed beer

veld – (pronounced 'felt') open grassland; variations include lowveld, highveld, bushveld, sandveld and sourveld

venison – if you see this on a menu it's bound to be some form of antelope, usually springbok

vienna – smaller version of the russian sausage

vlei – (pronounced 'flay') any low open landscape, sometimes marshy

VOC – Vereenigde Oost-Indische Compagnie (Dutch East India Company)

Voortrekkers – the original Afrikaner settlers of the Orange Free State and Transvaal who migrated from the Cape Colony in the 1830s

waterblommetjie bredie – a traditional Cape Malay stew of mutton with faintly peppery water-hyacinth flowers and white wine

weg – literally 'way' but translated as 'street' or 'road'; eg, 'Abelweg' means 'Abel Rd'

Where do you stay? – 'Where do you live?' not 'Which hotel are you staying at?'

yah well no fine – yes-no-maybe-perhaps

you must – Sometimes it sounds as though everyone's ordering you around: 'You must sit over there'; 'You must order from the waiter'. But they aren't. 'Must' is a fairly neutral word in South Africa, and doesn't have the 'bossy' connotations that it does in other English-speaking countries. Think of 'You must ...' as a less polite version of 'Please ...'.

zol – marijuana, also known as *dagga*

Behind the Scenes

THE LONELY PLANET STORY

The story begins with a classic travel adventure: Tony and Maureen Wheeler's 1972 journey across Europe and Asia to Australia. There was no useful information about the overland trail then, so Tony and Maureen published the first Lonely Planet guidebook to meet a growing need.

From a kitchen table, Lonely Planet has grown to become the largest independent travel publisher in the world, with offices in Melbourne (Australia), Oakland (USA), London (UK) and Paris (France).

Today Lonely Planet guidebooks cover the globe. There is an ever-growing list of books and information in a variety of media. Some things haven't changed. The main aim is still to make it possible for adventurous travellers to get out there – to explore and better understand the world.

At Lonely Planet we believe travellers can make a positive contribution to the countries they visit – if they respect their host communities and spend their money wisely.

THIS BOOK

This 4th edition of *Cape Town* was researched and written by Simon Richmond. Simon wrote the 3rd edition with Jon Murray, who also wrote the first and second editions. This guide was commissioned in Lonely Planet's London office and produced in Melbourne. The project team:

Commissioning Editors Fiona Christie, Will Gourlay, Emma Koch & Kalya Ryan
Coordinating Editor Lucy Monie
Coordinating Cartographer Jacqueline Nguyen
Coordinating Layout Designer Adam Bextream
Assisting Editors & Proofreaders Susannah Farfor, Thalia Kalkipsakis & Tom Smallman
Cover Designer Brendan Dempsey
Managing Cartographer Shahara Ahmed
Managing Editors Bruce Evans & Darren O'Connell
Layout Managers Adriana Mammarella & Kate McDonald
Project Manager Rachel Imeson
Language Content Coordinator Quentin Frayne (with thanks to Peter Finn for his help and feedback)
Regional Publishing Manager Kate Cody
Cover photographs Wave at Noordhoek Beach, Paul Kennedy/ Lonely Planet Images (top); Alfred Basin and Table Mountain, Walter Bibikow/Getty Images/Taxi; Flower seller on Trafalgar Place, Ariadne van Zandbergen/Lonely Planet Images
Internal photographs Ariadne van Zandbergen/Lonely Planet Images. All images are the copyright of Lonely Planet Publications unless otherwise indicated. Many of the images in this guide are available for licensing from Lonely Planet Images: www.lonelyplanetimages.com.

THANKS
SIMON RICHMOND
A huge round of applause, as always, goes to the dynamic Sheryl Ozinsky and her fabulous staff at Cape Town

Tourism. The 'grand dames' Lee and Toni were also their usual hospitable and opinionated selves. Kim Wildman very kindly gave me a great base from which to work. Steve and Jeremy opened up a few doors in the Waterkant as did Brent Meersman into the worlds of the arts and politics. Many thanks to Anne Wallis Brown, Patricia Davidson and Estelle Jacobs for their advice and assistance.

OUR READERS

Many thanks to the travellers who used the last edition and wrote to us with helpful hints, useful advice and interesting anecdotes. Your names follow:

Gavin Pearce, DK & Sue Adams, Garth Angus, Hugh Annand, Zafer Babur, Polly Bagnell, Helen & Paul Bates, Valentina

SEND US YOUR FEEDBACK

We love to hear from travellers – your comments keep us on our toes and help make our books better. Our well-travelled team reads every word on what you loved or loathed about this book. Although we cannot reply individually to postal submissions, we always guarantee that your feedback goes straight to the appropriate authors, in time for the next edition. Each person who sends us information is thanked in the next edition – and the most useful submissions are rewarded with a free book.

To send us your updates – and find out about LP events, newsletters and travel news – visit our award-winning website: www.lonelyplanet.com.

Note: We may edit, reproduce and incorporate your comments in Lonely Planet products such as guidebooks, websites and digital products, so let us know if you don't want your comments reproduced or your name acknowledged. For a copy of our privacy policy visit www.lonelyplanet.com/privacy.

Bojanic, Eileen Booth, DJ Briers, Patricia Buck, Catherine & Keith Buxton, Susan Cartwright, Louke & Jeanette Charpentier, Mieke Clerx, Viviana D'Alto, Rob Davidowitz, Julie Davies, Frouke de Groot, Dylan Edwards, Kris Engle, Hans Ermel, Ole Eskesen, Jane Evans, Norman & Pat Farnworth, Bryan & Sonja Fraser, Mike French, Natasha Gale, Kosty Gilis, Michael Goff, Maria Gotmalm, Vasily Grebennikov, Sarah Greenfield, Stefan & Jeanine Gunter, Penny Hall, Elisabeth Hansen, Derek Huby, Anthony Hulton, David Hunt, Hans Husum, Paul Kilfoil, Sarah Kirton, Karen Kjeldsberg Pihl, Margriet Krijgsman, M Kruger, Sandy Lam, Comari Lategan, Chris & Aileen Lea, Angela Leeding, Mary Lindsey, Gaby Lipscomb, Richard Lonmon, Amanda Lyons, Bernard Madigan, Chris Magnuson, Richard Mahoney, Ilya Marritz, David & Sally Martin, Sean & Michelle McDiarmid, Noelle McGrady, Markella Mikkelsen, Natasha Milijasevic, Giorgia Naccarato, Amanda Norman, Sarah Nouwen, Ken Park, Mike Parkin, Nina, Kiran & Maya Patel, Moonsamy Pelay, Paul Pellizzari, Lynne Plenderleith, Tibor Poelmann, Peter Ras, Ian Reason, Peter Reinhold, Leslie Robin, Keith Rodwell, Walter Rogoff, Sebastien Salze, Christian Schwarz, Jim & JoElle Scott, Christopher Scoville, Chris Seavell, Ulrike Seidel, Max Slade, Ervin Staub, Silje Marita Strand, Dominic Symons, Richard Townsley, Karen Treanor, Rune Utne Reiten, Clementina van der Walt, Alex von Furstenberg, Jennifer Walker, Gemma Watmough, Joachim Wehner, Phil Whitchurch, Linda White, Michael Ziemba.

Notes

Index

See also separate indexes for Drinking (p192), Eating (p192), Shopping (p193), Sleeping (p193) and Wineries (p194).

000 map pages
000 photographs

SLEEPING

SHOPPING

WINERIES

Index

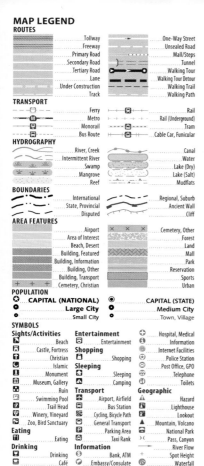

MAP LEGEND

ROUTES
.... Tollway
.... Freeway
.... Primary Road
.... Secondary Road
.... Tertiary Road
.... Lane
.... Under Construction
.... Track

.... One-Way Street
.... Unsealed Road
.... Mall/Steps
.... Tunnel
.... Walking Tour
.... Walking Tour Detour
.... Walking Trail
.... Walking Path

TRANSPORT
.... Ferry
.... Metro
.... Monorail
.... Bus Route

.... Rail
.... Rail (Underground)
.... Tram
.... Cable Car, Funicular

HYDROGRAPHY
.... River, Creek
.... Intermittent River
.... Swamp
.... Mangrove
.... Reef

.... Canal
.... Water
.... Lake (Dry)
.... Lake (Salt)
.... Mudflats

BOUNDARIES
.... International
.... State, Provincial
.... Disputed

.... Regional, Suburb
.... Ancient Wall
.... Cliff

AREA FEATURES
.... Airport
.... Area of Interest
.... Beach, Desert
.... Building, Featured
.... Building, Information
.... Building, Other
.... Building, Transport
.... Cemetery, Christian

.... Cemetery, Other
.... Forest
.... Land
.... Mall
.... Park
.... Reservation
.... Sports
.... Urban

POPULATION
○ **CAPITAL (NATIONAL)**
● **Large City**
● Small City

◉ **CAPITAL (STATE)**
● **Medium City**
○ Town, Village

SYMBOLS

Sights/Activities
.... Beach
.... Castle, Fortress
.... Christian
.... Islamic
.... Monument
.... Museum, Gallery
.... Ruin
.... Swimming Pool
.... Trail Head
.... Winery, Vineyard
.... Zoo, Bird Sanctuary

Eating
.... Eating

Drinking
.... Drinking
.... Café

Entertainment
.... Entertainment

Shopping
.... Shopping

Sleeping
.... Sleeping
.... Camping

Transport
.... Airport, Airfield
.... Bus Station
.... Cycling, Bicycle Path
.... General Transport
.... Parking Area
.... Taxi Rank

Information
.... Bank, ATM
.... Embassy/Consulate

.... Hospital, Medical
.... Information
.... Internet Facilities
.... Police Station
.... Post Office, GPO
.... Telephone
.... Toilets

Geographic
.... Hazard
.... Lighthouse
.... Lookout
.... Mountain, Volcano
.... National Park
.... Pass, Canyon
.... River Flow
.... Spot Height
.... Waterfall

Map Section

Kuilsrivier

To Paarl (42km);
Johannesburg
(1400km)

To Somerset
West (20km);
Strand, R44 (24km);
Gordon's Bay, Nottentots
Hollandberg (30km);
Hermanus (90km);
Port Elizabeth (750km)

Khayelitsha

Bellville

R300

Kuilsrivier

Parow

Cape Town
International
Airport

Mitchell's Plain

To Cederberg,
Springbok
(550km)

Goodwood

Monte
Vista

Goodwood

Crossroads

Nyanga

Guguletu

Strandfontein

Milnerton

Koeberg

Acacia
Park

Kensington
Maitland
Ndabeni
Pinelands

Langa
Langa

Athlone

Rondebosch

Lansdowne

Rondevlei
Nature
Reserve

Strandfontein
Sewage Works

To Bloubergstrand,
The Blue Peter
(7km)

Jan Smuts

Hazendal

Klipfontein

Athlone
Crawford

Wetton
Ottery

Diep River

Retreat
Steenberg
Lakeside

Vaalbaai

Vanguard

Marine

Deep River

Maitland

Observatory

Salt River

Woodstock

Cape Town

Esplanade

Mowbray

Rosebank
Rondebosch
Newlands
Claremont

Wynberg

Wynberg
Plumstead

Steurhof

Main Rd

See Cape Town & Southern Suburbs Map (p198-9)

Table
Bay

Vredehoek

Table
Mountain

Cape Peninsula
National Park

Bishopscourt

Constantia

Steenberg Rd

Steenberg

Ferry To
Robben
Island

Signal
Hill

Sea Point

Main Entrance
to Kirstenbosch

Ryecroft Gate
Entrance to
Kirstenbosch

Ladies' Mile

Main Rd

Tokai

Clifton

Camps
Bay

The Twelve Apostles

Constantiaberge

Constantia Nek Rd

Imizamo Yethu

Constantiaberg

Noordhoek

Minor Roads Not Depicted

ATLANTIC
OCEAN

Wreck of
Romelia

Llandudno

Victoria Rd

Hout Bay

Sandy
Bay

See Hout Bay (p210)

Hout Bay Main Rd

Chapman's Peak Dve

Duiker
Island

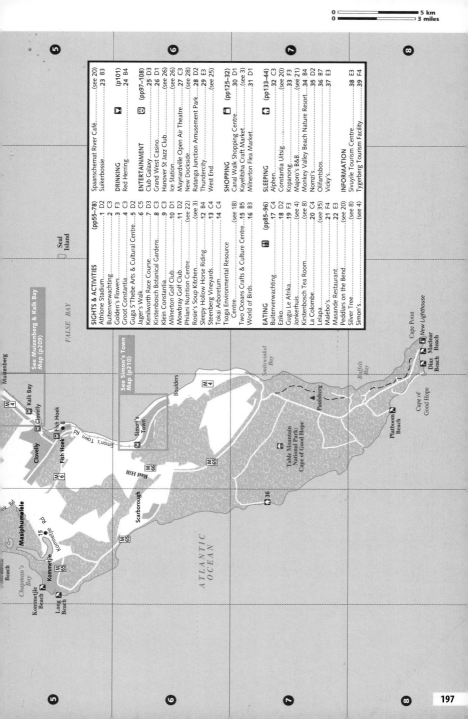

0 — 5 km
0 — 3 miles

SIGHTS & ACTIVITIES (pp55–78)
Athlone Stadium	1 D2
Buitenverwachting	2 C3
Golden's Flowers	3 F3
Groot Constantia	4 C3
Guga S'Thebe Arts & Cultural Centre	5 D2
Jager's Walk	6 C5
Kenilworth Race Course	7 D3
Kirstenbosch Botanical Gardens	8 C3
Klein Constantia	9 C3
Milnerton Golf Club	10 D1
Mowbray Golf Club	11 D2
Philani Nutrition Centre	(see 22)
Rosie's Soup Kitchen	(see 3)
Sleepy Hollow Horse Riding	12 B4
Steenberg Vineyards	13 C4
Tokai Arboretum	14 C4
Tsoga Environmental Resource Centre	(see 18)
Two Oceans Crafts & Culture Centre	15 B5
World of Birds	16 B3

EATING (pp85–96)
Buitenverwachting	17 C4
Eziko	18 D2
Gugu Le Afrika	19 F3
Jonkerhuis	(see 4)
Kirstenbosch Tea Room	(see 8)
La Colombe	20 C4
Lelapa	(see 35)
Malebo's	21 F4
Masande Restaurant	22 E3
Peddlars on the Bend	(see 20)
Silver Tree	(see 8)
Simon's	(see 4)

Spaanschemat River Café
Spaanschemat River Café	23 B3
Suikerbossie	(p101)

DRINKING
Red Herring	24 B4

ENTERTAINMENT (pp97–108)
Club Galaxy	25 D3
Grand West Casino	26 D1
Hanover St Jazz Club	(see 26)
Ice Station	(see 26)
Maynardville Open Air Theatre	27 C3
New Dockside	(see 28)
Ratanga Junction Amusement Park	28 D2
Thundercity	29 E3
West End	(see 25)

SHOPPING (pp125–32)
Canal Walk Shopping Centre	30 D1
Kayelitsha Craft Market	(see 3)
Milnerton Flea Market	31 D1

SLEEPING (pp133–44)
Alphen	32 C3
Constantia Uitsig	(see 20)
Kopanong	33 F3
Majoro's B&B	34 B4
Monkey Valley Beach Nature Resort	35 D2
Nomzi's	36 B7
Olifantsbos	37 E3
Vicky's	

INFORMATION
Sivuyile Tourism Centre	38 E3
Tygerberg Tourism Facility	39 F4

See Muizenberg & Kalk Bay Map (p209)

See Simon's Town Map (p210)

Seal Island

FALSE BAY

Muizenberg
Kalk Bay
Clovelly
Fish Hoek
Simon's Town
Boulders

Sandwiekel Bay
Bufiels Bay

Smitswinkel Bay

Table Mountain National Park: Cape of Good Hope

Paulsberg

Cape of Good Hope

Platboom Beach

Cape Point
New Lighthouse
Maclear Beach
Diaz Beach

ATLANTIC OCEAN

Scarborough

Red Hill

Simon's Town Rd

Masiphumelele

Kommetjie

Long Beach
Kommetjie Beach

Chapman's Bay

Chapman's Beach

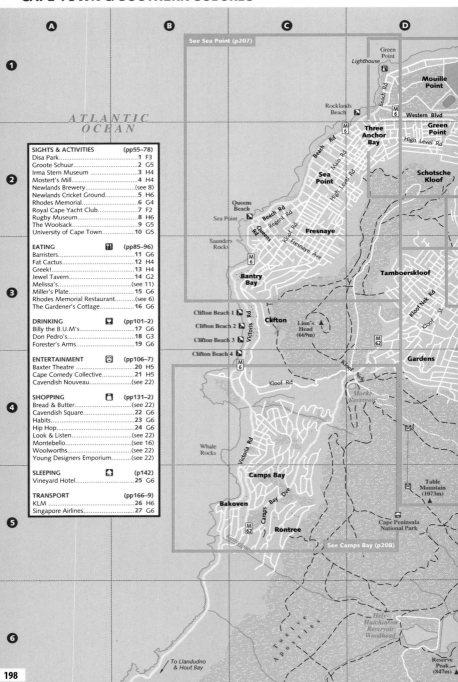

SIGHTS & ACTIVITIES		**(pp55–78)**
Disa Park	1	F3
Groote Schuur	2	G5
Irma Stern Museum	3	H4
Mostert's Mill	4	H4
Newlands Brewery	(see 8)	
Newlands Cricket Ground	5	H6
Rhodes Memorial	6	G4
Royal Cape Yacht Club	7	F2
Rugby Museum	8	H6
The Woolsack	9	G5
University of Cape Town	10	G5
EATING 🍴		**(pp85–96)**
Barristers	11	G6
Fat Cactus	12	H4
Greek!	13	H4
Jewel Tavern	14	G2
Melissa's	(see 11)	
Miller's Plate	15	G6
Rhodes Memorial Restaurant	(see 6)	
The Gardener's Cottage	16	G6
DRINKING 🍷		**(pp101–2)**
Billy the B.U.M's	17	G6
Don Pedro's	18	G3
Forester's Arms	19	G6
ENTERTAINMENT 🎭		**(pp106–7)**
Baxter Theatre	20	H5
Cape Comedy Collective	21	H5
Cavendish Nouveau	(see 22)	
SHOPPING 🛍		**(pp131–2)**
Bread & Butter	(see 22)	
Cavendish Square	22	G6
Habits	23	G6
Hip Hop	24	G6
Look & Listen	(see 22)	
Montebello	(see 16)	
Woolworths	(see 22)	
Young Designers Emporium	(see 22)	
SLEEPING 🏠		**(p142)**
Vineyard Hotel	25	G6
TRANSPORT		**(pp166–9)**
KLM	26	H6
Singapore Airlines	27	G6

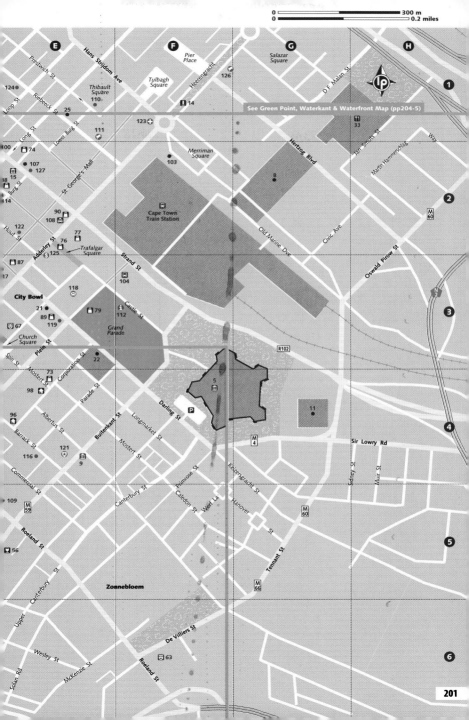

See Green Point, Waterkant & Waterfront Map (pp204-5)

E
Prestwich St
124
Loop St
Riebeeck St
25
111
100
74
107
127
15
Long St
Lower Burg St
St-George's Mall
Burg St
114
90
108
122
Hout St
76
77
87
125
Adderley St
17

Hans Strijdom Ave
Thibault Square
110
123
Merriman Square
103
Cape Town Train Station
Trafalgar Square
Strand St
104

F
Pier Place
Tulbagh Square
Heerengracht
14
126

G
Salazar Square
Hertzog Blvd
8

H
D F Malan St
Jan Smuts St
33
1

Martin Hammerschlag Way
M 60
2

Oswald Pirow St
M N
3

City Bowl
21
89
119
67
Church Square
Spin St
73
98
96
Barrack St
109
M 59
Roeland St
56

118
79
112
Grand Parade
Plein St
22
Mostert St
Corporation St
Parade St
Albertus St
Buitenkant St
121
116
9
Commercial St

Castle St
Darling St
P
Longmarket St
Mostert St
5
R102
11

Old Marine Dve
Civic Ave
M 4
Sir Lowry Rd
Sidney St
Muir St
4

Primrose St
Caledon St
Weir La
Canterbury St
Hanover St
Keizersgracht St
M 60
Upper Canterbury St
Roeland St

Zonnebloem
De Villiers St
63
Wesley St
McKenzie St
Solan Rd
Tennant St
M 66
5

6

300 m
0.2 miles

Ⓐ   Ⓑ   Ⓒ   Ⓓ

①

See Sea Point Map (p207)

Mouille
Point

Green
Point

②

Mouille Point

Lighthouse 🏛

Beach Rd

Bay Rd

🏛 19

Metropolitan
Golf Course

Stephan Way

Green
Point
Common

Beach Rd

Fritz Sonnenberg Rd

Vlei Rd

③

Bill Peters Dve

Green
Point
Stadium

Three
Anchor
Bay

M 6

Western Blvd

Green Point
Track

Main Rd

M 61

Western Blvd

56 🏛   68 ⊙   16 🏛

18 20 25

④

Glengariff St

Mutley Rd

St Bedes Rd

Richmond Rd

Antrim Rd

Hill Rd

St Georges Rd

Clyde Rd

Pine Rd

Wigtown Rd

53 🏛

**Green
Point**

York Cavalcade Rd

Upper Portwood Rd

Main Rd

Vesperdene Rd

Braehal Rd

57 🏛

50 🏛

High Level Rd

Ocean View Dve

⑤

Main Dve

Ocean View Dve

Springbok Rd

Merriman Rd

Twelve   Apostles

4 ●

Viewpoint 🏛

21 🏛

Signal
Hill
(350m) 🏛

**Schotsche
Kloof**

Longmarket St

⑥

See City Bowl Map (pp200-1)

Military Rd

Voetboog Rd

Astana St

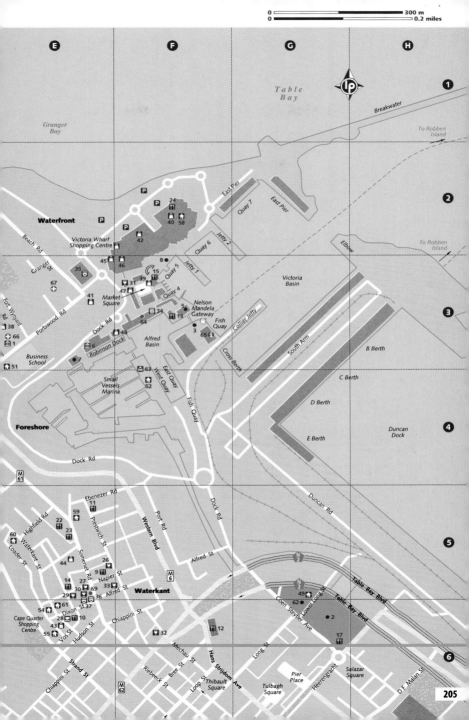

0 —————————— 300 m
0 —————————— 0.2 miles

Table Bay

Breakwater

Granger Bay

To Robben Island

Waterfront

East Pier

Quay 7

East Pier

To Robben Island

Beach Rd

Victoria Wharf
Shopping Centre

24
40 58
42

Quay 6

Jetty 2

Elbow

Granger St

Fort Wynard Rd

35
67

45
46
15
39
31
47

8

Quay 5
Quay 4
Jetty 1

Victoria Basin

Market Square

41

Portswood Rd

Dock Rd

64
34
5
13

Nelson Mandela Gateway

Collier Jetty

South Arm

B Berth

Business School

38
66
1

51

48
6
7

Robinson Dock

Alfred Basin

3
65

Fish Quay

Cross Berth

C Berth

D Berth

63
52

Small Vessels Marina

East Quay
West Quay

Fish Quay

E Berth

Duncan Dock

Foreshore

Dock Rd

M 61

Dock Rd

Duncan Rd

Ebenezer Rd

11
59

Highfield Rd

22
23

60

Prestwich St

Western Blvd

Port Rd

Dock Rd

Alfred St

N 2

Louder St

Waterkant St

44

Somerset St

26

Napier St

M 6

N 2

Table Bay Blvd

49

14
30
29
69
36
33

Alfred St

Waterkant

62

Lower Long

Coen Steytler Ave

Table Bay Blvd

54
61
28
10

Dixon St

2

Cape Quarter Shopping Centre

43
55

Vos St

Hudson St

Chiappin St

32

12

17

Mechau St

Long St

Heerengracht

Chiappini St

Strand St

Riebeeck St

Bree St

Loop

Hans Strijdom Ave

Thibault Square

Pier Place

Tulbagh Square

Salazar Square

D F Malan St

M 62

SIGHTS & ACTIVITIES	(pp55–78)
Bertram House	1 B2
Cape Town Holocaust Centre	(see 4)
Delville Wood Memorial	2 C1
Great Synagogue	(see 4)
Nazareth House	3 D3
Old Synagogue	(see 4)
South African Jewish Museum	4 C1
South African Museum & Planetarium	5 C1
South African National Gallery	6 C1

EATING	(pp85–96)
Arnold's	7 B2
Aubergine	8 C2
Café Gainsbourg	9 B2
Café Riteve	(see 4)
Cape Colony	(see 44)
Manolo	10 B1
Maria's	11 C2
Melissa's	12 B2
Naked on Kloof	13 B1
Nelson's Eye	14 C1
Ocean Basket	15 B1
Vida e Caffé	16 B1
Yindee's	17 B2
Yum	18 C4

DRINKING	(pp97–108)
Cafe Bardeli	19 B1
Cohibar	(see 19)

Planet	(see 44)
Stag's Head Hotel	20 C2

ENTERTAINMENT	(pp97–108)
Ashoka, Son of Dharma	21 B2
Drum Café	22 D2
Hectic on Hope	(see 20)
Jam	23 D2
Labia Cinema	24 B2
Labia on Orange	(see 30)
Little Theatre	25 B1

SHOPPING	(pp125–32)
Afrogem	26 B1
Cape Union Mart	(see 27)
Gardens Centre	27 C2
Heartworks	28 B2
Heartworks	(see 27)
Hotchi-Witchi	29 B2
Icuba	(see 27)
Lifestyles on Kloof	30 B1
Pick 'n' Pay	(see 27)
The Photographers Gallery	31 B2
Woolworths	(see 27)

SLEEPING	(pp133–44)
Amsterdam Guest House	32 B4
Ashanti Lodge	33 B2
Backpack	34 B1
Belmont House	35 C3

Cape Milner	36 B1
Cape Town Hollow	37 C1
Dunkley House	38 C2
Fritz Hotel	39 B1
Hemingway House	40 C2
iKhaya Guest Lodge	41 C2
Kensington Place	42 A3
Montague House	43 A3
Mount Nelson Hotel	44 B2
Oak Lodge	45 C3
Parker Cottage	46 B1
Table Mountain Lodge	47 A1
Villa Belmonte	48 B3
Villa Papillon	49 C2
Zebra Crossing	50 B1
Zindigo Lodge	51 C3

TRANSPORT	(pp166–9)
Downhill Adventures	52 B1
Le Cap Motorcycle Hire	53 B1
Mountain Club of South Africa	54 C2

INFORMATION	
Africa Travel Centre	(see 34)
Computicket	(see 27)
Flight Centre	(see 27)
French	55 C1
German	56 C1
Italian	57 C1

SEA POINT

0 ⸺ 300 m
0 ⸺ 0.2 miles

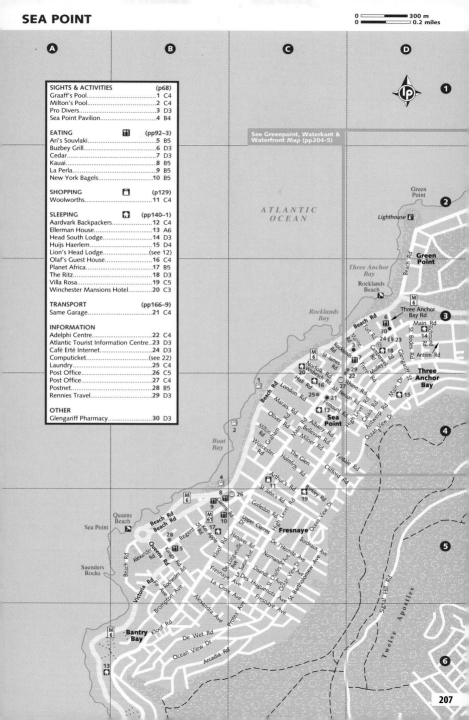

ATLANTIC OCEAN

See Greenpoint, Waterkant & Waterfront Map (pp204–5)

Green Point

Lighthouse

Three Anchor Bay

Rocklands Beach

Rocklands Bay

Green Point

Three Anchor Bay Rd

Three Anchor Bay

Boat Bay

Sea Point

Fresnaye

Queens Beach

Sea Point

Saunders Rocks

Bantry Bay

Twelve Apostles

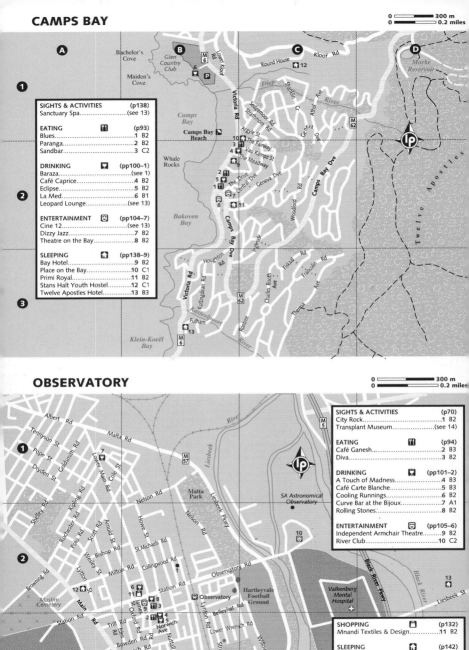

CAMPS BAY

0 ——— 300 m
0 ——— 0.2 miles

SIGHTS & ACTIVITIES	(p138)
Sanctuary Spa	(see 13)

EATING	🍴	(p93)
Blues	1	B2
Paranga	2	B2
Sandbar	3	C2

DRINKING	🍷	(pp100–1)
Baraza	(see 1)	
Café Caprice	4	B2
Eclipse	5	B2
La Med	6	B1
Leopard Lounge	(see 13)	

ENTERTAINMENT	🎭	(pp104–7)
Cine 12	(see 13)	
Dizzy Jazz	7	B2
Theatre on the Bay	8	B2

SLEEPING	🏠	(pp138–9)
Bay Hotel	9	B2
Place on the Bay	10	C1
Primi Royal	11	B2
Stans Halt Youth Hostel	12	C1
Twelve Apostles Hotel	13	B3

OBSERVATORY

0 ——— 300 m
0 ——— 0.2 miles

SIGHTS & ACTIVITIES	(p70)
City Rock	1 B2
Transplant Museum	(see 14)

EATING	🍴	(p94)
Café Ganesh	2	B3
Diva	3	B2

DRINKING	🍷	(pp101–2)
A Touch of Madness	4	B3
Café Carte Blanche	5	B3
Cooling Runnings	6	B2
Curve Bar at the Bijoux	7	A1
Rolling Stones	8	B2

ENTERTAINMENT	🎭	(pp105–6)
Independent Armchair Theatre	9	B2
River Club	10	C2

SHOPPING	🛍	(p132)
Mnandi Textiles & Design	11	B2

SLEEPING	🏠	(p142)
Green Elephant	12	A2
Lighthouse Farm Lodge	13	D2

INFORMATION	
Groote Schuur Hospital	14 A3

MUIZENBERG & KALK BAY

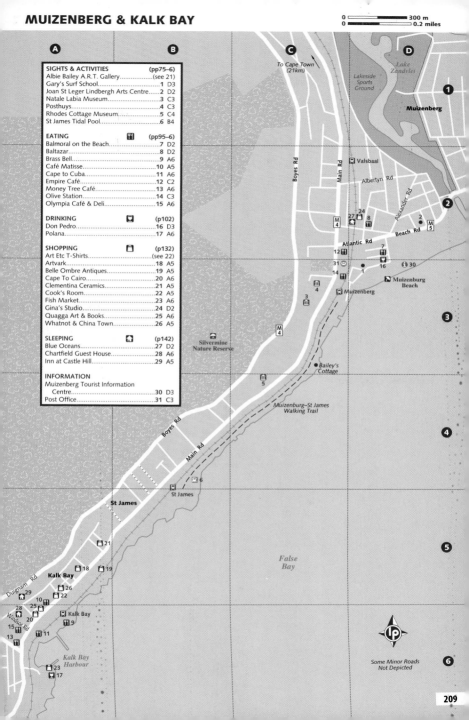

To Cape Town
(21km)

Lake
Zandvlei

Lakeside
Sports
Ground

Muizenberg

Boyes Rd

Main Rd

Valsbaai

Albertyn Rd

Alexander Rd

Beach Rd

Atlantic Rd

Muizenberg

Muizenberg
Beach

Silvermine
Nature Reserve

Bailey's
Cottage

Muizenburg–St James
Walking Trail

Boyes Rd

Main Rd

St James

St James

Kalk Bay

Duignam Rd

Windsor Rd

Kalk Bay

Kalk Bay
Harbour

*False
Bay*

Some Minor Roads
Not Depicted

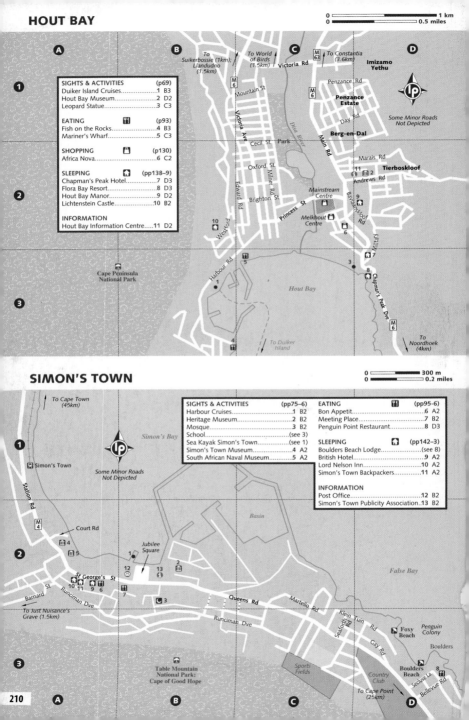

0 ——————— 1 km
0 ——————— 0.5 miles

SIGHTS & ACTIVITIES (p69)
Duiker Island Cruises...............1 B3
Hout Bay Museum....................2 D2
Leopard Statue..........................3 C3

EATING (p93)
Fish on the Rocks......................4 B3
Mariner's Wharf........................5 C3

SHOPPING (p130)
Africa Nova...............................6 C2

SLEEPING (pp138–9)
Chapman's Peak Hotel...............7 D3
Flora Bay Resort.......................8 D3
Hout Bay Manor........................9 D2
Lichtenstein Castle..................10 B2

INFORMATION
Hout Bay Information Centre.....11 D2

SIMON'S TOWN

0 ——————— 300 m
0 ——————— 0.2 miles

SIGHTS & ACTIVITIES (pp75–6)
Harbour Cruises..........................1 B2
Heritage Museum........................2 B2
Mosque......................................3 B2
School......................................(see 3)
Sea Kayak Simon's Town..........(see 1)
Simon's Town Museum................4 A2
South African Naval Museum.......5 A2

EATING (pp95–6)
Bon Appetit...............................6 A2
Meeting Place............................7 B2
Penguin Point Restaurant............8 D3

SLEEPING (pp142–3)
Boulders Beach Lodge...........(see 8)
British Hotel..............................9 A2
Lord Nelson Inn......................10 A2
Simon's Town Backpackers......11 A2

INFORMATION
Post Office..............................12 B2
Simon's Town Publicity Association.13 B2